Love, Joy, and Sex

†

STUDIES IN WORLD CATHOLICISM

Michael L. Budde and William T. Cavanaugh, *Series Editors*

Karen M. Kraft, *Managing Editor*

Other Titles in This Series

Love, Joy, and Sex

African Conversation on Pope Francis's *Amoris Laetitia*
and the Gospel of Family in a Divided World

EDITED BY
Stan Chu Ilo

WITH A FOREWORD BY
Cardinal Anthony O. Okogie

CONTRIBUTORS

Vincent E. Arisukwu
Stan Chu Ilo
Eunice Kamaara
Leonida Katunge
Emily Kerama
MarySylvia Nwachukwu

Richard Rwiza
Nicholaus Segeja
Barnabas Shabayang
Gabriel Tata
Bonaventure Ugwu

 CASCADE *Books* • Eugene, Oregon

LOVE, JOY, AND SEX
African Conversation on Pope Francis's *Amoris Laetitia* and the Gospel of Family
in a Divided World

Studies in World Catholicism 6

Cascade Books
An Imprint of Wipf and Stock Publishers
199 W. 8th Ave., Suite 3
Eugene, OR 97401

www.wipfandstock.com

PAPERBACK ISBN: 978-1-5326-1895-6
HARDCOVER ISBN: 978-1-4982-4489-3
EBOOK ISBN: 978-1-4982-4488-6

Cataloguing-in-Publication data:

Names: Ilo, Stan Chu, editor. | Okogie, Anthony Olubunmi, 1936–, foreword.

Title: Love, joy, and sex : African conversation on Pope Francis's *Amoris Laetitia*
and the gospel of family in a divided world / edited by Stan Chu Ilo ; foreword
by Cardinal Anthony O. Okogie.

Description: Eugene, OR : Cascade Books, 2019 | Series: Studies in World Catholi-
cism 6 | Includes bibliographical references and index(es).

Identifiers: ISBN 978-1-5326-1895-6 (paperback) | ISBN 978-1-4982-4489-3 (hard-
cover) | ISBN 978-1-4982-4488-6 (ebook)

Subjects: LCSH: Catholic Church.—Pope (2013– : Francis).—Amoris laetitia. |
Marriage—Religious aspects—Catholic Church. | Christianity—Africa. | Chris-
tian sociology—Africa—Catholic Church.

Classification: BX1753 .L70 2019 (print) | BX1753 .L70 (ebook)

Manufactured in the U.S.A.   JULY 9, 2019

This book is specially dedicated to my brother, Prince Jude Udo Ilo, and his wife, Nkem Ilo, and to Princesses Ziva and Ariella as we keep alive and eternal the memory of Princess Natasha Ilo who left too soon to watch over us from our eternal ancestral home. I also offer this book as a prayer to all mothers who have lost a child.

Contents

List of Contributors

Vincent E. Arisukwu is a Catholic priest of the Archdiocese of Owerri, Nigeria. Currently, he is studying in the U.S. and working for the Archdiocese of Baltimore, Maryland. He is a blogger on family matters and the founder of the Family Apostolate Ministry at Christ the King Church, Glen Burnie, MD, which provides pastoral support and spiritual guidance to married couples and families in general. He holds an MA in communications from Notre Dame of Maryland University, Baltimore. He writes regularly at www.familypriest.com.

Stan Chu Ilo is a research professor at the Center for World Catholicism and Intercultural Theology, DePaul University, Chicago, and the president of the Canadian Samaritans for Africa. His research areas include religion and social justice, African Christianity, World Christianity, Catholic ecclesiology, religion and development, intercultural mission, etc. He has authored or edited over seven books including, most recently, *The Church and Development in Africa*; *A Poor and Merciful Church: The Illuminative Ecclesiology of Pope Francis*; *Discover Your Divine Investment*; and *The Church as Salt and Light*. In addition to several essays in peer-reviewed journals and book chapters, his op-ed essays have appeared in many channels including *Toronto Star, Toronto Sun, Catholic Register, National Catholic Reporter, Chicago Tribune, CNN.com, CTV.com, Huffpost, The Hill*, etc.

Eunice Kamaara is professor of religion at Moi University, Kenya and international affiliate of Indiana University Purdue University, Indianapolis (US). Her research interest is largely in interpretive methods with interdisciplinary perspectives to religion and development. She is keen to translate research findings into practical development through policy influence and community research uptake. She is a founder member of ACIP.

Leonida Katunge is a member of the Sisters of St. Joseph of Mombasa. She holds a licentiate and PhD in sacred liturgy from the Pontifical Atheneum of St. Anselm, Rome. Currently she is a lecturer at the Catholic University of Eastern Africa (CUEA), Tangaza University College, and Don Bosco Utume in Nairobi. She is also pursuing her LLB at CUEA.

Emily Kerama is associate professor of Christian ethics at Moi University's School of Arts and Social Sciences, Kenya. She uses both Christian and African theological resources to respond to the social and ethical challenges that face the church in Africa. She is among the founding members of the African Christian Initiation Program (ACIP).

MarySylvia Nwachukwu is a member of the Daughters of Divine Love Congregation. She holds a BA in philosophy, licentiate in sacred Scripture, and a PhD in biblical theology. She is a member of many international and national biblical and theological associations and has authored two books and several articles. She teaches biblical languages and Scripture, and is the director of Planning and Quality Control at Godfrey Okoye University, Enugu, Nigeria.

Richard Rwiza is an associate professor and head of the Department of Moral Theology at the Catholic University of Eastern Africa (CUEA), Nairobi, Kenya. He holds licentiate degrees (STL) in moral theology from CUEA and in theology from the Catholic University of Leuven, Belgium. He has a PhD in theology (STD) from Leuven University. Rwiza is the author of *Formation of Christian Conscience in Modern Africa* (Paulines Africa, 2001) and *Ethics of Human Rights: the African Contribution* (CUEA Press, 2010). Fr. Rwiza served as Secretary General of the Catholic Archdiocese of Arusha, Tanzania, between 2003 and 2007.

Nicholaus Segeja is a priest of the Archdiocese of Mwanza, Tanzania, chair and professor of pastoral theology at the Catholic of University of Eastern Africa, and a member of International Theological Commission, Rome.

Barnabas Shabayang is a priest of the Diocese of Kano, Nigeria and is currently lecturing at the Veritas University (The Catholic University of Nigeria), Abuja where he is the acting dean of Student Affairs. He holds a doctorate in sacred theology from the Angelicum University, Rome.

Gabriel Tata is a Catholic priest from the Republic of Benin. He holds doctoral degrees in moral theology and theological anthropology. Professor of social ethics at the Faculty of Theology of the Pontifical Urban University, his research perspective is the analysis of the anthropological structures and specific ethical problems in social life.

Bonaventure Ugwu is the rector of Spiritan International School of Theology (SIST), Attakwu, Enugu, Nigeria. He holds degrees in sociology, religion, and a doctorate in dogmatic theology from the Gregorian University, Rome with a specialization in pneumatology. He has written a good number of articles and books and is currently the chief editor of the *African Journal of Contextual Theology*.

Acknowledgments

This book is the fruit of a collaborative effort. It would not have been possible to assemble such a collection of essays from a diverse body of African scholars without the cooperation of the authors of the chapters in this volume. I wish to thank all the contributors to this volume for their professionalism and collaborative spirit. The idea for this volume was conceived at Catholic University of Eastern Africa in the spring of 2016, and I wish to thank all the scholars who took part in the lunch conversation that gave birth to this project.

I thank Cardinal Anthony O. Okogie, who even in retirement continues to follow the developments in theology, church, and society in Africa as expressed in his inspirational foreword to this volume.

I thank my colleagues, Francis Salinel and Karen Kraft, at the Center for World Catholicism and Intercultural Theology, DePaul University, Chicago for their support, and Bill Cavanaugh and Mike Budde for their inspiration and guidance. The same thanks go to the entire faculty of the Catholic Studies Department at DePaul, especially our chair, Emanuele Colombo, for the spirit of collegiality and friendship.

I am grateful to Tony and Elaine Pangan, Joe and Ann Clark, Jan Cloud Mose and family, Terri Simeoni and family, and Fr. Collins Ekpe, Fr. Emmanuel Katongole, Fr. Paulinus Odozor, and Fr. Dezie Chibuko for their friendship and support as I worked on this project. My thanks flow in profusion to Fr. Ken Simpson, Fr. Simon Kim, John Hoffman, Bill Tchuck, and the Sisters of St. Joseph at La Grange Park with whom I have had wonderful conversations on the gospel of the family.

I cannot forget the love and friendship of my mother, Lolo Igwe Rose Ilo, who this past year has borne so much pain and suffering as a result of the death of my father, His Royal Highness, Igwe Vincent Ilo, and the tragic death of my niece, Natasha. Through my mom's heroic suffering, total trust in God, dedication to her children and grandchildren, and her presence with me in the fall of 2016, I gained enormous strength and new hope to carry on with this project and many others.

I dedicate this book to the eternal memory of my niece, Princess Natasha Ilo, who died suddenly at the tender age of two, and to my brother Udo, his wife Nkem, and Natasha's elder sister, Ziva, who in the midst of this terrible pain and loss have shown incredible faith, hope, and courage. We carry in our hearts so many families who are going through the pain of losing a child through violence, accidents, poverty, natural disasters, or any number of other causes. May the gospel of the family proclaimed by Pope Francis be for all families on earth a source of light, joy, and hope, especially when the day is too dark and the night too long.

Stan Chu Ilo

Foreword: The Role of African Theologians 50 Years after Vatican II

HIS EMINENCE CARDINAL ANTHONY O. OKOGIE

Introduction

It is not an easy task to discuss the future of Catholicism in Africa or anywhere else because the future can be so unpredictable nowadays. The world we live in is moving so fast that no one can predict with any kind of certainty what will happen from one day to another.

A second reason why it is so difficult to discuss the future of Catholicism in Africa, is the vastness and diversity of the continent. Africa is far from being a homogenous continent, where you find the same kind of people everywhere with an identical outlook on reality in general, and the place of religion in that reality. For instance, the inhabitants of the northern part of Africa have little in common with those of the sub-Saharan region in terms of respective histories and trajectory of development as nation states.

With the foregoing view, one can only hope to make some general comments that would be broadly applicable to as wide an area of the continent as possible, especially as African theologians and researchers are being called to be bold in making their voices heard in today's divisive debates in Catholicism and the World Church on many issues—marriage and family life, enculturation of the gospel, new forms of social media, authority, violence, religious persecution, and the relationship between the universal and local churches etc.

Before Vatican II

Before speaking about the future of Catholicism in Africa, it should be helpful to cast a cursory glance back on the period of time since the Second Vatican Council. When Pope John XXIII (1958–1963) announced his intention on January 25, 1959, to convoke a council, he expressed the hope that it would be a means of spiritual renewal, reconciliation, and service. At the convocation of this council, the Roman pontiff said:

> Today the church is witnessing a crisis underway within the society. While humanity is at the threshold of a new age, immensely serious and broad tasks await the church, as in the most tragic periods of her history. It is a question in fact of bringing the perennial life-giving energies of the gospel to the modern world, a world that boasts of its technical and scientific conquests but also bears the effects of a temporal order that some have wanted to reorganize by excluding God. This is why modern society is characterized by great material progress but without a corresponding advance in the moral sphere.[1]

Africa was well represented at the Second Vatican Council by bishops drawn from all over the continent. But those bishops were mostly expatriate missionaries from the older churches of Europe and North America. They were the spokespersons for the church in Africa at the Council.

It was thus the case, If there were to be a Third Vatican Council today, the situation would be totally different. Africa would be represented, mostly, if not entirely, by bishops who are indigenous sons of Africa. That is only one indication of the transformation that Catholicism has undergone in Africa since Vatican II. Similar scenarios can be painted for the rank of the clergy, consecrated persons, and the lay faithful.

It is thus the case, thanks be to God, that the Catholic faith has found a home in Africa. It is no longer perceived as an alien or imported religion meant for expatriate residents on the continent and those indigenous sons and daughters of Africa who have imbibed their ways of living and doing things. Indeed, the Catholic faith has become so well

---

1. John XXIII, *Humanae Salutis*,1.

established in some parts of Africa that they are now able to send missionaries to the very countries that first sent missionaries to evangelize their own continent.

Since Vatican II, the Catholic population in Africa has risen astronomically. For instance, CNN recently put the percentage of increase in the Catholic population of Africa since 1980 at 228 percent. This exponential increase is unique to the continent of Africa and reflects that the Christian faith is bearing fruit in this continent and has the seeds of hope for the future of the continent and the world.

Our Success

One may ask, to what should we ascribe the kind of "success" that Catholicism has witnessed in Africa since Vatican II? The first obvious answer is divine providence. Yes, Paul planted, Apollos watered, but it was the Lord who gave the growth, to use the well-known statement of Paul in I Corinthians 3:6. Yes, we African Catholics owe a huge debt of gratitude to God for the phenomenal growth of Catholicism on our continent since Vatican II.

But we must give due credit to the Pauls and Apolloses, too, the missionaries from outside our continent who toiled day and night to see that the faith was proclaimed in every nook and cranny of Africa. They did so in the midst of unspeakable hardship and at the cost of the lives of many of them. Their courage and zeal for the task of evangelization was truly legendary.

We must pay equal tribute to the indigenous catechists, interpreters, and service leaders who worked side by side with the missionaries in planting the faith on our continent. All too often the contribution of these sons and daughters of Africa is overlooked. But it is only fair to say that the task of the missionaries would have been made many times more difficult without the support and assistance of those indigenous workers.

Way Forward for Our Catholic Theologians

Where will Catholicism go from here? It depends on the task ahead of it and how well it responds to that task. In my view, the main task before Catholicism in tomorrow's Africa is one of deepening the faith of the masses that have embraced it. Theology in Africa must go beyond academic exercise in the comfort of our studies, libraries, and chanceries. We must step into the depths with our people and work on the frontiers of human experience so that our theologies can become incarnate in the very cultural, social, and spiritual context of our people. The Catholic theologian must lead the way in this regard so that the concrete context of African theologies will be, to a large extent, the realization of the synthesis of theory and praxis, deep faith and active witnessing in the public square and in the social context. In a letter to the theological faculty of the Pontifical Catholic University of Argentina, Pope Francis said: "the good theologians, like the good shepherds, smell of the people of the road and, with their reflection, pour oil and wine on the wounds of humankind."[2] Since the fiftieth anniversary of the closing of Vatican II, there has been an irreversible movement of renewal that comes from the gospel. The pontiff states that theologians

> now, must go forward. How, then, to go ahead? Teaching and studying theology means living on a frontier, one in which the gospel meets the needs of the people to whom it should be proclaimed in an understandable and meaningful way.[3]

He writes further, "we must guard ourselves against a theology that is exhausted in the academic dispute or watching humanity from a glass castle. You learn it to live: theology and holiness are an inseparable pair."[4] To separate theology from holiness is to cripple the power of theology. While a mathematician can teach mathematics without living a mathematical life, a theologian cannot teach theology without living a holy life.

If the truth must be told, the vast majority of those who have embraced the Catholic faith in Africa today have done so only superficially. Yes, they have been baptized; yes, they go to church and receive the sacraments; yes, they belong to religious societies and pious associations. But how well grounded are they in knowledge of the Catholic faith? How well grounded are they in knowledge of Scripture, sacred tradition, the teaching of the magisterium, and in particular the moral and social teachings of the Church?

2. Pope Francis, "A Letter to the Theological Faculty of The Pontifical University of Argentina," March 3, 2015.

3. Pope Francis, "A Letter to the Theological Faculty of The Pontifical University of Argentina," March 3, 2015.

4. Pope Francis, "A Letter to the Theological Faculty of The Pontifical University of Argentina," March 3, 2015.

It has been said in some circles that many Catholics in Africa have only been sacramentalized without being truly and properly evangelized. For them, religious formation terminated with the catechism classes that they attended prior to receiving the Sacrament of Confirmation at the age of fourteen or thereabouts, or with the last class that they attended in a Catholic primary or secondary school. As a result, while they may have attained phenomenal heights in their academic and/or professional formation, they have remained underdeveloped in their religious formation. On account of this, when their religion is challenged in the face of difficulties or other narratives of faith, they crumble like a pack of cards. Before you know it, they are calling the doctrines of their Catholic faith into question, if they do not repudiate them altogether.

Another area of concern is the extent to which African Catholics allow their faith to impact their daily lives: their family, profession, social life, and especially, public office. It seems that many African Catholics operate with two different sets of principles: one set for Sunday within the church premises; the other set, from Monday to Saturday, outside the church premises. That is the situation that has often bred active church-goers who are nevertheless prepared to compromise when it comes to making moral choices. It is a well-known fact, sadly enough, that many of the high profile cases of corrupt enrichment and outright theft of public funds in many African countries, including my own country of Nigeria, have been perpetrated by otherwise loyal sons and daughters of the Church. You wonder: where was their Catholic faith when they were committing such heinous crimes against their countries and their people?

Theology and Mercy

Pope Francis goes further and makes a very strong connection between theology and mercy: "theology may be an expression of a church which is a 'field hospital', which lives its mission of salvation and healing in the world. Mercy is not just a pastoral attitude, but it is the very same substance of the gospel."[5] Thus, "without mercy our theology, our law, our pastoral care run the risk of collapse into bureaucratic pettiness or

5. Pope Francis, "A Letter to the Theological Faculty of The Pontifical University of Argentina," March 3, 2015.

ideology, which of itself wants to tame the mystery."[6] This is very significant, because to understand theology is to understand God, who is love and merciful. This makes a distinction between a Catholic theologian and a theologian of the museum. The theologian of the museum accumulates data and information on revelation without really knowing what to do with it. The true Catholic theologian accumulates knowledge for mission in truly human dimensions. Theologians must, therefore, open their eyes to the signs of times to avoid making pronouncements in an academic vacuum.

The example of great African theologians and philosophers like Saint Augustine of Hippo and the great fathers of the church like the African bishops, Cyprian of Carthage and Cyril of Alexandria (to mention but a few), remind us of what it means to be a true Christian scholar. In the lives of the fathers of the church, shone real perfection—they were theologians, committed to Christ and his church. Sometimes when I look at their lively examples, I see how little we do in our time—next to nothing. We know so much about God, and yet so little of him; we speak so much about God, but seldom speak to him. What we do not know is that, if we keep speaking about God without speaking to him, it is only a matter of time; God will stop speaking through us.

Let us take a cue from our forebears. Although they weren't scholars, they were the saints and friends of Jesus. They served our Lord in hunger and in thirst, in cold and in nakedness, in labor and in weariness, in watching, in fasting, in prayers and meditations, in frequent persecutions and reproaches. They waged valiant battles to subdue their imperfections. What purity and straightforwardness of purpose kept them towards God! By day, they labored; they were far from leaving mental prayer. They renounced all dignities, honors, and kindred. They hardly took what was necessary for life. They were poor in earthly things but rich in grace and virtue. They were holy men and women. In them we find a beautiful synthesis of theology, holiness, and mercy.

The Task Ahead

In view of the foregoing, the task before Catholicism in Africa is, first and foremost, catechesis: deepening the faith of huge flock that providence

---

6. Pope Francis, "A Letter to the Theological Faculty of The Pontifical University of Argentina," March 3, 2015.

has gathered from the four corners of the continent. It is a task, first of all, of growing their knowledge of the Catholic faith to the extent that it can be said to be mature, adult, on par with the level of their academic and/ or professional formation. It is a task, secondly, of fostering a genuine conversion of hearts that will eliminate "the crass dichotomy between life and faith in many of our Christians," mentioned by the pastoral exhortation of the Catholic Bishops Conference of Nigeria, *The Church in Nigeria: Family of God on Mission.*[7]

The bishops had earlier said that, in order to evangelize, the Church herself must first be evangelized. "She needs to meet the challenge raised by this theme of the church, which is evangelized by constant conversion and renewal, in order to evangelize the world with credibility."[8]

I believe that the "success " or "failure" of Catholicism in Africa in the future will be measured by how well it responds to the double task of catechesis and conversion of the hearts of its adherents on the continent. This will bear eloquent testimony in marriage and family life, our communities, and our politics and social life. If Catholicism succeeds in achieving this double task among the majority of its adherents, not only will its numbers continue to soar, but the faith itself will take firm, unshakable root in the African soil. The specter of adult Catholics who are unable to provide rational justification for their beliefs in the face of criticism by people of other faiths and denominations will become a thing of the past. Similarly, the cases of "crass dichotomy between life and faith in many of our Christians," will be drastically reduced.

Conclusion

The future of Catholicism in Africa looks bright enough. More and more sons and daughters of the continent will continue to embrace the faith. One cannot predict how long this bright picture will endure. It all depends on how long the Catholics in Africa will be able to withstand the daily bombardment of their consciousness by negative propaganda from outside the continent, notably from the Western media. It is no secret that a sizable section of the Western media has an undeclared agenda to force certain unacceptable moral choices down the throats of the African

7. *The Church in Nigeria: Family of God on Mission* (Abuja, Nigeria: Catholic Secretariat of Nigeria, 2004) 102.

8. *The Church in Nigeria*, 101.

people. Those practices are largely in the area of sexual morality, such as contraception, abortion, homosexuality, same-sex marriage, divorce, and re-marriage. Sometimes, they issue threats of grave consequences if Africans do not embrace their ideology. Yes, that is what it is: an ideology, and an obnoxious one, at that. This is why it is commendable that these African theologians have taken up, in this significant volume, the task of providing an African commentary to the papal exhortation, *Amoris Laetitia*. The insight in this volume is rich and significant and demands the attention of all Catholics in Africa and the world at large.

Thus far, the people of Africa, including our governments, have been able to resist the pressure being brought to bear on them. But how long will they be able to continue to do that, when one considers the burden of crushing poverty that is weighing heavily on many African nations?

The fact remains that pure, unsullied Catholicism will be firmly entrenched on the African continent and continue to grow in numerical strength to the extent that it succeeds in catechizing the Catholic faithful and eliciting a genuine conversion of their hearts. That is the future that Catholicism should be looking forward to on the African continent.

Prayer

I pray that this work will contribute to the growth of the Church, in holiness and fidelity to the Lord's will and mission to families and all God's people for the building of God's kingdom. I commend all of your efforts to the loving intercession of Mary, mother of Good Counsel, who "through the same faith which made her blessed . . . is present in the Church's mission, present in the Church's work of introducing into the world the kingdom of her son."[9] May her prayer accompany you as you strive to extend the kingdom of Christ in obedience to the prompting of his Holy Spirit. To all of you involved in faithful theological inquiry and publication, thinking and working with the Mother Church and your local communities especially in many hidden corners of the continent, I cordially impart my blessing.

9. John Paul II, *Redemptoris Mater*, 28.

Introduction: African Conversations on Pope Francis and the Debate on Marriage and Family Life

Stan Chu Ilo

The vocation of doing theology can at times be a difficult labor of love, especially in environs that do not appreciate the ongoing search for God because of the clearly mistaken idea that the God-and-Christ-questions have long been answered and that, therefore, the theological quest involves merely finding and repeating the responses proposed in times past by certain individuals, synods, and councils. To some extent this is true, but there is equally a sense in which it is not. The quest for God is ever new and endless: the divine presence in new circumstances raises new questions which require new answers or, at least, new understandings. Herein lies the vocation of the theologian. Thanks to the cultural Christianity that was introduced into the African continent as well as the rapid changes now taking place, theology as an endless quest is especially incumbent upon the African theologian.[1]

—Laurenti Magesa

1. Laurenti Magesa, "Endless Quest: The Vocation of an African Christian Theologian," 24. In *Endless Quest: The Vocation of an African Christian Theologian, Essays in Honor of Laurenti Magesa.* Edited by J.N.K. Mugambi and Evaristi Cornelli. Nairobi: Acton, 2014.

Amoris Laetitia (AL) will probably be Pope Francis's most discussed document for years to come. AL deals with some of the most divisive moral questions in modern Catholicism, especially in the West. The debate has also gained traction with African theologians but for different reasons and with a different focus. Africans are debating AL with a view to drawing out some key principles which will nourish the pastoral ministry of the church in Africa as the family of God.[2]

The strength and ultimate influence and success of AL as a papal exhortation will depend on how the pastoral proposals in the text are brought to life in diverse contexts of church life across the globe. This genuine attempt to understand the principles at work in AL and how to appropriate them in Africa have been the focus of theological discussions on AL in African Catholicism. Pope Francis did not set out in this document to redefine church teaching. This is not the purpose of Apostolic Exhortations, which are usually given as a teaching and encouragement to a faithful living out of the faith for Christians in the world. Exhortations are given as the fruits of deliberation and dialogue from a synod. They are thus meant to inspire and nourish the whole church to renewal and Christian witnessing around a particular theme or aspect of the church's mission chosen for the synod.

In *Amoris Laetitia*, Pope Francis answers three key questions: (i) How can one understand the identity, nature, and mission of the family in the uncertain world of today? (ii) What are the current challenges facing the family and how should the church interpret and understand the diverse situations of families in today's world? (iii) What pastoral praxis will better meet these challenges which will provide families with concrete pastoral responses to some of the new questions emerging from the new context of faith and life in the midst of dizzying cultural currents and social change?[3]

There are two movements which are operative in AL. *The two movements are from understanding the nature and identity of the Church to*

2. On why the African Synod chose the image of "the family of God" for the church in Africa at the African Synod of 1994 and its implications for the renewal of the church and society in Africa, see Agbonkhianmeghe E. Orobator, *Theology Brewed in an African Pot* (Maryknoll, NY: Orbis, 2008), 88.

3. On how social change is affecting the Christian family in Africa, see Nehemiah M. Nyaundi, "The Contemporary African Family in the Light of Rapid Change Theory" in Nahashon W. Ndung'u and Philomena N. Mwaura, ed. *Challenges and Prospects of the Church in Africa: Theological Reflections of the 21st Century* (Nairobi: Paulines Africa, 2005), 71–87.

understanding the nature and identity of the family; and from an under-
standing of the challenges facing today's family to understanding the chal-
lenges facing the Church today. Francis is obviously speaking to the family
from the heart of the Church, but at the same time he is speaking to the
church and the world from the heart of the family.

On the surface, one may read this as an exhortation to the family
only (especially chapters 4 and 5) or get lost in the polemics over whether
Pope Francis is traditional or innovative in this document with regard to
the contested moral questions and pastoral challenges facing the modern
family. No Pope can resolve moral questions simply by publishing a document or by issuing instructions. This, at least, has been the experience
of modern Catholicism since the publication of *Humanae Vitae*. Thus
resolving the moral and legal contestations around same-sex relations,
polygamy, separation, divorce, and remarriage was not the intention of
Pope Francis in *Amoris Laetitia*.

There is the need to deepen an understanding of the principles at
work in AL so as to appreciate the beauty of this document. There is a
further need of a contextual application of these principles to pastoral life
in diverse human and cultural contexts with sensitivity to the experiences
of families, especially those experiencing pain and bearing suppurating
wounds. Catholics who are used to "yes" and "no" authoritative answers
to all problems from the Roman center are being invited in AL to enter
into dialogue with the infinite mystery of complex human and moral
situations and limitations in our personal and family lives, which often
unsettle our sense of order and normalcy.

This volume has gathered seminal commentaries on AL by African
Catholic theologians, social scientists, and pastoral workers. They offer
African theological and pastoral responses to the principles and practices
proposed by Pope Francis in AL. Each chapter addresses a specific chapter of AL, however, the chapters in this book are not numbered according
to the chapters of AL except for chapters one through three.

Each chapter is divided into three broad parts: the first part is a
textual commentary on a chapter of AL; the second part is an African
reflection on the text of that chapter; the third part is an attempt by each
writer to show the strengths and limitations of the chapter being analyzed
in developing a pastoral ministry to families in Africa and the worldwide
church.

All the contributors to this volume draw from the African context
and show the portrait of faith and life in Africa through the narratives of

everyday life of ordinary African Christians in their marriage and family. In addition, they also employ theological and social scientific methods in gathering and analyzing the stories from the everyday experiences of African families. What is on offer in these pages are different approaches to living the message of Pope Francis in AL, which can speak both to the African pastoral situation and social conditions as well as to other contexts of faith and life outside Africa.

This is the first such attempt to engage AL from a specific region of the church.[4] There are three main reasons which motivated us to undertake this project:

A Wounded World and a Divided Church Need to Learn from the African Experience of Faith and Life

There is something to be learned from the African continent and churches in Africa about how to live joyfully and hopefully in the midst of suffering, conflicts, ambiguity, and the experience of the mystery and power of faith in daily life. African churches are showing that it is possible to hold in balance contending and contrasting realities—suffering and smiling, sickness and health, war and peace—with patience, hope, and joy.

This is an attitude to life through a faith which embraces marginality as an ingress into the expanding space of hope being opened by the God of the African ancestors through the daily appeal of many people today in Africa to Jesus Christ in their churches and daily prayers. This, African Christians believe, will help individuals and communities—as long as they live a virtuous life—to overcome the forces of evil which diminish the participation of people in the bond of life. This religio-cultural belief, by moving away from dualism—that is, the casting of reality usually in oppositional terms, for example the secular-sacred divide, the liberal and conservative gulf, and so on—in thinking and acting, secures for

4. One attempt to address some chapters of AL and the context in which it was born through the synods of 2014 and 2015 was a series of interviews of some Western church hierarchs and lay theologians by Italian journalist Giovanni Panettiere in *La Famiglia Allo Specchio: Il Racconto del Cammino Sinodale con Brani Scelti da Amoris Laetitia* (Rome: Gabrielli Editori, 2016). See the collection of essays by African bishops before the second Synod on the family, Michael J. Miller, trans. *Christ's New Homeland—Africa: Contribution to the Synod on the Family by African Pastors* (San Francisco: Ignatius, 2015). See also the commentary on chapter 8 by Francesco Cardinale Coccopalmerio, *Il Capitolo Ottavo Della Esortazione Apostolica Post Sinodale Amoris Laetitia* (Vatican City: Libreria Editrice Vaticana, 2017).

the African believer the possibility of a unity of faith in making sense of the complexities of life. This approach to integrating all things through the lens of God and faith is central to understanding the reason why the Christian faith is exponentially growing in Africa today. African Christianity is offering African Christians the instruments with which to live beyond marginality towards integration through their unique experience of the Lordship of Jesus Christ.

It is in this light that I argue that beyond the romantic idealization of African spirituality or the triumphalism which may sometimes characterize the narrative of the exponential Christian expansion in Africa, there lies a deeper treasure in Africa which could provide "a third way." This is particularly needed in the discussion today on the future of the family—for example, how to deal with formation of couples before marriage and how to mentor young families after marriage, the various African approaches to resolving marital disputes, the African reverence for children and care for the elderly, the African sense of community and family life, and the inclusiveness of African meals, hospitality, and sharing that could help the church overcome the exclusionary practices in our churches with regard to reception of Holy Communion, etc.

Unfortunately, African positions on moral issues with regard to marriage have often been dismissed as irrelevant, dated, conservative, unscientific, or simply a-historical. The most surprising of such dismissive attitudes was that of Cardinal Walter Kasper at the Synod in 2014. The German prelate was quoted in an interview as saying with regard to African positions on marriage, divorce, same-sex relations, etc., that "Africans should not tell us too much of what we have to do."[5] The good news today is that African theologies have come of age and the voices of African churches are offering new narratives of faith and life, which can help expand the range of intellectual and paradigmatic approaches to some of the debates on some of the contested moral issues in the worldwide church.

What we have done in this volume is to provide African solutions—historical, cultural, anthropological, biblical, ecclesiological, etc.—which we believe offer different ways of looking at marriage and family life following the teaching of Pope Francis in AL.

---

5. https://www.firstthings.com/blogs/firstthoughts/2014/10/dont-listen-to-the-africans-says-catholic-cardinal.

Telling the African Christian Story through the African Family

AL speaks to the church from the family and to the family from the church. This volume also contains many stories about the challenges and joy of family life in Africa which illustrate the diverse and changing faces of the church and experiences of faith in Africa. In a sense, through these essays, we tell the stories of faith and society in Africa. In doing this, the contributors also bring out aspects of the challenges facing African families, societies, and churches that were ignored both at the synods and in AL.

Many Africans felt that the issues which were discussed at the synods and in AL were dominated by social and cultural conflicts in the West, dictated by contending versions of modernity and contrasting interpretations of the teaching of Vatican II. Contributors here argue that framing the challenges facing Christian families narrowly through a Western prism marginalized Africa and the Global South. As a result, it robbed Africa and the universal church of the opportunity to hear the stories of courage and hope from Africa about how families and African societies are joyfully living the gospel of the family in the midst of many challenges and difficulties.

The greatest achievements of AL are the bold, creative, and prophetic principles and movements which it introduced in Catholic theological and pastoral approaches to marriage, family life, and the mission of the church. Whereas it does not specifically address some of the issues facing families in Africa brought forward by the Symposium of Episcopal Conferences of Africa and Madagascar (SECAM)—childlessness, subordination of women, polygamy, ancestral bonds, levirate marriages, bridal wealth, marriage in stages, and the urgency of accepting the validity of African rites and rituals of marriage that are more decisive in establishing a covenant between families prior to and above the requirements of church sacramental weddings, etc.—the church in Africa can work with these principles like all local churches have been encouraged to do, in order to formulate pastoral plans for families.

This is exactly what contributors to this volume have achieved here. The essays aim at "bringing down" the document to the daily narratives of the lives of ordinary African Christians as a portrait which can also guide the worldwide church. Miroslav Volf points out that public faith is a rich complex of changing Christian narratives, identities, and cultures, each with their partly overlapping, partly conflicting sets of beliefs and practices. I will argue in the light of Volf's characterization that World Catholicism seeks to understand how we can situate the diversities in world history within the bigger picture of God's dealing with creation and how God is redeeming people in their specific cultural contexts and moral complexities through the healing balm of mercy and grace. This is why the stories of the faith from Africa are of relevance not only to Africans but also to non-Africans. It is also the reason why I argue that telling that story by those who live it, and through multiple lenses—as we have done in this book—offers a better approach to a fuller understanding or total picture of African Christian religion.[6]

Celebration of Diversity in the Catholic Church

I see a relation between what took place at Vatican II and what happened during the two synods on the family: the church's commitment to dialogue at all levels was on full display. Pope Francis invited the church to journey together especially with those who suffer. The church is called to provide the illuminative path, which will guide many people in a wounded and divided world into the truth, which saves, and grace, which brings abundant life. The synods on the family and the recommendations of AL are different forms of invitation to all Christians and the world to embrace diversity and inclusion.

There is a growing need in the Catholic Church for diversity in both theological formulation and the way the Catholic faith is celebrated. There is also a growing consciousness that an essential part of dialogue in the worldwide church today should be to listen to the laments of those who are suffering in our churches, those whose voices are not being heard and whose faces are not often seen in our churches. This is necessary because as Bradford Hinze argues, if we listen to laments in the church—especially the marginalized voices—we can "discover ways to learn from the frictions, frustrations, and failures present in the church, and how these have thwarted the intentions and aims of the church, or how these difficulties may reveal deeper aspirations and hopes behind, within, and in front of our sacred texts and traditions."[7] The affirmation of diversity in

6. Cf. Miroslav Volf, *A Public Faith: How Followers of Christ Should Serve the Common Good* (Grand Rapids, MI: Brazos, 2011), 85.

7. Bradford E. Hinze, *Prophetic Obedience: Ecclesiology for a Dialogical Church* (Maryknoll, NY: Orbis, 2016), 86.

the church is necessarily tied to a commitment to dialogue and plurality of expression and living out of the faith through pastoral practices, which reflect the cultural realities, and actual faith of people. At the same time, there is need, as the International Theological Commission highlighted, that our theological and ecclesiological models maintain some family traits, which highlight the unity of faith. [8]

I believe that the quest for a unitary method of inquiry on truth and the presupposition of a *theologia perennis* is a source of tension in the Catholic academy. This has created a gulf between pastoral ministry in parishes, the experiences of families at home, and the official teaching on faith and morals at many levels. It has also led in some cases to "double conscience" between clerics and laity who embrace different perspectives of Catholicism and morality which are in conflict with the official teaching of Rome or their local bishops.[9] Even though the Second Vatican Council tried to undo some of these unworkable structures of authority and centralization with a decisive historical approach to Catholicism, there is still within Catholicism today a strong rebuttal of any attempt to introduce diversity or dialogue to any of the doctrinal issues at the very heart of what mainline Catholicism will interpret as unchangeable and unchanging rule of faith or moral precepts.

For many Catholic hierarchs, laity, and religious who inhabit this classist mono-cultural narrative of Catholicism, there should be a homogenous canonical and moral teaching when it comes to same-sex marriage, communion for divorced and remarried Catholics whose previous marriages have not been annulled, the use of condoms to fight HIV/AIDs, birth control, celibacy, polygamy, and other burning issues of our times. This group will argue that what should be changed is the way the doctrine is presented and not its content or claims. They argue for a notion of sanctity and conformity to the Catholic faith which seems far removed from the actual faith and practice of many Catholics. The fear of mono-cultural Catholics is that the admission of diversity within Catholicism especially on some of these divisive moral issues will make her

8. "As it explores the inexhaustible Mystery of God and the countless ways in which God's grace works for salvation in diverse settings, theology rightly and necessarily takes a multitude of forms, and yet as investigations of the unique truth of the triune God and of the one plan of salvation centered on the one Lord Jesus Christ, this plurality must manifest distinctive family traits." *Theology Today: Perspectives, Principles and Criteria*, November 29, 2011, no. 2.

9. This is particularly evident with questions about marriage. See Walter Kasper, *The Gospel of the Family*. Translated by William Madges. (New York: Paulist, 2014), 20.

a denomination like other sister churches and ultimately lead to division, decay, and death of Catholicism as we know it.

There is also another important point which I want to draw attention to, that is, that while the faith and tradition of the church are grounded on some common beliefs and practices which give the church her form and identity, disagreement within the church in theology or pastoral life is not always a bad thing. Not having the answers to all questions is not bad because in a few instances the rush to give "authoritative answers" to complex questions have led the church to a certain rigidity even in matters which she and many Catholics have not fully understood. This is why dialogue, prayer, humility, patience, listening to the signs of the times, freedom of conscience, and a certain disagreement and silence are necessary in the church in dealing with the mysteries of God, world, and human nature.

Diversity presupposes disagreement and acceptance of multiple perspectives; it does not however mean confusion. The so called confusion and lack of consensus after the Synods on the family, or in AL, as well as the unresolved questions as to the reception and application of the teachings of the Second Vatican Council, are not a bad thing. In traditional society, the palaver in Africa never settles every matter; if we resolved all the questions about the faith today then what will the next generation do? And this seems to me to be a serious problem because often there is a quick approach to closing a matter through definitive answers and closing down further discussion and dialogue on certain moral issues even before the conversation had barely started.

The truth is that we are to grow into the mysteries of God. In addition, the daily moral choices which we make as Christians are directed to the ultimate purpose of the moral demand which require formation of conscience, discernment of right and wrong, God's grace, and the art of accompaniment and pastoral support and encouragement of one another, especially for those who do not live up to the ideals of faith and morality. It is true that understanding and making judgement on these mysteries is proper to magisterial teaching, the theological enterprise, and pastoral discernment. However, such judgements must be seen as open structures, always docile to the renewing light of the Holy Spirit who alone leads the church to all truths. We must be open as theologians and people of faith to the manifestations in new ways of the mystery we believe, profess, confess, live, and celebrate. This, I believe, is what Pope

Francis is inviting the church and the world to embrace in light of the challenges facing the church and families today.[10]

As then Cardinal Joseph Ratzinger so clearly demonstrated, history has shown us that no Council ever ended without disagreement and controversy. John Henry Newman for instance noted in 1870 before the First Vatican Council that "there has seldom been a Council without great confusion after it," citing five of the first ecumenical councils to validate his point.[11] Ratzinger writes about the comments attributed to Gregory of Nazianzus, a delegate at the Council of Constantinople in 381. That council added to the Nicaean creed the mention of the divinity of the Holy Spirit. Ratzinger reports that the deliberation had not ended when through the official Procopius; the Emperor invited Gregory, a significant voice in the church then for a kind of second session in 382. However, Gregory declined the invitation while responding to the emperor in these strong words: "To tell the truth, I am convinced that every assembly of bishops is to be avoided, for I have never experienced a happy ending to any council; not even the abolition of abuses...but only ambition and wrangling about what was taking place."[12] Gregory's friend, Basil, was even sharper in his criticism of what took place at the Council according to Ratzinger. Basil speaks of "the 'shocking disorder and confusion' of the council disputes, of the 'incessant chatter' that filled the whole church."[13] He argues further:

10. At the opening of the 2014 Synod on the family, Pope Francis asked the over 180 synod participants to speak freely in these words: "A basic general condition is this: to speak clearly. No one must say: 'this can't be said; he will think of me this way or that...' It is necessary to say everything that is felt with parrhesia. After the last consistory (February, 2014), in which there was a talk of the family, a Cardinal wrote to me saying: too bad that some Cardinals didn't have the courage to say some things out of respect for the pope, thinking, perhaps, that the pope thought something different. This is not good; this is not synodality, because it is necessary to say everything that in the Lord one feels should be said, with human respect, without fear. And, at the same time, one must listen with humility and receive with an open heart what the brothers say. Synodality will be exercised with these two attitudes. Therefore I ask you, please, for these attitudes of brothers in the Lord: to speak with Parrhesia and to listen with humility." https://zenit.org/articles/synod14-full-text-of-Pope-francis-opening-words/

11. Fergus Kerr, *Twentieth-Century Catholic Theologians* (Oxford: Blackwell, 2007), 204–5.

12. Cf. Joseph Ratzinger, *Principles of Catholic Theology: Building Stones for a Fundamental Theology*. Translated by Mary Frances McCarthy (San Francisco: Ignatius, 1989), 368.

13. Ratzinger, *Principles of Catholic Theology*, 369.

The Council of Nicaea, which formulated the definitive statement of the divine sonship of Jesus, was followed by a crushing
dispute that brought about the first great heresy in the Church,
that of Arianism, and, for a decade, rent the Church to her very
core. The same thing happened after the Council of Chalcedon,
which defined not only the true divinity but also the true humanity of Christ. The wound inflicted at that time is not closed
even today: the loyal heirs of the great Bishop Cyril of Alexandria felt that they had been betrayed by formulas opposed to
the tradition held sacred. As monophysite Christians, they form
even today a significant minority in the East, who by the very
fact of their existence, let us suspect something of the harshness
of the disputes of that time.[14]

Every genuine spiritual, pastoral, and theological insight is always
the fruit of deep discernment, which emerges in the purifying fire of
divine love, prayer, personal doubts, communal conversations, and questions, holy fear, and reverence. African theologians in this volume are
asserting that there are no easy answers to the questions about family life.
This is why they stretch the boundaries of theological conversation in our
churches and academies beyond the comforting reassertion of conclusions arrived at in different cultural and ecclesial settings, and challenge
the Eurocentric worldview of some of the timeworn answers to new
questions on contested moral issues.[15]

My contention is that we Africans want to worship God as Africans, not as Westerners; to think and talk about God as Africans, and to
live and celebrate the Christian faith and family life as Africans, in our
own words, in our voices, and in our own style. These are the only ways
through which the gospel comes alive for us. They also are manifestations
of the family traits of our Catholic faith and reveal the face of the God
of Jesus Christ and our ancestors while pointing to the eschatological
fruits of God's kingdom. The fifth gospel which reflects African types and
models of church as family of God and of faith and life may be strange

14. Ratzinger, *Principles of Catholic Theology*, 369.

15. "Africanisation réelle et cependant encore modeste—mais théologie propre
qui s'efforce de répondre aux questions posées par nos divers contextes historiques
et par l'évolution actuelle de nos sociétés: une pensée théologie a la fois fidèle a la
tradition authentique de l'église, attentive à la vie de nos communautés chrétiennes et
respectueuse de nos traditions . . ." Document produced as an appendix in Tharcisse T.
Tshibangu, *Le Concile Vatican II et L'Eglise Africaine: Mise en Œuvre du Concile dans
L'Eglise d'Afrique (1960–2010)*, 131.

to many outside Africa. However, in the stories of the daily struggles and joyful faith and strong hope of Africans in the trials and troubles and challenges facing African families, and in the hope which African mothers, fathers, and children display because of their faith in the Lord in the face of suffering and pain, one can see the revelation of God's presence and the surprises of the Holy Spirit.

Summary of Chapters

In chapter 1, MarySylvia Nwachukwu argues that AL should be read as a form of dialogue. Pope Francis, she proposes, is inviting us to a dialogue which begins not from our own places of comfort or unease, but from the perspective of God, the merciful and loving One. Nwachukwu uses the cultic setting of Psalm 128 to develop a biblical theology of marriage which invites us to enter into the original plan of God for marriage and the centrality and transcendence of love as both source and destiny of our Christian life, especially in the context of marriage and family life. She shows how this framework of dialogue, the movement from God to the human person, and from the human person back to God structures the chapters and message of AL.

Nwachukwu invites readers to go beyond divisive reading of AL to a deeper appreciation of the biblical depths which Pope Francis demonstrates in bringing out the beauty of divine love reflected in God's initiative toward us through the covenant. This is the dynamic which is at work in AL. It is important to understand this biblical dynamic so as to see marriage and family life from the perspectives of God and how our human context can be understood as intimately connected to God's plan for each person. This helps us, she argues, to see what gifts God has offered humanity and the church for healing a divided and wounded world. AL is an apostolic exhortation that gets its inspiration from the life and virtues of God. It proposes moral choices for individuals and families and pastoral plans that correspond with God's dream, which is captured in AL through the language of mercy, encouragement, and hope.

Gabriel Tata (chapter 4 of AL) and Barnabas Shabayang (chapter 5 of AL) address the theological, epistemological, moral, and anthropological foundations of Christian marriage. Tata in chapter 5 shows that love has an anthropological and communitarian foundation in the African world and is a pulsating dynamic in Africa today, which requires a greater appreciation. He draws from Yoruba culture in West Africa to show that Christian humanism when translated into African context is about relationship and abundant life. Family as the primary center for Christian humanism is characterized by relationships which help to build and bind relationships in the wider community. He proposes that deepening the relationship in families should be a central pastoral concern. Such an approach cannot be conceived without at the same time deepening the relationship in the church and wider society in such a way that the pains of the family become the pain of the church.

In chapter 6, Barnabas Shabayang explores the wealth of African Christian life and how this shapes African consciousness on the sociocultural celebration of the uniqueness of a child's birth. The gift of a child in Africa can be gleaned from the naming rituals in African traditional society and the celebration of the Eucharist in African churches as the divine meal of community. Just as people share the sacred meal of the Eucharist as a communion of love and friendship between humans themselves and between them and God, so is the sharing in the joy of the birth of a new child a Eucharistic moment in African societies. This, he points out, has serious implications for how building up families and the transmission and bestowal of divine and ancestral blessings could lead to love made fruitful in child bearing. He proposes how the African communal DNA of family life could be introduced into the appropriation of AL. This could be achieved by developing a deeper anthropological foundation of marriage, rooted in the Trinitarian life, Eucharistic spirituality, and in joyfully welcoming children through a culture of life and strong practices of prayer and faith formation for children.

In the second commentary on chapter 3 of AL, Bonaventure Ugwu develops an African theology of the body as a starting point for recovering the intimate connection between married couples themselves, their children, the church, the wider community, and the world. Love is more than a word. In this light, Ugwu grounds the development of family values and the foundation of love and family on this anthropology of incorporation and bondedness in the life of each other and in God. This is why childlessness seen as the inability to generate life is a serious challenge for families in African communities. Ugwu's recommendations on how to build relationship in the midst of social changes in African families, how to meet the challenges of poverty ravaging many families, and a pastoral commitment to initiating children and married couples deeper into the mysteries of the faith and ongoing formation are worthy of consideration.

Central to the discussion of the chapters in this volume is a constant return to the cultural questions and how cultural forces effect marriages in Africa and in the world. Along the same line is the concern on how to translate the teachings of the church so that they can capture the cultural imagination of people and inspire them to make sound moral judgments to meet these challenges. This is the backdrop of the commentaries by Nicholaus Segeja (chapter 2), Vincent Arisukwu (chapter 4), and Eunice Kamaara and Emily Kerama (chapter 7).

Segeja identifies three interrelated realities that Pope Francis correlates when discussing the challenges of families. Reading the signs of times seems to be the key source and point of departure in understanding the truth and hope that the church should communicate in relation to the challenges of families today. It is precisely this source that also determines the self-understanding of the church as it relates to the variety of situations and challenges afflicting marriage and family life today. Thus, in Segeja's opinion, Pope Francis proposes a new method and attitude, essentially pastoral in its nature and basically open to African insights that would require a different way of approach to the challenges of the families in concrete situations. He argues that meeting the challenges of families today will require "a reverential-dialogue approach," and an honest and committed search for effective pastoral approaches to challenges facing families in their concrete life situation.

Vincent Arisukwu, who runs a family life ministry in the Archdiocese of Baltimore, develops his approach to the cultural questions by an impressive survey of the teaching of the church on the family since the Second Vatican Council. He identifies the continuity and development of the church's teaching on marriage and family life. Drawing from experiences of families in the US, Europe and Africa, he shows how cultural forces affect contemporary families and the distinctive features of African approaches to addressing these challenges which can act as models for the World Church. His essay shows how marriage and family life are seen among different cultures in Africa and how the images of the family in Christianity relate to these cultural images and perfect them. Amidst all the challenges of contemporary cultures, Arisukwu sees in the family the hope for humanity and grounds this assertion in theological and cultural foundations while giving a road map of what a pastoral approach to family ministry would look like in World Christianity.

In chapter 7, Eunice Kamaara and Emily Kerama two outstanding African lay female theologians and social scientists with interests in religious studies, marriage, gender issues, and poverty complement from very experiential perspectives what is often a terrain of discourse on marriage and family life dominated in Catholicism by unmarried men and women (clergy and religious). They identify some neglected topics in chapter 7 of AL that are pertinent issues of concern to Africa including, but not limited to, condom use—especially in the context of HIV/AIDS—polygamy, celibacy of priests, corruption, youth unemployment, and radicalization, among others. However, they agree with Pope Francis's project on the future of the family, especially on creativity and contextualization of family apostolate with concrete pastoral actions which appeal to specific cultural contexts and values. For the African context, they propose a move beyond theoretical discussions on inculturation to practical integration of African traditional values with Christian values and they share a model from Kenya, the African Christian Initiation Program (ACIP). ACIP is a pastoral formation and care program that supports adolescents to effectively transition into responsible adult members of the society. It is a practical reconstruction of traditional rites and rituals through which the values of relationships and community are inculcated to integrate them with Christian values.

Richard Rwiza (chapter 8), Stan Chu Ilo (chapter 9) and Leonida Katunge (chapter 10) comment on chapters 7, 8, and 9 of AL. Dr. Rwiza focuses on the education of children. He points at the centrality of children in traditional African families and the place accorded to them in the church and society. He proposes that the integral education of children in Africa will require integrating different theories of social development and cultural approaches to socialization in African culture and the church's own diverse means for faith formation. What is clear from Rwiza's chapter is a commitment to holistic formation, and a sensitivity to the challenges facing child upbringing today, especially the cultural, social, and economic pressures on family. In addition, he calls on the church in Africa to work towards providing the family with all the means for meeting these challenges, and also the need to explore deeper the riches of Catholic educational traditions in shaping future citizens.

Stan Chu Ilo discusses chapter 8 of AL. Many people have pointed out that this is the most controversial chapter of AL and it is the one that has drawn so many comments, commendations, and criticisms including the *dubias* sent by Cardinal Burke and a few other cardinals. Ilo argues that this chapter offers the hermeneutic for reading the whole of the document because here Pope Francis develops the logic of integration and the logic of mercy. These follow the see-judge-act structure through three steps: discerning the difficulties in people's lives; accompanying them in those difficulties with compassion and care; and pastoral ministry which is able to integrate them into the community. The goal of AL, Ilo proposes, is an invitation to pastoral discernment and praxis which is capable of healing the wounds of sin and division, and restoring people's dignity and appreciation of their calling as members of God's family. It is within this logic of integration, love, and mercy that Ilo develops a theology of accompaniment which could be enriched with the African sense of community, participation, and *ubuntu* in overcoming the contentious issues around annulment, and communion for divorced and separated Catholics, polygamists, and those in same-sex unions.

Sr. Katunge's chapter is spiced with stories of the everyday living realities of families in Africa. Like Pope Francis, she shows how African spirituality can both grow from the experience of suffering and hope in the daily struggles of the family, and bring about transformational pastoral ministry of healing and hope to families. African Christian spirituality, Katunge proposes, can help address the many unresolved questions in Africa today on polygamy, dignity and rights of women, communion, fidelity, divorce, and hospitality, preparation for marriage, taboos in family, funeral rites, same-sex unions, and barrenness.

Katunge calls for a more experiential approach to entering into people's stories similar to what she and many other pastoral agents, especially those working with the small Christian communities (scc), do in their daily encounter with people in their homes and places of pain and hope. She proposes a pastoral approach of dialogue and listening to those in difficult situations rather than a quick and negative judgment about their situation. She points to the challenges of annulment in African families and emphasizes the need to strengthen families through formation and ongoing pastoral support to equip families with the moral and personal virtues and strength for meeting the challenges and cultural pressure facing modern families.

These essays are hopeful and pastoral. They are offered as a beginning of a conversation rather than conclusive statements and generalizations about faith and life. They are also illustrative in nature, moving from the concrete experiences of families, to designing a portrait of how pastoral ministries to families will look like in following the principles of AL. They are an invitation from Africa to African Christians and the worldwide church to look beyond divisive debates to a renewal of faith and life in the church today in the spirit of Vatican II, as translated in the priorities and practices of Pope Francis. It is a courageous call to people to enter into the spirit of the illuminative ecclesiology of Pope Francis. It is, finally, a humble invitation from Africa to the worldwide church to behold the emerging light of hope which is shining from the beautiful continent of Africa in the way her Christians celebrate marriage and family life with joy and fidelity even though they are often surrounded by uncertainty, puzzling life situations, and complex social conditions.

Stan Chu Ilo
Divine Mercy Sunday, April 23, 2017

1

Marriage and Family in the Light of the Word of God: Interpreting the First Chapter of *Amoris Laetitia*

M A R Y S Y L V I A   N W A C H U K W U

Introduction

The title of the papal Apostolic Exhortation, *Amoris Laetitia* (AL),[1] resounds and recalls the joy that love awakens in a couple. The vibrations of the heart, the focus on the object of love which accompany the neglect of other realities, the total gift of self and the joy of every new encounter with the loved one; all these describe the joy of love. In this exhortation, Ps 128 and Gen 1:26–28; 2:24 are singled out as key interpretive texts,[2] and with the leading idea that the husband and wife image God in many ways, Pope Francis invites couples in love to consider these joyful sentiments and expressions as invitations to enter into the heart of love, which is God's life.

The interpretation of this chapter is done here in five sections. After this introduction, section one explains the story line of the chapter.

1. Henceforth, *Amoris Laetitia* is represented with the acronym AL in the body of the text.

2. 1 Cor 13 will become a key interpretive text in the fourth chapter of the exhortation.

The second section is biblical-theological interpretation of the chapter through a broadened description of backgrounds of Ps 128 and of themes drawn from the story line of the chapter. A better appreciation of the strength and weakness of AL is shown in the third and fourth sections where this first chapter is read within the context of the entire exhortation and of previous papal documents on the theme of family. The last section concludes this essay with some proposals for pastoral action in Africa.

The Biblical Foundation and the Story Line of the Chapter

The first chapter of AL titled "In the Light of the Word" exposes the biblical foundations on which Pope Francis proposes a way of life for families in the light of contemporary challenges. It is an interesting commentary on biblical texts that are given as foundational to marriage and to the family. Of all encyclicals and exhortations dedicated to marriage and family since *Casti Connubii* of Pius XI in 1930, AL is the only one that has a chapter dedicated to the biblical foundation of marriage and the family. More interesting is a handling that makes the entire Bible look like a book on marriage and the family. This depiction of the Bible strikes the reader immediately at the very first paragraph of the chapter (AL 8). According to Pope Francis, the Bible's first two chapters (Gen 1–2) usher in family stories of birth, love, and crises which fill the Bible, and the stories culminate in the presentation of the wedding feast of the bride and the Lamb (Rev 21). From this description, the family appears in the Bible as the first gospel and the first stage of God's plan of salvation.[3] By showing that family stories and images introduce and conclude the Bible, Pope Francis clearly underlines the vital place and importance of marriage and family in God's plan.[4] This presentation gave impetus to a reinterpretation of biblical texts in AL from the perspective of family.

Ps 128 provides the story line of the chapter. The thematic content of this psalm is used in AL to divide the chapter into different sections. The psalm develops five themes: the blessedness of a man (Ps 128:1, 4), which reverberates on four fundamental relationships: his relationship with the

3. See the first chapters of the Old and New Testaments (Gen 1–2; Matt 1:18–25; Luke 1–2).

4. In biblical interpretation and exegesis, this literary device is called enveloping. When a symbol, image or text is found at the beginning and end of a scriptural unit, it is important for the interpretation of the entire unit.

soil (Ps 128:2), his relationship with his wife (Ps 128:3a), his relationship with his children (Ps 128:3b, 6a), and his relationship with the society (Ps 128:5, 6b). Chapter 1 of AL reflects these themes in the thirteen paragraphs of its six sections (i) the liturgical setting for marriage in which the man is pronounced "Blessed" (AL 8), (ii) the man and his wife (AL 9–13), (iii) the couple and their children (AL 14–18), (iv) the dignity of human labor and family crises (AL 19–23), and (v) labor and societal development (AL 24–26). These five sections end with some concluding remarks on renewed call to discipleship (AL 27–30).

The second key interpretive biblical text is Gen 1:26–28 and 2:24, introduced with the principal idea that "the human couple" is the image of God. With this text, Pope Francis explains the various ways in which the relationship of the human couple provides the means for understanding and describing the mystery of God (AL 11).

Biblical-Theological Interpretation of the Chapter

The Interlocutor

In presenting the biblical foundation, Pope Francis meant to dialogue with an interlocutor, a real, not an imaginary married couple, when he invited all "to enter one of those houses . . . to cross the threshold of this tranquil home . . ." (AL 8, 9). This dimension of the exhortation to dialogue with historical persons with specific identity is very necessary, given the different definitions of marriage today by diverse ideological movements in contemporary times. One of such definitions is explicitly mentioned in chapter 2 (AL 56): "Yet another challenge is posed by the various forms of an ideology of gender that "denies the difference and reciprocity in nature of man and a woman and envisages a society without sexual differences, thereby eliminating the anthropological basis of the family.""

Among other observations, Pope Francis could be making a strong but silent statement against the growing popularity of same-sex marriages being adopted by even nations with deeply Christian roots. Matt 19:4, which the pontiff cites at this stage, proves this point and reaffirms God's original plan that a married couple is necessarily composed of two persons of the opposite sex, male and female, united as one flesh (Gen 2:24). The couple in question is real, not imaginary, because they have a personal story of love that is historical. Their story makes them more interlocutors than addressees. This historical note changes the tone of the entire exhortation.

I will note here that Pope Francis, rather than insisting on doctrine, concentrates on a pastoral message of encouragement, consolation and hope to all families, especially those that are undergoing suffering. As interlocutors and not listeners, the couple contributes in no small measure to the development of the discussion with their life experiences.[5] Here, one notes immediately the experiential dimension of this exhortation. Pope Francis is inviting the entire church to enter into the daily stories of modern families and allow these stories to open our eyes and senses to the presence of God in the daily realities of family, even in the brokenness we may find in these stories. The diversity and nature of these stories are to be noted, especially when we see them in the light of the Trinity which is the source, foundation and goal of all families.

Psalm 128 and Its Background

This section of the work exposes the different backgrounds of the key text Ps 128, in order to highlight the rich and varied meanings they add to the discussion on family and marriage.

The Cultic Setting of Psalm 128

At the beginning of chapter 1 of AL, Ps 128 is introduced as a hymn that leads the wedding procession, which "resounds in Jewish and Christian wedding liturgies." As a characteristic "Song of Ascents," Ps 128 is replete with family motifs and it appears like a hymn of blessing to a couple about to enter into wedlock. Although the original setting of the psalm is cultic,[6] it was not originally intended for wedding ceremonies.[7] It is possible that this post-exilic psalm,[8] with its concern for family, came

5. The historical experiences of the couple is the topic of the second chapter of AL.

6. This is the view of some scholars, for instance, Lipinski, "Macarismes et psaumes," 347–48. For the various views, see Allen, "Psalms 101–150," 183.

7. In the psalter, Ps 128 forms a pair with Ps 127, and both, with clear wisdom motifs, serve didactic functions. Both share common family motifs, being connected especially through the idea of "building a house" in verse 1: "If the Lord does not build the house . . ." which refers metaphorically to raising a family.

8. The incorporation of the "shalom" formula in verse 6b and the mixed form of the psalm support its post-exilic context. See Westermann, *Genesis 12–36*, 184.

to be used also for wedding liturgies as scheme for building a blessed home.[9] Of all papal encyclicals or exhortations dedicated to the family, AL is unique in using this psalm as an invitation to embrace marriage according to God's original plan. Implicitly, the use of this psalm, with its setting in the liturgy, draws attention to the meaning of marriage as primarily a religious institution. Therefore, the first line of the psalm is used here to encourage couples to begin their married life with the divine blessing which the liturgy mediates. By doing this, they are led to accept God's original design for marriage.

The *ashre* formula ("Happy is . . .") at the beginning of the psalm performs a number of functions in its cultic setting.[10] Composed as a beatitude, the psalm served a pedagogical tool for teaching from concrete human experience,[11] and as an implicit exhortation that refers to an ideal to emulate.[12] Specifically, Ps 128 is a wisdom teaching to pilgrims who participate in a religious festival in Jerusalem. On arrival at the sanctuary, the pilgrim is welcomed with congratulatory greetings (verses 1–3), and verse 4 is a rubric (*This is how a man is blessed*)[13] that introduces the blessing conferred on the pilgrim (verses 5–6).[14] In the first part of the psalm (verses 1–3), the double beatitude in verses 1–2 hangs on the fulfilment of two important conditions, that is, to fear the Lord and walk in his ways. In the Wisdom Literature, the expression, "fear of the Lord" means a person's proper and obedient response to God. The other terminology, "walk in his ways," is a language for personal relationship not strictly defined by obedience to concrete individual laws. A similar expression is found in Gen 17:1 (⊠*ālāk lipnê*—literally, "walk before me"),

9. As AL says at the beginning of the first chapter, "Let us now enter one of those houses, led by the Psalmist with a song that even today resounds in both Jewish and Christian wedding liturgies" (AL 8).

10. In the Old Testament, the formula occurs more frequently in the Psalms and the book of Proverbs where it refers to one who has received God's favor or blessing, the sanctuary being the place where blessing is mediated. Together with another motif ("*derek*"—way), *ashre* is an important wisdom motif that makes Ps 128 a traditional wisdom psalm. See Allen, "Psalms 101–150," 185.

11. Crenshaw, *Old Testament Wisdom*, 23–26.

12. See W. Janzen, "AŠRÊ in the Old Testament," 215–26; Perdue, *Wisdom and Cult*, 328.

13. See a similar rubric in Num 6:23.

14. The phrase "the man who fears the Lord" in verses 1 and 4 are indicators of beginning of separate strophes. See "Division of the Psalm" in Allen, "Psalms 101–150," 183–84.

where it presents God's instruction to Abraham to live in such a way that every of his single steps is made with reference to God.[15] The meaning of these two terms shows that they relate in a synonymous manner. To fear the Lord is to walk in his ways, and obviously, to "walk in his ways" is to adopt a way of life in conformity with God's design.[16] One could conclude that the two expressions point to a religiously motivated life, a fundamental option to adhere to God's ways. Such a life would surely attract achievement in the basics of life which the psalm describes: fertility, good harvest and general wellbeing.

It is important to explain how the *ashre* formula relates to the language of blessing in the second part of the psalm. The structure of the psalm shows a correspondence between the God-fearer who is proclaimed happy (verses 1–2) and the one who is blessed (verse 4).[17] In biblical tradition, the language of blessing spells out both the invitation to share in God's life and the mission such a status confers on the beneficiary.[18] The sign of such relationship with God is fruitfulness, evidenced in the continuation of the person's generation, through whom God promotes his project, and their general wellbeing. This is evident in both the patriarchal and Mosaic traditions where God's blessing is connected to the promise of innumerable seed and wellbeing in God's land.[19] In the Wisdom tradition, as Ps 128 shows, the context for blessing is cultic, being connected to the sanctuary or Zion (verse 5) as the earthly link to Yahweh and a medium of the bestowal of such blessing.[20] The cultic setting implies that God, in deed, is the origin of the fortunes of the God-fearer. This explains the goal of Ps 128 as a psalm of pilgrimage. The second part of the psalm further shows that the continuation of blessing depends on the survival of the holy city with its religious traditions (verse 5) and the unbroken chain of the community from generation to genera-

15. This priestly tradition represents a period in which God's commands are no longer passed on as concrete instructions but are directed to a person's entire life and existence in relation to God. See Westermann, *Genesis 12–36*, 259.

16. The emphasis is more on lived life rather than observance of specific laws.

17. The double beatitude in verses 1–2 corresponds with the double language of blessing in the second part of the psalm (verses 4–5).

18. In the creation account of Gen 1:1–2:4a and in the account of the call of Abraham in Gen 12:1–3, the language of blessing fulfills these two functions.

19. See Gen 12:1–3; Deut 6:18; 11:8–9. Explicit connection between blessing and progeny is found in Deut 7:13, "I will bless you and give you increase."

20. See Allen, "Psalms 101–150," 185.

tion (verse 6).[21] Therefore, the holy city and its cult have vital roles to play in the assurance of God's blessing for the people.

The content of the exhortation of Ps 128 also draws attention to a Deuteronomic background.[22] In addition to having the exhortatory tone of the Deuteronomic tradition, Ps 128, with its concern for family, also uses the language of Deuteronomy to describe the blessings which obedience to God attracts—fruitfulness of the womb (Ps 128:3; Deut 7:12), fruit of human labor (Ps 128:2; Deut 8:7–10), general wellbeing and long life in the land (Ps 128:5; Deut 5:33; 6:2). In its verse 2, the psalm repeats a purpose clause which is typical of Deuteronomy, "so that it may go well with you" (Deut 6:3,18; 12:28). In fact, the psalm represents the Deuteronomic teaching according to which fear of the Lord and obedience are the essence of religion and condition for inheritance of blessing and wellbeing (Deut 5:29 and 10:12).[23] The teaching of Ps 128 and its cultic setting seem, therefore, to be part of the concerted effort of the post-exilic Jewish community to exhort families on a life lived in total conformity with God's law.

The Deuteronomic Background and Didactic Function of Psalm 128

The didactic function of Ps 128 is more comprehensibly seen from its Deuteronomic background. Biblical texts connected to this background share similar goals with Deuteronomy, which is to interpret the meaning of the exodus event, to exhort on the blessings of obedience to God's law in a time of gross infidelity in the land and to endorse the teaching office of Moses and his successors.[24] Texts such as Deut 4:14; 5:23–31; 29:1; 31:19,28 highlight the position of Moses as custodian and teacher

---

21. Since the psalm is post-exilic, this could be an aspect of the reward for obedience to God. Therefore, "Zion" and "Jerusalem" in verse 5 being references to the sanctuary and the city respectively.

22. Ps 128 encloses certain recurrent themes which are found in Deuteronomy and Wisdom Literature. These are: fear of the Lord (Prov 1:7; Job 28:28), pedagogical function in the areas of cultic teaching on the law (Deut 6:4–9) and transmission of faith to the children (Deut 6:7; 9:20–25; 11:19; Prov 2:1; 2:1; 4:1). See Mayes, *Deuteronomy*, 151.

23. See Mayes, *Deuteronomy*, 151, 179; Fuhs, "Yārēh," 313–14.

24. AL does not discuss the teaching office of the church as previous papal documents on the family do, but it does it implicitly by using Ps 128 as key text. See the paragraph on "*Amoris Laetitia* and Previous Papal Documents . . ." below.

of the sacred traditions and laws which God gave to the people.[25] Within the book of Deuteronomy, a text like Deut 6:31 is very significant in this regard. God tells Moses, ". . . I shall tell you all the commandments, the laws and the customs which you are to teach them and which they are to observe in the country which I am giving them as their possession." At the end of his ministry, Moses committed the teaching of Israel's sacred traditions to the care of Levites (Deut 31:24) and of heads of families (Deut 32:45–47). He did this amidst fears that the Israelites might abandon the ways of the Lord after his death (Deut 4:25–26; 31:27, 29). With this, the transmission of Israel's most sacred traditions was ensured from generation to generation. Such transmission also happened around night gatherings and during festivals as elders and professional story tellers handed over those traditions to the younger generation (see Deut 6:20–25). Given the focus on the family, the cultic setting in which this psalm is used was part of a systematic catechesis to Israelite families on God's law and Israel's sacred traditions. Ps 128 shows further that one of the contexts for such teaching is the marriage ceremony.

The Content of AL's Teaching on Marriage

The exposition of the cultic and Deuteronomic backgrounds of Ps 128 highlights very important ideas which are not immediately deducible in AL,[26] and which would enrich the understanding of the entire exhortation. These backgrounds draw attention to an age of gross infidelity to God's law which made necessary a catechetical project on Israel's sacred traditions in liturgical contexts. The psalm's backgrounds, therefore, bring out more clearly both the teaching office of the church as custodian of God's law and the content of that teaching. In using Ps 128 as a key text in AL, Pope Francis shares a similar goal with the Deuteronomic tradition when he speaks of the presence of ideologies that devalue marriage and family, and of a cultural decline which encourages extreme individualism and fails to promote love and self-giving (AL 33–39). While the cultures of same-sex marriage and single parenthood continue to grow in popularity, with so much being proposed under the guise of individual

25. The admonition to listen (Deut 4:1; 6:3,4; 7:12; 9:1; 27:9) underscores the pedagogical context.

26. Ideas such as (a) defense of the teaching office of the church; (b) the church as legitimate custodian of sacred traditions revealed by God; (c) the faithful transmission of these sacred traditions from generation to generation.

or civil rights, the pope sees the need to redirect and situate the dialogue on marriage in its proper context—the word of God which explains God's design from the beginning of creation (Gen 1:26–28). The use of Ps 128 in this exhortation further establishes the function of the liturgical setting of marriage as an occasion for teaching the couple and the people of God the specific vocation of the family within God's creative and salvific design. While the pope used this psalm to renew divine blessings of obedience for anyone who would embrace marriage according to God's original design, he draws the content of that teaching from these two key texts as the paragraphs below show.

Genesis 1:26–28 and 2:24: The Married Couple as Image of God

The presence of similar themes in Ps 128 and Gen 1 and 2 prove that the psalm is a re-interpretation of the message of Genesis for post-exilic Israelite families. Both texts share similar concerns, which is to mediate divine blessings to families who live according to God's plan. They are used here as foundational texts, which disclose the profound meaning upon which the institution of marriage is founded. After crossing "the threshold of this tranquil home," the very first text Pope Francis addressed himself to is Gen 1:26–28. According to him, this text "presents the human couple in its deepest reality" (AL 10). The first founding statement about the couple is that God created them in his image (Gen 1:26). As important as it is in the interpretation of the relationship between God and human beings, the image motif in Gen 1:26 has received various and varied interpretations.[27] Primarily, this motif functions to distinguish human beings from other creatures, having been created to have a special relationship with God which serves the wellbeing of other creatures. From this primary meaning derives the interpretation that human beings, created male and female, are God's representative or regent in a manner that reflects the actions of God.[28] From the beginning, therefore, the significance of marriage is grounded in the meaning disclosed by the word of God, whereby the married couple become a special means of

27. See interpretations by W. Brueggemann, *Theology of the Old Testament*. G. J. Wenham lists five main proposals of interpretation: natural qualities in man, mental and spiritual faculties, physical resemblance, representational function, and relational capacity. See Wenham, *Genesis 1–15*, 29–31.

28. For the many views of scholars on this topic, see Nwachukwu, *Creation–Covenant Scheme*, 61–64.

representing God in the world. This implies that the primary task of the couple is to live in a manner that replicates God's life as a unique communion of persons and as life giving principle. Pope Francis's interpretation of these texts in AL 10–13 reveals ways in which the human couple is the image of God:

a) The image of God is the human couple, composed necessarily as male and female (Gen 1:27). This statement is made against any sexist interpretation of God's nature or any prejudice to God's transcendence. It simply underscores the constitution of the human couple as essentially male and female. Any marital union short of this human constitutional differentiation, which symbolizes their completeness,[29] is not a reflection of God's image. Matt 19:4 is Jesus's confirmation of this divine design for marriage.

b) The human couple is also truly the image of God in their fruitfulness, that is, their ability to open themselves and their love to new life. The fruitfulness of the couple is in many ways a visible sign of God's creative act and symbol of God's inner life. The triune God is family, constituted of father, Son and Spirit, a communion of love … (AL 11). Here, the idea of fruitfulness corresponds with the terminology of blessing in Ps 128:4–5, which in biblical tradition is connected both to progeny and to God's project in the world.

c) Thirdly, Gen 2:24 evokes the marital union between the couple in their voluntary self-giving in love, and as united as one flesh. Herein lies the joy and the burden of the marital union, the aptitude for reciprocal self-surrender. According to Pope Francis, the couple image God most in their capacity for self-surrender. Both creation and salvation are possible, thanks to God's act of self-giving. The direct encounter and union of hearts and life between the couple also reflects our union with God, because the man clings to his wife just as the human soul clings to God (AL 12–13). In clinging to his wife, the man realizes that the full meaning of life is achieved through communion; that is, through relationship in which one exists with and for someone. Citing also Eph 5:21, Pope Francis implies that what is required here is the mutual submission of the couples.

---

29. Gen 1 is a wisdom text which characteristically designates reality as the pairing of opposites: darkness and light, heaven and earth, day and night, male and female, tree of good and evil. These opposites designate totality and completeness.

The foregoing interpretation of Gen 1:26–28 within the liturgical context suggested by Ps 128 is an assertion of the most fundamental meaning of marriage. It underlines that through the liturgical ceremony, the couple is inserted sacramentally into the life of the Trinity, and in the occasion, they are given the mission to participate in God's creative project and to build a union nurtured by reciprocal self-giving. The couple's capacity to build communion through total self-gift to each other is the essence of their reflection of God's image. In underscoring these dimensions of the image motif, Pope Francis justifiably and by implication exhorts against attitudes and cultural practices which contradict them, such as, unions contracted without the blessing of the liturgical setting, unions that reject openness to new life, and cultural practices that place more value on the couple's ability to bear children rather than on their capacity for reciprocal self-surrender and communion. In order to explain how the couple, having been inserted in God's life, participate in God's creative project, Pope Francis returns to the message of Ps 128.

The Home: Your Wife, Your Children, and The Labor of Your Hands

The presence of children invites other responsibilities conferred on them through blessing.[30] Blessing gives human beings the ability to guide all created realities to their respective purposes in God's plan, "be fruitful, multiply, fill the earth and subdue it" (Gen 1:28). Therefore, in AL 14–18, the Pontiff describes the different ways in which God's blessing gives the human couple specific roles towards others and towards the society.

The Home of the Blessed: A Domestic Church

Ps 128 depicts a concrete home where husband and wife are seated at table with children, who represent the foundations of that home.[31] The use of symbols of the vine and the olive to describe this home are clear references to the community of God's people.[32] This home, with a divinely

30. See notes 18 and 19 above. In Gen 1:27–28, God's blessing for human beings differ from the blessing given to animals. True to its biblical meaning, God's blessing does not only confer the power to procreate; it also confers a sense of mission.

31. See Ps 127:1–5.

32. The prophets use these symbols to describe Israel's relationship with God. See notes 33–34 below.

oriented goal is a domestic church, a home filled with God's blessing, a setting for the Eucharist, a home in which children receive their first lessons in the faith.[33] The psalm safeguards the role of parents in the transmission of God's way of life to their children (Deut 4:9; 6:7,20).[34] The symbols by which this domestic church is depicted are further interpreted in the paragraphs below.

Your Wife Like a Fruitful Vine (Psalm 128:3a)

The vine is frequently mentioned in the Bible as a known cultivated plant in Israel. Every element of this plant is useful: the leaves are edible; the sweet and juicy fruits, which grow in large clusters, may be consumed fresh or dried as raisins and currants. Wine or vinegar is made from its juice, while the remainder of the plant is used for fodder. The prophets considered the vine as a symbol of peace and prosperity,[35] and of Israel as a nation.[36] This symbol draws attention to the many traits in the woman by whose resourcefulness the home thrives and is sustained in peace. It refers not only to her fertility but also to her unitive relevance as a woman. The Wisdom Literature recommends this image of the ideal wife as an important pedagogy for building peaceful and meaningful homes.[37] Like the vine, the woman spends all that she is for nurturing her family, and through her unreserved attention and commitment to every member and every aspect of the family.[38]

This description offered here of a woman's domestic role is growing very unpopular, thanks to the activities of individuals and institutions that broke the chains which confined women solely to the domestic sphere.[39] The efforts of these institutions have empowered women to

---

33. This insight is drawn from Ps 128:4–5, "Thus shall the man be blessed who fears the Lord. The Lord bless you from Zion." See AL, 15 and 16.

34. A major item in the great commandment is respect for and submission to parental guidance and authority, "Honor your father and your mother" (Deut 5:16).

35. See Mic 4:4; 1 Kgs 4:25.

36. See Jer 2:21; Ezek 15:6; Hos 10:1.

37. See Prov 31:10–31.

38. AL 24 appraises the labor of mothers.

39. Until the twentieth century, women's roles were defined in procreative terms, confined to the home, and made object of pleasure and exploitation. John XXIII lists the sudden entry of women into public life among the signs of the times. See John XXIII, Encyclical Letter, *Pacem in Terris*, 22. As the modern society experience the

build up an image and status that enable them to contribute to the development of the human society and to participate successfully in different spheres of life, areas that were previously reserved only for men.[40] This breaking of barriers is welcomed in modern society as progressive. While commitments in defense of women's rights and interests continue, I suggest here that every investigation into the plan of God about marriage should also include what constitutes women's role in that divine plan. I find this stated in the narrative of the second account of creation.

The second account of creation (Gen 2:4–25) is like a drama of two scenes (verses 15–17 and 18–24), introduced by a long preface (verses 4–16) and a short conclusion (verse 25). The first scene represents the woeful attempt to run the affairs of the human family without the involvement of the woman. The second scene begins with a divine assessment of the inappropriateness of this earlier attempt, "it is not good . . ." (verse 18), which is a divergence in the divine evaluation that concludes the first creation account, "God saw all he had made, and in deed it was very good" (Gen 1:31).[41] Although the drama of the second scene is presented as an after-thought in God's plan,[42] the story is told to draw attention to what is proper to a woman's mission according to God's plan, which is, that the good or overall wellbeing of creation is not complete without her.[43] Moreover, as "the mother of all the living" (Gen 3:20), every human institution, especially the human family, needs to be blessed by the touch of a woman's maternal instinct in order to experience wholeness.[44]

---

gradual collapse of sex-determined roles, the role and position of women in the church still remains one of the most controversial issues, a challenge with great pastoral implications.

40. See Scaraffia, "Socio-Cultural Changes in Women's Lives," 15–22.

41. In the first and second creation stories, the Hebrew word "tov" (translated as "good") designates what corresponds with the cosmic order and what is in harmony with God's original design for creation. See Nwachukwu, *Creation-Covenant Scheme*, 58.

42. A similar literary device is found in Gen 6:5, which says that God is sorry to have made mankind. The story that follows this divine evaluation represents the view point that accords with God's plan.

43. The meaning of the text will elude anyone whose interpretation is guided by any form of cultural bias. This text should be understood in the light of the Yahwist attempt to explain the origin of the frustrations which human beings encounter in life.

44. According to John Paul II, "the presence of the feminine element, alongside the male element and together with it, signifies an enrichment for man in the whole perspective of his history, including the history of salvation." See John Paul II, *The Theology of the Body*, 49.

Herein lies an evident weakness in the message of AL. The interpretation of the symbol of the vine that is offered here complements the almost lack of attention given to it in AL. The exhortation contains only but a very brief appraisal of woman's labor in its twenty-fourth paragraph. A more generous appreciation of the feminine genius would not have been out of place in an exhortation located in an extraordinary Jubilee year of Mercy,[45] especially since the message of the jubilee projected women's natural capacities, such as their maternal solicitude, ability to live the values of compassion, tenderness and care of life in all of its forms.

Your Children Like Olive Shoots (Psalm 128:3b)

The second part of chapter 1 (AL 14–18) speaks of children as the sign of continuity of the family from generation to generation. Children, described as olive shoots or branches, are a sign of growth in the life of the couple and of the domestic church. The olive tree is known for being ever green through all seasons, with its numerous branches clustering around the main trunk. As a figurative representation of children, the olive shoots symbolize God's provision of life, health, fruitfulness and wholeness to the family. Therefore, as branches that spring from and derive nutrient from the olive trunk, children depend on parents to achieve the purpose of their existence.[46] By implication, the olive branch depicts a task to be accomplished. The required pruning of the branches in order for them to bear much fruit, and the crushing of the fruit and its seed to produce oil; all these describe the great and sensitive tasks involved in the proper upbringing of children and their education in faith traditions. Like the olive trunk, the couple is expected to remain ever green in order to withstand challenges that might present themselves.[47] In a parent-child relationship, children also learn to respect their parents

45. The terminology of mercy in Francis's *Misericordiae Vultus* describes God's maternal solicitude for creation (1–18).

46. The olive tree also points beyond itself. It is used for lighting the Temple, the anointing of kings, the anointing of the sick and for the blessing of God's people for various purposes. See Ps 92:10; Isa 10:27; Mark 6:13; Rom 10:17; Jas 5:14–15. Insights in this paragraph are taken from Trever, "Olive Tree."

47. See Exod 12:26–27; 13:14; Deut 6:20–25; Ps 78:3–6; 148:12. The pedagogical responsibility of parents is brought out more clearly in the book of Proverbs, a biblical sapiential book that is dedicated to the transmission of wisdom to the young. See Prov 3:11–12; 6:20–22; 13:1; 22:15; 23:13–14; 29:17.

and to fulfill family and social commitments.[48] In the life of Jesus, we see a confirmation of divine arrangement of these parent-children responsibilities in his own life. Without neglecting the obedience he owed his parents,[49] Jesus showed that a child's life is an essential part of God's project for his kingdom in the world.[50]

By the Labor of Your Hands (Psalm 128:2)

Human labor is a necessary requirement for the building of a home. According to the foundational text of Gen 2, work is not an option for humans; it is part of the essence of being human and a requirement for human dignity and wellbeing (Gen 2:15).[51] The wellbeing of society also depends very much on human labor. Ps 128:2 introduces the *pater familias*, a laborer who sustains the family wellbeing through the work of his hands: "You shall eat the fruit of the labor of your hands; you shall be happy, and it shall be well with you." This hope expressed in the context of marriage ceremony belongs to the original divine mandate to humans to develop themselves, the family and the human society through labor.[52] The essential nature of labor for human dignity and development unveils the evil of life deprived of labor. The document puts forward biblical examples of people and families affected by the evil and effects of unemployment,[53] of the abusive ravaging of nature[54] and of injustice.[55]

An appreciation of chapter 1 of AL is enhanced when this chapter is placed in diachronic analysis and relationship with other chapters of the documents and in comparative relationship with other papal documents on marriage and the family. These two relationships are the topic of the next paragraphs.

---

48. Exod 20:12; Sir 3:3–4; Mark 7:11–13.
49. Luke 2:52.
50. See Luke 2:48–50; 8:21.
51. See Prov 31:10–31; Acts 18:3; 1 Cor 4:12; 9:12; 1 Thess 3:10; 4:11.
52. See Ps 128:5–6.
53. For instance, Matt 20:1–16.
54. Gen 3:17–19.
55. 1 Kgs 21; Luke 12:13; 16:1–31.

Meaning of the Biblical Foundation for the Development of Other Parts of the Document

In developing the biblical foundation for the institution of marriage, the first chapter of AL also introduces pertinent themes that are developed in the different chapters of the papal Apostolic Exhortation. This first chapter presents the couple, the interlocutor, as seated at a festive table, surrounded by their children, and with their personal stories of love and experiences. These experiences become the topic of discussion in the second chapter, which projects the situation of married people and their families in its lights and shadows, valuing them as the seed bed for divine revelation. Chapter 2 is like the description of challenges that inspired both the choice of the foundational texts of chapter 1 and the unique interpretation they are given in this exhortation. Of these challenges, special mention is made of those that affect and/or detract the biblical foundation of marriage. These are: the individualistic cultures that erode the marriage bond and family unity, a flourishing ideology of gender which makes human identity the choice of the individual and which denies the anthropological basis of the family, and human procreation technologies which manipulate the reproductive act, making it independent of the sexual relationship between the man and the woman.

Chapter 1 of AL lays much emphasis on marriage as a special way of sharing in the life of the Trinity. This leading idea is developed in chapter 3, which further elaborates on the aim of pastoral activity for married people, that is, to help them to enter more deeply into the mystery of the Father's infinite love revealed in Christ. Should married couples, therefore, seek for models of love to emulate, this chapter refers them to the example of Jesus Christ, the Incarnate Son of God, who is the model of self-immolation and mutual self-giving. Jesus is also at the heart of many stories which reveal the deepest truth about human relationships and the deeper meaning of marriage in God's plan. Chapter 4 further provides a basis for nurturing the love of the spouses through a path of fidelity and mutual self-giving. This chapter links with the first chapter, especially because it develops the connection which the first chapter makes between human labor and family crisis. Since the linking of family crisis to human labor is also found in the key text, Gen 2–3,[56] the implication is that crisis in marital union is an aspect of the elemental disorderly reality

---

56. In Gen 3:17–19, human labor and suffering are punishment for sin, even though Gen 2:15 shows that labor is consequential to the human vocation in general.

that constantly threatens the good of creation.[57] The relationship of the couple is subject to complex realities that affect the unity and peace of the family. Crises seem to break in upon the pleasant relationship of the couple, threatening the foundation upon which marriage is founded. In fact, Jesus's teaching about marriage is given in the context of a discussion about divorce, an outcome of the original flaw in human relationship.[58]

Chapter 4 develops concrete ways of healing family wounds through its detailed explanation of the behaviors which love demands, as they are presented in 1 Cor 13. The last part of this fourth chapter presents the compassionate attitude that heals families in crisis, the tenderness of an embrace. It also suggests, with the use of Ps 131, an attitude that the couple must shun, that is, haughty or scornful attitude and conceited self-concepts that promote self-love. An interpretation of the demands of love in 1 Cor 13 in this chapter serves this purpose.[59]

The fifth chapter returns to the topic of the responsibilities of the couple to the primary task of being God's image, especially in relation to children. Chapters 6 and 7 speak of the different ways in which the family is a great asset for building up the church and a setting for education and social integration of their children. An Apostolic Exhortation that gets its inspiration from the life and virtues of God would, by implication, propose action plans and modes of behavior that correspond with its original propositions. The last chapters of the document do this with the language of mercy, encouragement and hope.

Amoris Laetitia and Previous Papal Documents on Family and Marriage

Marriage and the family is a frequently visited topic in papal encyclicals and exhortations through the centuries. It is important to locate this within the wider teaching ministry of the pope. Recognizing the great importance of the family as the foundation of both the society and church, the church through the centuries, has expressed the deepest desire and task of the church to protect it from ever new ideologies that promote perverse, life-threatening and family-endangering forms of morality. The

57. According to Gerhard Von Rad, chaos is the threat to everything created and the abyss of formlessness that lies behind all creation. See Von Rad, Genesis, 51.

58. AL 19–21. See Gen 3:16; Matt 19:3–9.

59. This chapter prepares for the ideas about conjugal love (see AL 120).

task to protect families from all negative teachings, morality and ideologies, as well as from all forms of social experimentation, led the church through the years to vindicate the divine institution of marriage, to illumine the heart of all people with the true doctrine regarding marriage in God's plan and to enable married people to act in conformity with that plan. All papal documents on marriage and family[60] defend the essential aspects of marriage—its place in God's plan, the union of the couple, its sacramental nature, love for and education of children and the dignity of work. All these ideas are defined and sustained with texts from the Bible, the canon law, Vatican II, the Fathers and the church's liturgy.

There are salient ideas which receive elaborate attention in previous papal documents, but which are only deducible from the text of AL and/ or not easily evident in it. These ideas are: moral norms guiding sexuality in marriage, indissolubility of marriage, the dignity of human life, influence of government or public authorities on decision regarding their children, use of contraception, sex education and the church as legitimate custodian and teacher of truths revealed by God. Although resembling previous documents in many ways, AL registers a very unique identity in having its first chapter entirely dedicated to explaining the biblical foundation of marriage. It is also important to point out that of all papal documents on the family since the *Casti Connubii* of Pius XI in 1930,[61] the letter *Gratissimam Sane* (GS)[62] of John Paul II in 1994, is closest to AL in style and content. Both documents are also similar in being located historically in Jubilee years, where the concern for family is proposed as essential step towards a fruitful preparation and celebration of the Jubilee.[63]

---

60. Since *Gaudium et Spes* of Vatican II, the most outstanding papal documents on marriage and family are: *Humane Vitae* of Paul VI (July 25, 1968); *Familiaris Consortio* of John Paul II (November 22, 1981); *Gratissimam Sane* of John Paul II (February 2, 1994); *Deus Caritas Est* of Benedict XVI (2005), *Africae Munus* of Benedict XVI (2011), *Lumen Fidei* of Pope Francis (2013); and *Amoris Laetitia* of Pope Francis (March 19, 2016).

61. *Casti Connubii* of Pius XI, given on December 31, 1930. Another significant papal document on marriage and family before this date is *Arcanum* of Leo XIII given in 1880.

62. Represented as GS in this work from here henceforth.

63. See GS 3; "This exhortation is especially timely in this Jubilee Year of Mercy . . . it seeks to encourage everyone to be a sign of mercy and closeness wherever family life remains imperfect or lacks peace and joy" (AL 5).

At the beginning of the exhortation, Pope Francis is similarly motivated as John Paul II to address a real interlocutor, with the gesture of "knocking and entering a home,"[64] in order to share in their joys, hopes, sorrows and anxieties (GS 1).[65] By addressing a historical interlocutor and their challenges, both documents express similar aims while affirming the character of God's word as encounter with concrete people in history, "the word of God is not a series of abstract ideas but rather a source of comfort and companionship for every family that experiences difficulties or suffering."[66]

In both documents, the key interpretive principle is the biblical idea of "the human being as image of God" (Gen 1:26–27). Both documents interpret Gen 1:27 as the creation, not of single human persons, but of the community of two physically different human subjects, male and female, with qualities of communion and complementarity.[67] Pope Francis followed Pope John Paul II in seeing this biblical text as a reference to the family, and saying that the family stands at the beginning of human existence, whose primordial model is the Triune God, the eternal mystery of communion and life. Lastly, AL and GS also meet in the importance they give to 1 Cor 13 and its lessons on the truth and virtues of love, marital fidelity, and both derive from this text the teaching about indissolubility of marriage.[68]

Concluding Remarks and Pastoral Application

The goal of this final part of the essay is to show how the light of God's word, which shines in the first chapter of AL, offers a pastoral plan of action on behalf of families in Africa.

---

64. Similarly, Pope Francis, "Let us cross the threshold of this tranquil home . . ." (AL 9).

65. The first family-related situation he mentioned is that of those who did not experience at birth the loving care and embrace of a family, and who thereby develop an anguished sense of pain and loss which burden their entire life (GS 2).

66. AL 22; see GS 2.

67. See GS 6, 8; "It is striking that the "image of God" here refers to the couple, "male and female"" (AL 10).

68. AL, chapter 4; GS 14 calls it the "Civilization of Love."

The Ministry of Mercy for Families

The historical location of AL in the context of Jubilee adds a significant flavor to the message of the exhortation. In the biblical sense, every Jubilee is a time of grace and of return to the Lord.[69] Consequently, the publication of AL in the Year of Mercy places every family in the forefront of the pilgrimage towards the "Door of Mercy." By placing family concerns within mercy, the church invites all couples and all families to approach the throne of God's mercy with their stories of joy and pain, so that they could experience the profound richness of the mystery of God's love for his people.[70] This note of mercy seems to exert considerable weight in the exhortation, to the almost neglect of moral laws guiding marriage which received so much attention in previous documents on the family. This certainly presents enormous challenge to the church and its leaders, who must bear practical witness to this gospel through courageous gestures that reflect the values of God. This involves especially rejecting a self-concept defined by exclusion, but bearing witness to the unity of God's people, to compassion, generosity and to forgiveness that heals. Every local church is thereby challenged to devise ways of being present to the families as the "soothing balm of mercy" and to minimize the punitive measures that keep them away from the sacraments.

A Church in Dialogue with Families

Although known as an essential ingredient for the achievement of peace and wellbeing among parties and peoples, dialogue is still very far from being brought to bear practically on relationships between parties because human beings tend to guard their boundaries from what they consider eccentric and unfamiliar. The God-human relationship, which the Bible presents, offers human beings in the church a model of relationship to adopt. God is not ashamed to choose as dialogue partner weak and stubborn human beings whose ways are different from God's, and God makes human experiences of joys and sorrows the preferred backdrop for divine revelation. The entire Bible show that God's merciful ways is the

---

69. See Lev 25:13.

70. See *Misericordiae Vultus*, 18.

dimension of relationship that turned the biblical stories of families in crises[71] into stories of salvation.

The dialogical character of salvation inspired the tone of AL. In presenting the exhortation as a conversation with a historical interlocutor, AL draws attention to the experiential dimension which should underlie both pastoral plans in the church and relationships among different groups in the church. This dialogue is most necessary in the modern society, where various forms of ideology also claim the right to define questions concerning human life, gender, parenthood and education of children. Many families find themselves at the crossroads between faith and other relativizing options. In responding to this situation, Pope Francis counsels against an excessive idealization that makes Christian marriage uninteresting and undesirable. Pertinently, he asks, ". . . have we always provided solid guidance to young married couples, understanding their timetable, their way of thinking and their concrete concerns. At times, we have also proposed a far too abstract and almost artificial theological ideal of marriage, far removed from the concrete situations and practical possibilities of real families" (see AL 36–37).

In today's Africa, many more families are affected by challenges never experienced before, caused by political and socio-economic factors. On the increase are cases of divorce, single-parenting and conflicts that rupture family unity. The church will find in these contexts a rich mine of human experiences, family stories that are raw materials for a narrative theology. The narrative method is not foreign to the African; rather, it has served as a means for articulating African religious and ethical worldview. Theology in Africa should exhaust the benefits of this method, bringing it to bear on African ecclesiology. In fact, the church's renewal and enrichment depends a lot on the options it makes on behalf of the "weak and overburdened."[72] This narrative method is recommended because in both biblical and African thought, narrative as a literary *genre*, presents the characters of a story as they are, without judging them (see AL 296); it includes the good and the bad in its comprehensive vision of reality; and in biblical thought, it is more open to God's grace.

71. The stories of the families of Adam, Abraham, Isaac, and Jacob all begin with crisis.

72. The church experiences renewal through openness to the weak. See Dowling, "Bishops as Theologians," 3.

Reconsidering Marriage Customs in the Light of God's Word

A strong focus on families in Africa has been on how they are affected by marriage cultural practices, especially practices that encourage divorce, polygamy, exploitation of women and neglect of the education of children. These negative realities point to the need to positively consider what the founding vision of marriage says to the rich culture and customs of marriage which have served the local people of Africa for a long time. The liturgy should feature more clearly those aspects of the African vision of marriage which reflect the biblical vision; for instance, marriage as creator of perpetual bonds and lasting friendships, promoter of solidarity between families and communities, the invaluable contribution of the woman to the wellbeing of the family, and marriage as a means for perpetuating the chain of humanity.[73] The purpose should be to promote the image of family which reflects the triune God as a communion of love (see AL 11) and to reflect a family image where every member is helped to experience growth in their human dignity as human beings made in God's image. Moreover, with the collapse of cultural structures in Africa, which previously encouraged male dominance and their traditionally conceived status of the man as "bread winner," the contribution of women to the family is coming to greater light. Many families are surviving today thanks to the resourcefulness of women and their commitment to both the education of children and care of the more elderly members of the family unit. This is another "sign of the time" which the church should preach by discouraging customs opposed to the biblical vision, especially those that promote selfishness, exploitation of women and negation of their human right.

More Committed Catechesis for the Family

Amoris Laetitia is almost a year old, yet many families in some local churches are ignorant of its existence. The same thing holds for some

73. These basic ideas about how life's chain is continued during and after a person's historical existence recapture the idea of immortality, which is found in creation stories of ancient peoples. So long as a deceased person is still remembered and recognized by name by relations who knew him, he or she is a living dead. He is in a state of personal immortality, which is externalized through reincarnation, sharing of symbolic meals and libation and obedience to instructions they had given. The process of dying is completed when no family member could perform these memorial acts on behalf of the dead. See Mbiti, *African Religions and Philosophy*, 24–25.

previous papal exhortations and encyclicals which address either the entire church or some members of it. In most cases, the people of God are uninformed and ignorant of church teaching on marriage and the family. While growing up, I experienced a church in which the priest is personally committed to teaching the people of God, especially at evening Sunday schools. This practice is eroding or is almost absent in some local churches. The crises of faith into which individuals and families are plunged stem from ignorance and lack of guidance. In some cases, also, this lack of knowledge is pervasive, extending even to those who should teach the people. For this reason, the proposed dialogue with families should include the following: (a) efforts to improve the reading culture and interests of agents of evangelization, (b) efforts directed towards faithful transmission of received doctrine, and (c) a thoroughgoing catechesis for families on the content of the church's teaching on marriage. These pedagogical efforts serve for building the capacity of the dialogue partners. Moreover, the African continent, with its rich cultures, offers various festive moments which the church should consider as favorable setting for teaching. Occasions which necessitate family re-unions, such as traditional and church weddings, child-dedication ceremonies, blessing of a new house, initiation rites of different kinds, and so on; all these are advantageous for interpreting the inherent values of these family-related rites in the light of the gospel. Today, more than previously, given the dangers to which families are exposed due to the presence of teachings and ideologies that contradict faith, the church must not relent in her mission to educate people on the values of God.

Bibliography

Agbasiere, J. T. *Women in Igbo Life and Thought*. New York: Taylor and Francis Group, 2000.

Allen, Leslie C. "Psalms 101–150." In *Word Biblical Commentary*, vol. 21, edited by John D. W. Watts. Dallas: Word, 1983.

Brueggemann, Walter. *Theology of the Old Testament: Testimony, Dispute, Advocacy*. Minneapolis: Fortress, 1997.

Crenshaw, J. L. *Old Testament Wisdom: An Introduction*. Louisville: Westminster John Knox, 1998.

Dowling, Bishop Kevin. "Bishops as Theologians. Listening, Discerning and Dialogue." In *The Church We Want: African Catholics Look to Vatican II*, edited by A. E. Orobator. New York: Orbis, 2016.

Francis. *Amoris Laetitia: Post-synodal Apostolic Exhortation on Love in the Family*. Vatican City: Libreria Editrice Vaticana, 2016. http://w2.vatican.va/content/

dam/francesco/pdf/apost_exhortations/documents/papa-francesco_esortazione-
ap_20160319_amoris-laetitia_en.pdf.

———. *Misericordiae Vultus: Bull of Indiction of the Extraordinary Jubilee of Mercy*.
Vatican City: Libreria Editrice Vaticana, 2015. http://w2.vatican.va/content/
francesco/en/bulls/documents/papa-francesco_bolla_20150411_misericordiae-
vultus.html.

Fuhs, H. F. "Yārēh." In *Theological Dictionary of the Old Testament*, vol. VI, edited by G.
Johannes Botterweck, et al.. Grand Rapids: Eerdmans, 1990.

Janzen, W. "'AŠRÊ in the Old Testament." *Harvard Theological Review* 58 (1965) 215–
26.

John XXIII. *Pacem in Terris: Encyclical on Establishing Universal Peace in Truth,
Justice, Charity, and Liberty*. Vatican City: Libreria Editrice Vaticana, 1963.
http://w2.vatican.va/content/john-xxiii/en/encyclicals/documents/hf_j-xxiii_
enc_11041963_pacem.html.

John Paul II. *Familiaris Consortio: Apostolic Exhortation on the Role of the Christian
Family in the Modern World*. Vatican City: Libreria Editrice Vaticana, 1981. http://
w2.vatican.va/content/john-paul-ii/en/apost_exhortations/documents/hf_jp-
ii_exh_19811122_familiaris-consortio.html.

———. *Gratissimam Sane: Letter to Families*. Vatican City: Libreria Editrice Vaticana,
1994. http://w2.vatican.va/content/john-paul-ii/en/letters/1994/documents/hf_
jp-ii_let_02021994_families.html.

———. *The Theology of the Body: Human Love in the Divine Plan*. Boston: Pauline,
1997.

Lipinski, E. "Macarismes et psaumes de congratulation." *Revue Biblique* 75 (1968)
347–48.

Lonergan, B. *Method in Theology*. New York: Seabury, 1972.

Mayes, A. D. H. *The New Century Bible Commentary: Deuteronomy*. Grand Rapids:
Eerdmans, 1979.

Mbiti, John S. *African Religions and Philosophy*. 2nd ed. Johannesburg: Heinemann,
1989.

Nwachukwu, MarySylvia C. *Creation–Covenant Scheme and Justification by Faith*. (Tesi
Gregoriana Serie Teologia, 89.) Rome: Gregorian University Press, 2002.

Paul VI. *Humanae Vitae: Encyclical Letter on the Regulation of Birth*. Vatican City:
Libreria Editrice Vaticana, 1968. http://w2.vatican.va/content/paul-vi/en/
encyclicals/documents/hf_p-vi_enc_25071968_humanae-vitae.html.

Perdue, L. G. *Wisdom and Cult: A Critical Analysis of the Views of Cult in the Wisdom
Literatures of Israel and of the Ancient Near East*. Missoula: Scholars, 1977.

Pius XI. *Casti Connubii: encyclical on Christian marriage*. Vatican City: Libreria Editrice
Vaticana, 1930. http://w2.vatican.va/content/pius-xi/en/encyclicals/documents/
hf_p-xi_enc_19301231_casti-connubii.html.

Scaraffia, Lucetta. "Socio-Cultural Changes in Women's Lives." In Pontificium
Consilium Pro Laicis, Study Seminar on *Men and Women: Diversity and Mutual
Complementarity*. Rome: Libreria Editrice Vaticana, 2006.

Trever, J. C. "Olive Tree." In *The Interpreter's Dictionary of the Bible*, vol. 3, edited by
George Arthur Buttrick, et al. New York: Abingdon, 1962.

Von Rad, Gerhard. *Genesis*. Philadelphia: Westminster, 1972.

Wenham, G. J. *Genesis 1–15: Word Biblical Commentary*, vol. 1. Dallas: Word, 1987.

Westermann, C. *Genesis 12–36: A Commentary*. London: SPCK, 1985.

2

The Experiences and Challenges of Families in Africa

NICHOLAUS SEGEJA

Summary

From the African and pastoral perspective, our commentary and reflection on chapter 2 of *Amoris Laetitia* on the experiences and challenges of marriages affirms that marriage and family life is a vital basis both for the success of the church and society. However, there is an urgent need for personal and communal concerted effort, operating from the grassroots level, to respond to the challenges affecting the family today due to the socio-political, economic, and cultural changes taking place, especially those resulting from a globalized and secularized world. We realize that the original and true image of the family has drastically changed, affecting the couples and their children to make it remain a living manifesto of reverential, dialogue-based new evangelization.

Introduction

The Apostolic Exhortation *Amoris Laetitia* (AL) by Pope Francis is a result of the thirst to respond to the challenges of the family today. Thus, chapter 2 of AL answers one of the key concerns Pope Francis addresses, namely: the challenges facing the family in the world today and how the church should interpret and understand the diverse situations of families in today's world.[1] Perhaps this is the heart and hub of the document. This work, therefore, from the pastoral and African perspective attempts to make a commentary and some reflections on the experiences and challenges of families in the light of the second chapter of AL. The rationale and purpose is to contribute towards an effective, efficient, and relevant implementation of the document. This, of course, is done while maintaining the purpose and context of the whole exhortation in its totality as a pastoral document. In all these, we argue that marriage and family life is a vital basis both for the success of the church and society, particularly in the African context. However, there is an urgent need for personal and communal concerted effort, operating from the grassroots level, to respond to the challenges affecting it today so as to make it remain a living manifesto and agent of reverential, dialogue-based new evangelization.

Understanding the Experiences and Challenges of Families

Due to socio-political, economic, and cultural changes taking place, especially those resulting from a globalized and secularized world, the original and true image of the family has drastically changed, affecting the couples and their children. Providentially, AL by Pope Francis has eventually come out as a result of the great need to respond to the challenges of the family today. Thus, chapter 2 of AL, consisting of twenty-seven articles and mainly divided into two sections—besides discussing the current reality of the family—also exemplifies, though briefly, at least three interrelated features and some challenges, especially those commanding special attention from the church and society.

1. See Francis, *Amoris Laetitia*. The author responds to at least three issues or rather key questions: (i) How can we understand the identity, nature, and mission of the family in the uncertainties of our world today? (ii) What are the challenges facing the family in the world today and how should the church interpret and understand the diverse situations of families in today's world? (iii) What pastoral praxis will better meet these challenges which answer some of the new questions emerging from the new context of faith and life in the social changes of today?

Anthropological-Cultural Volatility

It is worth mentioning here that Pope Francis wishes to reflect on concrete concerns about marriage and family life as a point of departure. In fact, as he opens chapter 2 of AL, the Holy Father cogently says that we do well to focus on concrete realities, since "the call and the demands of the Spirit resound in the events of history," and through these "the Church can also be guided to a more profound understanding of the inexhaustible mystery of marriage and the family" (AL 31).[2] Thus, besides his own experience, the Holy Father articulates and makes use of the understandings of the situation of the families worldwide as examined by the Synod Fathers. This precisely echoes the call and spirit of the Second Vatican Council (Vatican II) to read the signs of the times.

Observing what is happening, almost globally, Pope Francis confirms the presence of substantial anthropological-cultural changes. This is manifested, for example, in the less support received today by individuals in personal and family life from social structures than in the past (AL 32). The autonomy of the individual is exaggerated and not guided by realities beyond the self, hence, in most cases ends up considering each member of the family as an isolated unit (AL 33). Related to this situation, the Holy Father reiterates, as the Synod Fathers also confirmed, that "cultural tendencies in today's world seem to set no limits on a person's affectivity," hence frustrate the individual's growth to personal maturity (AL 41).

In a situation where individualistic culture and the volatility of life propelled by globalization and advances in science and technology, take precedence the tendency is to esteem the present at the expense of the future. Thus, marriage and family life is reduced to the level of *material objects and the environment: everything is disposable; everyone uses and throws away, takes and breaks, exploits and squeezes to the last drop. Then, goodbye* (AL 39). This situation has eventually graduated to what Pope Francis refers to as a "culture of the ephemeral"—a kind of mindset which asserts minimal chances for a person's affectivity to grow to maturity. Consequently, it weakens family bonds, hence, sending a pastoral alarm. In fact, this opens to an overly individualistic culture—a culture caught up with possessions and pleasures desired and limited to individuals. Intolerance and hostility in the family, attitudes of constant

2. Unless mentioned otherwise, the numbers in brackets refer to the articles of the exhortation, *Amoris Laetitia*, by Pope Francis.

suspicion, fear of commitment, self-centeredness, and arrogance are but some of the symptoms of this culture.

A Freedom Void of Transcendental Values

Without being judgmental, Pope Francis further illustrates that today's fast pace of life does not only result into anthropological-cultural changes that in most cases leave each member of the family as an isolated unit, but also substantially influence one's ability to make decisions (AL 33). This is when freedom becomes void of transcendental values, and as such, easily confused with the idea that each individual can act arbitrarily, as if there were no truths, values, and principles to provide guidance, and everything were possible and permissible (AL 34). In fact, in this situation one becomes a measure and standard of what is good. Such a situation eventually yields to uncertainty and ambiguity, particularly when conflict of personal interest and desires take their cause, militating against permanent decisions. This can foster attitudes of constant suspicion, fear of commitment, self-centeredness, and arrogance. What provokes concern for the life and mission of the church, at least from the pastoral perspective, is precisely not only the fact that the reality of *koinonia* is frustrated but also the whole spirit of genuine *diakonia* and of the sense of the sacred are impeded: hence, life then tends to become desperate and futile.

Freedom that is void of transcendental values eventually degenerates into an inability to give oneself generously to others. And before such a pervasive culture, marriage and family life are not spared. No wonder evidences show that in many countries where the number of marriages is decreasing, more and more people are choosing to live alone or simply to spend time together without cohabiting. Perhaps this is what Francis names as a "crisis of communal commitment." It mitigates the exercise of human freedom for the common good and in line with the will of God. In fact, when the human person closes and hides in one's individualistic interests, passions, and desires, s/he then falls into a trap of exercising his or her freedom by avoiding others and God, especially when this demands a reaching out to the other through services which do not necessarily generate immediate personal gains. Negative ethnicity, the practice of witchcraft, and materialism can be ascribed to this tendency. Perhaps this also explains the predisposition among many today in marriage and family life to hide in sensational satisfactions with the use of the omnipresent

powerful radio, television, iPad, and mobile phone.[3] One can also add
here, as the Synod Bishops also noted, the current "spread of pornography and the commercialization of the body, fostered also by a misuse of
the internet" (AL 41). In fact, this reflects the very inner tendency of the
human person to hide from God and his will reflected in the Scriptures.[4]

When the individual becomes almost the sole criterion to understand the mystery of life, including human sexuality and freedom, the
whole logic of living according to the gospel counsels, expressed through
the demands of marriage and family life, is frustrated. Instead of marriage and family life being a call to a personal relationship with Jesus
Christ, it becomes like a private effort for each member of the family
considered as an isolated unit.[5] Consequently, the acceptance of the call
by an individual impairs the process of ongoing configuration to Christ's
grace, and one's mind fails to transcend the self and to be open to being
as he is who equated his relationship to the church to that between married people.[6] Thus, in this situation it becomes almost impossible to see
the importance of marriage and family as a vocation embracing mutual
assistance rather than an apparently exaggerated insistence on the duty of
procreation (AL 36). Nevertheless and providentially, as Pope Francis, in
line with the Synod Fathers observes, in various parts of Africa, secular-
ism has not weakened certain traditional values, and marriages forge a
strong bond between two wider families, with clearly defined structures
for dealing with problems and conflicts (AL 38). Consequently, it does
not look strange to find people who still value family relationships even
in the traditional set-ups.

Socio-political and Economic Strain

The anthropological-cultural changes happening at a vigorous pace are
also influenced by socio-political and economic stress for most of the
families. Perhaps, the youth are the most affected group by this situation
of stress. In such a situation and especially when freedom is not guided

3. See Bakka, *Talking to God*, 23.

4. See Gen 3:9–10. Adam and Eve had moved away from the garden, a place or
situation that would always remind them of God's will. This can also explain the tendency in society of pushing religion to the periphery.

5. See Segeja, "A Pastoral Reflection," 73.

6. See Phil 2:5; 1 Cor 2:16.

by values and principles of universal and transcendental nature, it becomes increasingly difficult to make decisions leading to a long-lasting
commitment like marriage and family life. This is because of the apparent
fear of losing freedom and independence. It is also a result of trying to
maintain a certain style of life essentially based on the self and private
desires and wishes. Such a situation makes families and especially the
youth, for example, vulnerable to ideologies which devalue marriage and
family (AL 40). Related to this, one may also include those "reprehensible
situations where people are forced into prostitution" (AL 41).

Economic strain and the looming reality of poverty condition
people to spend most of their time trying to earn a living. This is the situation of families living in dire poverty and great need that Pope Francis
is referring to in AL 48. Among others it includes lack of dignified or
affordable housing. In some cases, this had led to unconsciously or even
intentionally less preoccupation with matters pertaining to religion and
faith (AL 43). Besides leaving the members of the families isolated not
only from their beloved ones but also from God, a general feeling of pow-
erlessness in the face of socio-cultural realities estranges them from the
church and society in general. The increase of emotional problems and
outbreaks of violence are but some of the indicators of this socio-political
and economic strain. The phenomena of both single parenthood (AL 45)
and migration (AL 46) could also be the result of the socio-economic
strain and poverty if not the desire to exercise personal freedom and independence. In the context of the socio-political and economic strain
AL also reiterates the need for particular attention to "families of persons with special needs, where the unexpected challenge of dealing with
a disability can upset a family's equilibrium, desires and expectations"
(AL 47). One could also add here the negative attitude towards care of
the elderly which at times leads to the encouragement of euthanasia and
assisted suicide (AL 48). As Pope Francis explicitly says, these amounts
to another sign of the times to be faced and understood in terms of its
negative effects on family life.

The New Challenges

Looking at the great variety of the situations encroaching families today, especially the fast pace of life resulting in anthropological-cultural
changes, freedom that is void of transcendental values and socio-political

and economic strain, AL in chapter 2 sees the new challenges that they pose. In fact, such challenges are in addition to what already frustrates marriage and family life in the history of the human person. Among others this includes the challenge in raising children (AL 50), of having a proactive approach to reality and of the responsible use of the individual will impeded by relativism. The stress and tensions of life usually lead to other complications and new challenges. Escapism that goes with avoidance of responsibility is perhaps the most challenging reality expressed in the tendency to hide in the name of relaxation, or even consciously or unconsciously *taking flight from reality*, hence, having no time for others. Abuse of drugs as one of the phenomena scourging our times is just one example of the tendency to take flight from responsibly facing reality (AL 51). Related to drug abuse, one can also include alcoholism, gambling, and other addictions like television and the internet. Having no time for others can also explain, at least in some sense, the absence of a father in a family. Of course this is not always intentional. But in any case it gravely affects family life and the upbringing of children and their integration in society.

Escapism or taking flight from reality can lead to a destructive way of responding to reality, usually expressed in violence within families and beyond. It is in this context that the bishops of Mexico have pointed out that new forms of social aggression and tendency to a violent personality, especially in families where communication is lacking and a defensive attitude predominate, usually breed in resentment and hatred.[7] It suffices here, for instance, to mention as AL confirms the practice of a culture of *male chauvinism*. Besides considering women inferior, there is the exploitation and commercialization of the female body in the current media culture, this ranges from the shameful ill-treatment to which women are sometimes subjected to domestic violence, which includes verbal, physical, and sexual violence that some women endure in their marriages, genital mutilation, and lack of equal access to dignified work and roles of decision-making (AL 54).

There is still another new challenge related to marriage and family life. Generally speaking, one can allude to the *reality of relativism and indifferentism*. Concretely, as AL says, this is embraced in the failure to realize that only the exclusive and indissoluble union between a man and a woman has a plenary role to play in society as a stable commitment that

7. See Mexican Bishops' Conference, *Que en Cristo Nuestra Paz, México Tenga Vida Digna*, 67.

bears fruit in new life (AL 52). Perhaps the obvious expression of this failure is to equate same-sex unions, for example, with marriage. But one can also look at the practice of polygamy, living together, and cohabitation, without necessarily the intention to marry. What underlines all this is the tendency to adopt models based almost exclusively on the autonomy of the individual, hence, becoming short-sighted of substantial and complementary differences and roles. In all this, then the society lives as if there are no sexual differences, hence "eliminating the anthropological basis of the family" (AL 56). Thus, it makes human identity solely a choice of an individual, one which can also change over time. In this respect, personal freedom is exercised without reliable and lasting references, hence reducing the reproductive act to a private affair independent of the sexual relationship between a man and a woman, and making human life and parenthood modular and separable realities.

Looking at the variety of situations and the new challenges of the families, Pope Francis in his Apostolic Exhortation surely is not short-sighted of the witness of the positive and encouraging aspects. In fact he concludes chapter 2 by thanking God that many families, which are far from considering themselves perfect, live in love, fulfill their calling and keep moving forward, even if they fall many times along the way (AL 57). All in all, the pope attests that due to the present variety of situations and new challenges of the families, the church needs to seek new forms of missionary creativity for their pastoral care. It is in this context that Pope Francis wishes to speak both to the family from the heart of the church and to the church and to the world from the heart of the family. No wonder the Holy Father opens chapter 2 by clearly stating: "The welfare of the family is decisive for the future of the world and that of the church" (AL 31).[8]

Challenges of Families in Light of Faith: African and Pastoral Insights

There are three interrelated realities that Pope Francis correlates when discussing the challenges of families. Reading the signs of times seems to be key source and point of departure in understanding the truth and hope that the church should communicate in relation to the challenges of families today. It is precisely this source that also determines the

8. Francis, *Amoris Laetitia*, 31.

self-understanding of the church relevant to the variety of situations and challenges afflicting marriage and family life today. Thus, in our opinion, Pope Francis proposes a new method and attitude, essentially pastoral in its nature and basically open to African insights that would require a different way of approach to the challenges of the families in concrete situations.[9] Perhaps, in the African context, the challenge and key question that deserves serious examination would be: how would the church look for solutions together, as a family?

Evangelical Reading of the Signs of the Time

It is clear from the discussion of Pope Francis that experiences of families, even in moments of shadow and apparent brokenness should be the point of departure and pastoral focus. Key to all this is the ability to always discern the presence of God in daily practices and life. Much as this is the duty of the church, especially the *Magisterium*, Pope Francis sees it as a communal duty and vocation as well, to be practiced by all— the members of the church and in the world led by the Holy Spirit. In fact, this echoes the mind of Vatican II, which is all more the necessary nowadays when things change so rapidly and thought patterns differ so widely.[10] Discerning the presence of God in history is more than an approach. In fact, it has to be inculcated as a value and attitude, hence a way of thinking and doing.

It is perhaps important here to also emphasize that like any other Apostolic Exhortation, AL is essentially a pastoral document. The concern and focus of the Exhortation, therefore, is not first and foremost about confirming or defining a church doctrine, like on the family, but rather demonstrating its effectiveness, efficiency, and relevance; hence its practical application in a given context.[11] In the relation to what

9. We are aware, though, that in science, method and content although can be differentiated and distinguished, cannot be separated. In fact, every method implies an interest, a purpose, and an intention, hence, a message or teaching to communicate.

10. Vatican II, *Gaudium et Spes*, 44. The Council asserts that with the help of the Holy Spirit, it is the task of the whole people of God, particularly of its pastors and theologians, to listen to and to distinguish the many voices of our times and to interpret them in the light of the divine Word in order that the revealed truth may be more deeply penetrated, better understood, and more suitably presented.

11. The purpose of Apostolic Exhortations is not to teach new doctrine, but to suggest how church teaching and practices can be profitably applied today. Thus, the issue of context is crucial because it determines the needs, hence the themes to be discussed.

transpired in our discussion above, given the situation and conditions encroaching marriage and family life—the issue of context—hence evangelical discernment is crucial in any attempt to respond to the challenges of families today. Context, at least from the pastoral perspective, encompasses several notions.[12] Observed in their entirety/totality, notions constitute not only the immediate location (contact) of doing pastoral theology—a *locus theologicus*—but also the point of departure in responding to challenges like those of the families.[13]

Key to this aspect and of pastoral concern here is the fact that the church is thoroughly integrated within humanity and the contemporary history of the world. As a pilgrim church, though not identified with it, the church is like salt and light, but the world solely describes the reason of her existence, namely, the mission to evangelize. There are at least two related implications to marriage and family here. On one hand, the challenges of families should be understood in their respective concrete contexts, hence, the need to establish their root causes. This requires an aspect of socio-pastoral analysis, hence discernment. On the other hand, it requires that the analyzed situation concerning the challenges be understood in the light of the signs of times as related to the tradition of the church and the Holy Scriptures.

When a pastoral approach looks at context(s) and concrete situations in their entirety, it considers them as a God-given opportunity and a *graced reality*. Pastoral wisdom has it that the world, as desired by God, especially in terms of human relationships according to the mystery of creation, is graced. Of course one should also note at the same time that the world is broken and sinful as a result of the "fall." Redemption (Christ's event) extends grace to all humanity. Redemption is essentially linked to creation, which is integral. The pastoral approach also understands context(s) as *fragmentation in the search for unity and truth*. The contemporary world is marked with the reality of intellectual and cultural pluralism and modernity—hence, difference, like fragmentation, in terms of ideas and values. Difference presupposes unity—oneness or standard. As Robert Schreiter says: "It is only by beginning with otherness can we hope to build the kind of conversations that will lead to a harmonious society where difference is recognized and even celebrated

---

Consequently, Apostolic Exhortations would normally be devoted to different themes in a particular part of the world or universally.

12. See Segeja, "Contexts in Doing Theology," 47–71.

13. See Midali, *Practical Theology*, 145.

as a gift for the enrichment of human society."[14] To understand the dynamics of the emerging new contexts as immediate location and major
areas of apostolate, there is need to establish the causes—effects, coher-
ence, and discernment—socio-pastoral analysis and reading of the signs
of the times. This requires evangelical discernment and dialogue with
the other sources of revelation, namely, the Scriptures and tradition. This
would serve the church from succumbing to propaganda and interests of
some human sciences that may not be concomitant with the vocation of
marriage and family life.

As proposed in the next section the challenge, therefore, is to put in
place inclusive structures, both in the church and society that would engage all—states, agents, and stakeholders of human integral development
who essentially influence and even condition the human experiences
related to marriage and family life. Here, the thinking should not only be
global but inclusive and provoked by concrete experiences in the search
for the truth. It also requires a spirituality of communion extended to the
whole church as it relates to society and the world. It is in this context,
that we need new models and paradigms—ardor, methods, and human
expression in dealing with the challenges of the families today. In the
African context, inclusive thinking should place at the center of discussion or reverential dialogue the entire church in all she is and all she does
in relation to her spiritual and sacramental affairs, education, health care,
information technology, and communication. [15]

Church-Family Ecclesiology Contextualized

It is not difficult to detect the ecclesial features which are operative in
this chapter—and indeed in the whole document—and in Pope Francis's
other writings. In its understanding of the life of the church, Francis's
ecclesiology esteems the experience of marriage and family as the basis
and hope of the church. Perhaps this echoes what Pope Francis refers to
as the "logic of God," which proceeds from mercy and love and transfigures evil into good by entering into contact with sin as different from the
"logic of the scholars of the law."[16] The logic of scholars proceeds from

14. Schreiter, "Pastoral Theology as Contextual," 7.

15. See New Evangelization: Lineamenta, 5. See also Benedict XVI, Africae Munus,
133–46.

16. See Francis, The Name of God is Mercy, 66.

pre-conceived and rigid notions of truth and purity. It is in this context Pope Francis exhorts the whole church to adopt the logic of God, what he calls the "way of beauty" even in the contradictions and complexities of life.[17]

Consequently, according to Francis's understanding, the church should be a realization of the concreteness of God's loving presence in every human situation. Thus, the realities of sin, pain, suffering, and brokenness in marriage and family life are to be considered as invitations from God to see His presence—hence, open to the gifts of hope, and mercy. On the practical level: putting in place inclusive structures, both in the church and society that would engage all—states, agents, and stakeholders of human integral development who essentially influence and even condition the human experiences. Popular awareness/consciousness: invest in the spirituality of communion and integrate in it the social dimension of evangelization. Doing theology, therefore, much as it needs to be critical and creative, should also adopt strategic thinking as discussed in the next section.

Consequently, the parish should be renewed so as to be a source of genuine joy for all, especially those experiencing the pastoral challenges of the family. In the African context where the church is manifested as family, the parish should assume a reverential dialogue ministry and missionary outreach.[18] Thus, the parish should have a pastoral approach that is Christ-centered and community-oriented. This presumes that the parish really is in contact with the family amidst its pastoral challenges.[19] The parish in all its basic pastoral activities, therefore, should inclusively encourage and train all faithful to be evangelizers because of their mandate emanating from their baptism. The parish should be a sanctuary where those experiencing family pastoral challenges, like other thirsty faithful, come to drink through activities that foster their spiritual growth and apostolate. Thus the challenge is to renew the parish so that inclusivity may enable all the faithful to be of one heart and one soul, thus keeping their hope and joy vibrant in all life situations.[20]

17. See Francis, Evangelii Gaudium, 167.

18. Segeja, "Reverential Dialogical Ministry," 45. See also Lonema, "Structures of Participation in the Parish," 93; Karambai, Structures of Decision-Making, 21.

19. See John Paul II, Christifideles Laici, 26.

20. See Acts 4:32.

Reverential-Dialogical Approach

In the context where the church wishes to be engaged in the concrete situations families are experiencing today, and engaging all in the process of responding to the challenges, the dialogical approach is inevitable. In the context of the church as family, therefore, reverential-dialogical approach surfaces as a necessity. This is a unique type of dialogue, like that which happens in a good African family, where not only ideas are respected, but also the different functions and charisms are welcomed. In actual fact, this pertains to the prophetic nature of the church and is in line with the idea of integration as discussed by Pope Francis.[21] What prevails in all this is God's mercy and unlimited love to all. Thus, every time and in all conditions where love is expressed, like in marriage and family life, the presence of God is realized. Consequently, according to Pope Francis the approach to the challenges of families and even the language used should constantly listen and make reference to the love of God.

One then can easily see why Christ in the salvific event, the expression *par excellence* of the love of God, is the basis to always realize one's identity and the great wealth of the other, especially those in difficult situations. The marriage consent, being a sacramental expression of love of God, through Christ in the Spirit, therefore, does not only find its basis and meaning through Christ in the Spirit, but also becomes the source of strength of the life and mission of the church. This, therefore, affects the way the church should approach the challenges of the family as they always carry with them the expressions of the life of Christ and the dictates of the Spirit. In fact, the approach takes us beyond looking at the challenges just on the anthropological basis as affecting the human person. It situates us on a broader and integrated perspective putting the trinitarian relationship at the center.

Towards a Concerted Pastoral Response to the Challenges of Families

Looking at what is happening in relation to how the church responds to the challenges of the family at different levels, Pope Francis notes a great

---

21. See Hinze, *Prophetic Obedience*, 151–57. The author in chapter 6, and indeed in the whole book, discusses extensively prophetic obedience as related to ecclesiology for a dialogical church. Although his exposition is not directly referring to the African context, still most of his confirmations can equally be applied to this continent.

weakness. He points out that marital problems are "often confronted in haste and without the communal courage to have patience and reflect, to make sacrifices and to forgive one another" (AL 41). It is precisely this failure, according to him, that leads to new couples, new civil unions and new marriages, creating family situations which are complex and problematic for the Christian life.[22] In addition, such family situations are hardened not only by substantial current anthropological-cultural changes and the socio-economic strain, but also by popular trends emanating from the presence of a culture that promotes a freedom void of transcendental values. In all these, therefore, the focus is not on the doctrine as such but on how it can be concretely delivered given the new conditions and understanding. In light of AL and precisely in the African context, there is need to espouse a comprehensive *liberative* pastoral perspective based on mercy and reverential-dialogical approach. All this has to strategically take place in a parish set-up where the formation of small Christian communities (SCCs) is a pastoral priority and a way—perhaps the best—of being church today.

A Comprehensive Liberative Perspective

AL comes into existence while the church is in the period of celebrating the fiftieth anniversary of Vatican II. Its implementation, therefore, should recapture the spirit of communion of Vatican II that has led to the new self-understanding of the church and its mission in the contemporary world. In fact, after Vatican II, as William T. Ditewig points out, Pope Paul VI began speaking of a *novus habitus mentis*—a new way of thinking.[23] A challenge here would perhaps be to understand this new way of thinking emanating from the spirit of communion of Vatican II and what would be its implications to the family in the parish set-up. As Ladislas Orsy says: "to acquire a new disposition of the mind means to enter into a new field of vision; that is, into a new horizon."[24] This is meant to influence the whole ordinary and natural as well as extraordinary and

22. See Third Extraordinary General Assembly of the Synod of Bishops, *Message*.

23. See Ditewig, "Novus Habitus Mentis," 142. Although the author makes reference to ordained ministry, which eventually led to the revision of the 1917 Code to reflect the vision of communion of Vatican II, the need for new thinking can as well be applied to all Christian faithful.

24. Orsy, "The Meaning of *Novus Habitus Mentis*," 431.

supernatural Christian life.[25] In fact, family life with its challenges today should in the first place make sense by adding value to ordinary life. In itself also, such life should be opening to the divine reality as its root and source. Thus, family life is eventually a learned recognition of actions, patterns of behavior, attitudes that ultimately become a habit, transcends the self, and surrenders to a relationship with God and his will.[26]

Consequently, the key challenge then is to develop *whole new habits* of thinking, being, and acting among family members and all Christians in general according to the signs of the times and obedient to the dictates of the Holy Spirit. In fact, developing *whole new habits* can only be possible when one puts a lot of trust in the *liberative* power and providence of the gospel message. No wonder, in the Year of Mercy (2016) while also celebrating the fiftieth anniversary of Vatican II, one gospel message Pope Francis called our attention to is when Jesus starts his public ministry, saying: "He has sent me to bring good tidings to the afflicted; to bind up the broken-hearted, to proclaim liberty to captives."[27] This suggests a new world view, a new vision, and a new horizon for the church and the world in response to the challenges of families and others.

Concretely, this would imply the whole church, especially at the local level, to translate the vision and spirit of the church as communion. In fact, the Assembly of the first Synod of Africa, in light of inculturation, already started this concerted effort by taking the church as God's family as its guiding idea or vision for the evangelization in Africa, hoped that the theologians in the continent would work out its corresponding theology.[28] This *liberative* vision is a new way of thinking and becoming a living sign of God's *liberative* work of salvation meant not only to affect and influence the family life but also the pastoral ministry of the church to people of the contemporary world.[29] No wonder: this vision emphasizes care for others, solidarity, warmth in human relationships, acceptance, dialogue, and trust. In fact, this is in line with the idea of

---

25. See William, *Novus Habitus Mentis*, 144. See also Nichols, *The Shape of Catholic Theology*, 13–14.

26. See Nichols, *The Shape of Catholic Theology*, 13–14.

27. See Luke 4:16–22. See also William, *Novus Habitus Mentis*, 149.

28. See John Paul II, *Ecclesia in Africa*, 63.

29. See John 14:6. Jesus made it clear to Phillip that to see him is actually to see the Father (John 14:8–11).

service according to Pope Paul VI, which has been central in the understanding of the church.[30]

Consequently, the self-understanding of the church-family does not
only reflect a new thinking but makes it become a living sign of the servant of God and savior of humanity who liberates—Jesus Christ. It is this
comprehensive communal and *liberative* perspective which is the source
and foundation of new thinking and at the same time a sign of ventur-
ing into the future with hope based on divine intervention.[31] It is very
unfortunate, however, that very few local churches in Africa have tried to
localize the vision of the church as family in their respective dioceses and
parishes. A recommended pastoral tool for doing this would have been
convening of diocesan synods. My research and experience in moderating diocesan synods, without going into details, seem to suggest that it
is only about 12 percent of the dioceses in Africa that have had diocesan
synods. In all this approach is far from being pastoral. Marriage life also
in most cases is not considered a determining factor in actualizing the
vision of the church as family.

What is of great interest to our discussion is precisely the understanding of marriage and family life as a call, just as the whole Christian
life, which requires listening to Jesus Christ, the face of the Father's mercy.[32] The life and mission of the church-family is a call to listen to Jesus
Christ. This was made very clear at the baptism and beginning of his
public ministry, just as it was during the event of Transfiguration which
was precisely meant to be a divine strategy and source of encouragement
and hope to the disciples.[33] Thus, localization of the self-understanding
of the church-family would help all those in marriage and family life
mold their personal and communal life, as to make it an expression of
the realization of God's appeal, namely, listening to Jesus Christ amidst
the challenges of today.

30. See Paul VI, *Hodie Concilium*, 57–64. See also Wood, *Sacramental Orders*, 1.
The author, as a theologian, picks from the idea of the servant church to advance a new
thinking about "ordained ministry" in the light of Vatican II.

31. See Segeja, *Perspectives for the Future*, 27–28. See also Mark 9:2–8; Matt 17:1–3;
and Luke 9:28–36.

32. The affirmation and appeal to listen to the beloved Son of the Father during
the event of Transfiguration echoes a scenario already experienced at Jesus's baptism
into His public ministry. See Matt 3:7; Mark 1:11; and Luke 3:22.

33. The disciples were terribly hurt to learn that Jesus was to die. See, e.g., John
1:14; 2 Pet 1:16–18.

Marriage and family life denote a specific nature of that stable form of Christian life built on listening to Jesus Christ.[34] This is precisely the reason for the contentment and joy, married persons find in their chosen state of life, despite the challenges they may face. Thus, married people should say by way of their life, that "It is beautiful (good, wonderful) for us to be here," to listen to Jesus, and therefore to live as married people. Since it is essentially linked to the truth, marriage and family life, when it is consciously lived, does not only set one free but also makes him or her grow in holiness, which is a personal and communal call. Thus, the issue is not the number and condition of sins or failures, but rather the joy that goes with the acceptance of the call for a change of life, hence, opening to the fullness of God's *liberative* love and mercy.[35]

Structural Family-based Renewal and Transformation

We therefore need renewed structures and forums, especially in the parish, where married people and all Christians together can experience God's mercy and *liberative* power as they listen to Jesus Christ and respond to the challenges of the families. In our opinion, for this to be realized, the parish as an expression of God's mercy through Jesus Christ should be a place where married people feel at home. The parish should encourage all to become agents of mercy, goodness, and tenderness built on understanding the situation and context of people, accompanying and restoring hope in them in their search for the truth and God.[36] It is in this line of thought Pope Francis insists that the way of the church is a way of beauty and encouragement realized in the concrete reality of each person's life despite his or her condition (AL 49).

The focus and attitude of Pope Francis concerning the approach to the challenges of the families in the context of mercy is even more amplified and assumes a unique concern in the African situation, where the church-family vision is distinctly considered as a priority.[37] As we discussed elsewhere, reverential dialogical approach perhaps echoes better

34. In fact, the other word for listening, which implies silence, is obedience. Originally, obedience was the only vow that those in consecrated life professed. But this is meant to be a living sign of all Christian practice and life.

35. In the parables of mercy, God is always presented as full of joy, especially when he pardons. See, for example, Matt 18:22.

36. See Francis, *Amoris Laetitia*, 92, 127, 291, 307–8, 311–12.

37. See John Paul II, *Ecclesia in Africa*, 63.

the focus and attitude exhorted by Pope Francis and the understanding
of the church as family.[38] In fact, we have always been registering the
same sentiment every time we engage in moderating diocesan synods
and even facilitating the formation of small Christian communities up to
date. It is this experience, for example, that triggered some of our publications, especially related to reverential dialogical ministry and small
Christian communities as a vital icon for new evangelization in the parish.[39] Reverential dialogical ministry in the first place embraces the value
of relatedness like among family members. In fact, relatedness embraced
in reverential dialogue guarantees marriage and family union. In this
line of thought, Uzukwu says: "relatedness is a fundamental principle—a
human person is essentially human because of other human beings."[40]
One should also quickly add here that in the African context, relatedness
embraces all the conditions affecting human life, environmental, material
and sacred. This is what Nyamiti calls *totemism*—the African's closeness
to nature and one's special intercourse with reality—particular plants and
animals, conditions their influence on human life.[41]

Lived experience and concreteness is another value promoted
through reverential dialogue. In the African perspective, family members collaboratively and as equals with different roles perceive new situations and experience personal as well as social transformation through
reverential dialogue.[42] All is shared in the neighborhood again through
reverential dialogue in different forums. In fact, reverential dialogue
makes use of experience and concreteness as a deep evocative value. It
usually starts from the most ordinary and totally interpersonal human
experience, like those of marriage and family life, into which those of the
church and society is inserted.[43] Since the formation of SCCs as a way of
being church in Africa commands not only a pastoral priority today but

38. See Segeja, *An Ecclesiology of Reverential Dialogue in the Family*. In the context of the Basukuma People and in light of *Ecclesia in Africa* by John Paul II, the author discusses an ecclesiology of reverential dialogue in the family, while also making
reference to other ecclesiologies in the context of Africa.

39. See Segeja, "*Reverential Dialogical Ministry*," 59–79.

40. Uzukwu, *A Listening Church*, 73.

41. See Nyamiti, "The Incarnation Viewed from an African Understanding of Person," 35.

42. See Segeja, *An Ecclesiology of Reverential Dialogue in the Family*, 7.

43. See Collins, *Models of Theological Reflection*, 35–43. The author explains experience as the primary locus of pastoral theological reflection. See also Vatican II,
Gaudium et Spes, 1, 4; *Optatum Totius*, 13–21.

also invests on the social and ecclesial importance of the family, it can then be utilized to meet the vocation and challenges of African families through a creative and transformative approach to pastoral ministry.

Related to reverential dialogue, openness to self-reconstruction and transformation is another African value amplified by Pope Francis in the second chapter of AL, as in the whole exhortation.[44] In the light of the Second Vatican Council, Pope Francis exhorts a dialogical approach to the challenges of the family rather than imposing rules by sheer authority. What is needed is a more responsible and generous effort to present the reasons, Christian beliefs, and motivations for choosing marriage and the family (AL 35–36). Furthermore, Pope Francis also highlights another pertinent African value, namely, family or communal consciousness and awareness. The presence of substantial anthropological-cultural changes, the socio-economic strain, and a culture that promotes freedom that is void of transcendental values provide new challenges. All these call for a renewed understanding and commitment to the reality of family life. In the family, such an understanding is constantly renewed through the ongoing process of reverential dialogue. Whether it is instructional, formative, or *liberative*, reverential dialogue eventually creates a communal consciousness that enables the members to participate responsibly in family life. We should, however, understand this in the context of Africa especially in light of the Post-synodal Apostolic Exhortation, *Africae Munus* of his Holiness Pope Benedict XVI. Reverential dialogue in Africa should lead the church to a common awareness of the demands of reconciliation, justice, and peace in favor of the vocation of the family and evangelization.[45]

The challenge then would be to come up with reverential dialogical parish forums and structures in favor of the vocation of the family and evangelization. In the African context, at least three related realities clearly surface. In our view, the formation of SCCs realized as a reverential dialogical reality can be of great help in promoting the vocation of the family amidst the challenges of the families today. Engaged in the

---

44. See Segeja, *An Ecclesiology of Reverential Dialogue in the Family*, 9.

45. See Majawa, "The Call to Use Power for Liberation and Integral Development of Africa," 159. The author, even before *Africae Munus*, comments that Africa will not accomplish her task of recreating the face of the earth and improving the quality of human life, unless each person devotes himself or herself, with renewed understanding and determination, to creating peace, respect for human rights and integral development.

basic pastoral activities, namely, evangelization in all facets—proclamation; witness; integral or holistic development; reconciliation, justice and peace; inculturation; communication; deeper and new evangelization; ecumenism and interfaith dialogue; catechesis; sacramental and liturgical life; and the spirituality of the faithful, family members through reverential dialogue in SCCs can grow in articulating the importance of a person's sense of fulfillment and participation in the Lord's paschal mystery (AL 48). Concretely, this can be promoted by establishing and fostering SCCs' councils.[46]

The second reality is the establishment and promotion of the parish pastoral council which, instead of wasting much of its energy and time on finances, should focus on enabling and facilitating a sense of shared responsibility in the parish.[47] A parish pastoral council, service-oriented and centered on the concrete needs of the people—as it should be—is a vehicle for the parish not only to develop a clear and deeper understanding of the need for all to share in the responsibility to carry on Christ's mission and message of mercy in the world, but also to propose ways on how to concretely respond to the challenges of families and others. Concretely and on daily basis, this would imply having a special ministry on marriage and family life both at the parish and SCC levels for promoting the vocation of marriage and family life.

We can talk as well about the practice of the church groups and associations, especially those which are pro-lay vocation, ministry, and apostolate. This is another reality ranging from lay movements and associations like Couples for Christ, Marriage Encounter, and others to the formation of Lay Apostolate Cells (LACs).[48] In our opinion, the formation of LACs is timely and a sign of our times fostering the vocation of marriage and family life for the new evangelization. This is precisely because through LACs the laity are enabled to discern their personal vocations in their everyday lives and continue to respond to the question—how is God calling each one of them to serve Him, to serve their neighbor, and to carry on the redemptive work of Christ? In the final analysis, LACs invest in the need for ongoing formation and growth towards maturity of conscience and cooperation with God's grace. It is here where the

46. Segeja, "Small Christian Communities," 26–34.

47. See Segeja, "Small Christian Communities," 17–19.

48. See Segeja, "Reverential Dialogical Ministry," 73–76. In the context of parish renewal for new evangelization, the author proposes the formation of lay apostolate cells based in parishes.

mutual support of Christians is crucial, especially today when the culture of indifferentism and relativism, propelled by an anthropological-cultural volatility, the socio-economic strain and the tendency to practice a freedom void of transcendental values are eroding the fiber of society and even of the church.

A comprehensive gaze at the current reality of the family, especially in relation to the principal tendencies in anthropological-cultural changes which lead individuals in personal and family life to receive less and less support from social structures than in the past, extreme individualism and today's fast pace of life and socio-economic stress reveals, among other factors a situation that militates against permanent decisions. Such a situation, as noted by Pope Francis, also encounters widespread uncertainty and ambiguity (AL 33). Thus, he exhorts that we need a more responsible and generous effort not only of presenting our Christian beliefs but also of explaining the reasons and motivations for choosing marriage and the family (AL 35–36). In all this, self-criticism both on the personal and communal levels becomes inevitable. Our approach to family challenges, therefore, requires in the first place understanding concrete challenges of the families with their respective situations, hence, a need to put in place a ministry, at least at the parish level, for socio-pastoral analysis and discernment. This requires a new thinking and doing in the spirit of communion of Vatican II. In this respect, listening should be fostered not only by communal life, but also by thinking together in the search for the truth.[49]

In this line of thought, therefore, strategic pastoral planning (SPP) as a tool towards effective, efficient, and relevant response to challenges of families is of paramount importance. If SPP is adopted, especially in the parish as a converging reality of the new evangelization at the family, SCCs, and the local church levels, more chances for fruitful response towards the challenges of families shall be scored.[50] In the first place for example, SPP being inclusive in its approach shall engage the youth. This will encourage them to reasonably and responsibly address their life instead of scaring and instigating fear among them about making a

---

49. See Canon Law, 619. Indeed, Vatican II in the spirit of communion, also ratified by the Code of Law, has already urged that authority must remain integral in those in positions of leadership since it is connected to their office, even if they can or must ask for an opportunity of cooperation.

50. See Segeja, "Reverential Dialogical Ministry," 67–88. The author discusses at length the importance of the parish in promoting reverential dialogical ministry.

commitment. Marriage and family life, while remains a demanding re-ality and vocation, through SPP, becomes reasonable and relevant. SPP also, when efficiently practiced, can encourage those already in married life not to feel impelled to divorce or to avoid having children.

Furthermore, SPP, especially when done in the parish set-up, will help address the challenge of poverty in more effective ways. It engages the church, especially at the grassroots level, to reflect on the mission of the church-family in Africa and its preoccupation or rather concrete and planned involvement in reconciliation, justice, and peace. For example, dedication and concern shown to migrants and to persons with special needs alike can be practiced through SCCs if SPP is properly done in the parish set-up following the model of the communities in the Acts of the Apostles. This is a sign of the Spirit. As Pope Francis clearly says, this is a test of our commitment to show mercy in welcoming others and to help the vulnerable to be fully part of our communities.

SPP shall also better position the church to persuade the state to promote the rights of family and not only those of individuals. For exam-ple, families have the right to "to be able to count on an adequate family policy on the part of public authorities in the juridical, economic, social, and fiscal domains."[51] One may add here other rights like family's access to adequate health care, education, cultural activities, and involvement in the life of society. All in all, SPP should maximize efforts to enable family members to gather together all parents to be with their children in such a way as to nurture their relationships each day.

Conclusion

According to Pope Francis, most of the challenges facing the family in the world today have become systemic. Much as a personal engagement would be required, there is need for concrete and communal concerted action on how the church should interpret and understand the diverse situations of families in today's world. One therefore understands why this chapter, like the whole document, does not consider the issues fac-ing families, especially in Africa, in view of proposing solutions. Neither does Pope Francis in this chapter, and indeed in the whole document, set out to redefine church teaching on marriage and family or to pro-pose immediate solutions to the challenges of the families. In fact, he

51. See Pontifical Council for the Family, *Charter of the Rights of the Family*, 9.

is not even directly responding to all the challenges facing the families. One realizes, for example, that in this chapter Pope Francis only makes reference to some of the issues facing families in Africa, especially those brought forward by the Symposium of Episcopal Conferences of Africa and Madagascar (SECAM)—like childlessness, subordination of women, polygamy, ancestral bonds, levirate marriages, bridal wealth, marriage in stages, and the urgency of accepting the validity of African rites and rituals of marriage which are more decisive in establishing a covenant between families prior to and above the requirements of church sacramental wedding. Rather than address all these, Pope Francis instead proposes a new focus and approach.

Consequently, the focus on reading the document would be rather on its greatest achievements. This is particularly in relation to the bold, creative, and prophetic principles and movements which it introduces in Catholic theological and pastoral approaches to marriage and family life. In doing so, Pope Francis has invited us all to enter deeper into embracing the mission of the church in Africa given the new conditions and situations encroaching marriage and family life today. The variety of situations and new challenges summons the church to revive its hope and to make it the source of prophetic visions, transformative actions and creative forms of charity in support of marriage and family life. The challenges of the families, therefore, should be understood and responded to in a broader context through a comprehensive *liberative* approach and structural family-based renewal and transformation. The challenges are integral to the very life and mission of the church, hence, requiring a concerted effort, hence SPP realized from the grassroots level of the church, namely, the parish as a church-family or community of SCCs built by families in the neighborhood.

Bibliography

Benedict XVI. *Africae Munus: Africa's Commitment*. Vatican City: Libreria Editrice Vaticana, 2011. http://w2.vatican.va/content/benedict-xvi/en/apost_exhortations/documents/hf_ben-xvi_exh_20111119_africae-munus.html.

Catholic Church. *Catechism of the Catholic Church*. Nairobi: Paulines Africa, 1994.

Francis. *Amoris Laetitia: On Love in the Family*. Vatican City: Libreria Editrice Vaticana, 2016.   http://w2.vatican.va/content/dam/francesco/pdf/apost_exhortations/documents/papa-francesco_esortazione-ap_20160319_amoris-laetitia_en.pdf.

————. *Evangelii Gaudium: The Joy of the Gospel*. Vatican City: Libreria Editrice Vaticana 2013. http://w2.vatican.va/content/francesco/en/apost_exhortations/documents/papa-francesco_esortazione-ap_20131124_evangelii-gaudium.html.

Hernandez, Victor. "The Spirituality of the Ecclesial Base Communities." In *Small Christian Communities: Fresh Stimulus for a Forward-looking Church*, edited by Klaus Kramer and Klaus Vellguth, 67–86. Quezon City, Philippines: Claretian, 2013.

International Theological Commission. *Texts and Documents 1969–1985*. San Francisco: Ignatius, 1989.

John Paul II. *Christifideles Laici: Vocation and Mission of the Lay Faithful*. Libreria Editrice Vaticana, 1988. http://w2.vatican.va/content/john-paul-ii/en/apost_exhortations/documents/hf_jp-ii_exh_30121988_christifideles-laici.html.

————. *Ecclesia in Africa: The Church in Africa*. Vatican City: Libreria Editrice Vaticana, 1995. http://w2.vatican.va/content/john-paul-ii/en/apost_exhortations/documents/hf_jp-ii_exh_14091995_ecclesia-in-africa.html.

————. *Ecclesia in Asia: The Church in Asia*. Vatican City: Libreria Editrice Vaticana, 1997. http://w2.vatican.va/content/john-paul-ii/en/apost_exhortations/documents/hf_jp-ii_exh_06111999_ecclesia-in-asia.html.

————. *Familiaris Consortio: The Family in the Modern World*. Vatican City: Libreria Editrice Vaticana, 1981. http://w2.vatican.va/content/john-paul-ii/en/apost_exhortations/documents/hf_jp-ii_exh_19811122_familiaris-consortio.html.

————. *Letter to Families: 1994, Year of the Family*. http://w2.vatican.va/content/john-paul-ii/en/letters/1994/documents/hf_jp-ii_let_02021994_families.html.

————. *Novo Millennio Ineunte: At the Beginning of the New Millennium*. Vatican City: Libreria Editrice Vaticana, 2001. http://w2.vatican.va/content/john-paul-ii/en/apost_letters/2001/documents/hf_jp-ii_apl_20010106_novo-millennio-ineunte.html.

————. *Pastores Dabo Vobis: I Will Give You Shepherds*. Vatican City: Libreria Editrice Vaticana, 1992. http://w2.vatican.va/content/john-paul-ii/en/apost_exhortations/documents/hf_jp-ii_exh_25031992_pastores-dabo-vobis.html.

————. *Redemptor Hominis: The Redeemer of Man*. Vatican City: Libreria Editrice Vaticana, 1979. http://w2.vatican.va/content/john-paul-ii/en/encyclicals/documents/hf_jp-ii_enc_04031979_redemptor-hominis.html.

Karambai, Sebastian S. *Structures of Decision-Making in the Local Church*. Bangalore: Theological Publications in India, 2001.

Lonema, Fabien. "Structures of Participation in the Parish." *African Christian Studies* 26:1 (March 2010) 93–118.

Njoge, Teresia. "Pre-marital Counselling and Its Contribution to Stability in Marriage." *African Christian Studies* 27:1 (March 2011) 60–80.

Nyamiti, Charles. "The Incarnation Viewed from the African Understanding of Person." *African Christian Studies* 6 (1990) 1–27.

Nyaundi, Nehemia M. "The Contemporary African Family in the Light of Rapid Social Change Theory." In *Challenges and Prospects of the Church in Africa*, edited by Nahashon W. Ndung'u and Philomena N. Mwaura, 71–87. Nairobi: Paulines Africa, 2005.

Ogbamicael, Lettedenghil. *Dynamics of Human Growth*. Nairobi: Paulines Africa, 2011.

Pontifical Council for Justice and Peace. *Compendium of the Social Teaching of the Church*. Nairobi: Paulines Africa, 2004.

Segeja, Nicholaus. *Perspectives for the Future in Light of the Synods of the Church in Africa: A Socio-Pastoral Reflection*. Nairobi: CUEA Press, 2012.

———. "Reverential Dialogical Ministry [Part I]." *African Christian Studies* 28:2 (June 2012) 42–66.

———. "A Pastoral Reflection on Single Parenthood in Vocations Animation." *African Christian Studies* 29:4 (December 2013) 62–83.

———. "Understanding *Amoris Laetitia* in the Light of *Evangelii Gaudium*: A Pastoral Perspective." *GOOD SHEPHERD, A Journal of Pastoral Theology* 1:2 (December 2016) 58–80.

Synod of Bishops XII Ordinary General Assembly. *The New Evangelization for the Transmission of the Christian Faith: Lineamenta*. Nairobi: Paulines Africa, 2011.

Vatican II. *Apostolicam Actuostatem: Decree on the Apostolate of the Laity*. November 18, 1965. http://www.vatican.va/archive/hist_councils/ii_vatican_council/ documents/vat-ii_decree_19651118_apostolicam-actuositatem_en.html.

———. *Gaudium et Spes: Pastoral Constitution on the Church in the Modern World*. December 7, 1965. http://www.vatican.va/archive/hist_councils/ii_vatican_ council/documents/vat-ii_cons_19651207_gaudium-et-spes_en.html.

———. *Lumen Gentium: Dogmatic Constitution of the Church*. November 21, 1965. http://www.vatican.va/archive/hist_councils/ii_vatican_council/documents/vat-ii_const_19641121_lumen-gentium_en.html.

———.*Unitatis Redintegratio: Decree on Ecumenism*. November 21, 1964. http:// www.vatican.va/archive/hist_councils/ii_vatican_council/documents/vat-ii_ decree_19641121_unitatis-redintegratio_en.html.

Vijay, Thomas. "Theological-Pastoral Foundations of DIIPA-Vision for Small Christian Communities." In *Small Christian Communities: Fresh Stimulus for a Forward-looking Church*, edited by Klaus Kramer and Klaus Vellguth, 293–328. Quezon City, Philippines: Claretian, 2013.

3

The Vocation of the Christian Family in Africa

V INCENT E. A RISUKWU

Introduction

The gospel of the family proclaims the vocations of the family life, namely that married couples look to Jesus, the incarnate Word of God, who took flesh in the Holy Family and thus, sanctified and ennobled marriage and family life. In this essay, I will discuss the content of chapter 3 of *Amoris Laetitia* (AL). I wish to draw from the richness of culture and faith of the African people to demonstrate how we can support, sustain, and promote marriage and family life after the mind of God, following the teachings of the church.

Marriage is a gift in African culture. This is seen from the various understanding of traditional marriages in Africa. The image of God is also a strong factor in African families portrayed in the trinitarian, ecclesiological, and anthropological understanding of this presence. The divine image in African families can best be understood through an authentic Afro-Christian faith and theology.

This chapter will draw from library materials, internet resources, telephone interviews, and one-on-one conversations with both ecclesiastical authorities and lay African faithful. I hope to propose in this essay what a family ministry should look like in Africa by suggesting a review of religious education, marriage formation programs, Catholic schools, establishment of tuition support, outbound evangelization, and an improved pastoral care for marriage and family life. In the words of Pope John Paul II, "Now is the time for each local Church to assess its fervor and find fresh enthusiasm for its spiritual and pastoral responsibilities, by reflecting on what the Spirit has been saying to the People of God."[1] Based on those words, I propose that some adaptations for marriage preparation programs be made from the U.S. to the African church taking into consideration the socio-cultural context and challenges specific to African peoples and ecclesia in Africa.

Marriage and Family in the Light of AL

Pope Francis presents several themes in chapter 3 of AL. He treats marriage and family life within the context of the "kerygma, 'that which is most beautiful, most excellent, most appealing and at the same time most necessary.'"[2] He envisions in the family God's message of love and tenderness, "a gift given for the sanctification and salvation of the spouses."[3] We shall treat some of the themes as follows:

a) Jesus as the restoration and fulfillment of God's plan: Gift of marriage

b) The family in the documents of the church

c) The Sacrament of Matrimony

d) Transmission of life and the rearing of children

e) The family and the church

Whereas, our goal here is to analyze the key themes above as presented by Pope Francis, we shall stress the idea of marriage and family as gift within the African milieu.

Affirming that Jesus is the restoration of God's plan in the family, the pope remarks that the incarnation of the Word in human form radically changed the history of the world. Thus, the beauty of family life is taking roots from Christ who became part of human history. In the mystery of Christmas, we contemplate the "Yes" of Mary and the "Yes" of Joseph. We contemplate the various encounters of Christ—the shepherds, the Magi,

1. John Paul II, *Novo Millennio Ineunte*, 3.

2. Francis, *Amoris Laetitia*, 58.

3. Francis, *Amoris Laetitia*, 72.

Zechariah, Simeon and Anna—as well as the various experiences that brought about the beauty of family life.[4]

Pope Francis references the history of the church to emphasize the beauty of marriage and the dignity of the family. He acknowledges the conciliar documents and the writings of his predecessors to promote the dignity of marriage and the family. These include:

- *Gaudium et Spes*: "defined marriage as community of life and love (48), placing love at the center of the family . . . True love between husband and wife involves mutual self-giving, includes and integrates the sexual and affective dimensions, in accordance with God's plans."[5]

- *Lumen Gentium* sees the Christian family as a domestic church through which spouses are consecrated and by means of a special grace build up the Body of Christ.[6]

- *Humanae Vitae*: Pope Paul VI emphasized the importance of conjugal love and the generation of life. He stressed that responsible parenthood enables couples to recognize their duties towards God, towards one another and towards the human society.[7]

- In his *Letter to Families, Gratissimam Sane*, Pope John Paul II paid attention to the catechesis on human love. The pope defined the family as "the way of the Church, offered a general vision of the vocation of men and women to love, and proposed guidelines for the pastoral care of the family and for the role of the family in society."[8]

- *Deus Caritas Est*: Pope Benedict XVI highlighted marriage based on an exclusive and definitive love which becomes an icon of the relationship between God and his people. He returned to the topic of the truth of the love of man and woman, which is fully illuminated only in the love of the crucified Christ.[9]

With the teachings of the church above, Pope Francis set the tone for the vocation of the Christian family as "the image of God who is a

---

4. Francis, *Amoris Laetitia*, 65.

5. Vatican II, *Gaudium et Spes*, 48.

6. Francis, *Amoris Laetitia*, 67.

7. Paul VI, *Humanae Vitae*, 10.

8. John Paul II, *Familiaris Consortio,* 13; Francis, *Amoris Laetitia*, 69.

9. Benedict XVI, *Deus Caritas Est*, 2; Francis, *Amoris Laetitia*, 70.

communion of persons."[10] Earlier, Archbishop Fulton Sheen stated that Christians view marriage as "a descent from God, or a gift from above."[11] When couples come together to express their consent to each other, they engage in both physical and spiritual exchange. Christ says, "They are no longer two, therefore, but one flesh" (Matt 19:6).

AL sets out to enlighten humanity on the mystery of the Christian family in the light of the Father's love revealed in Christ. Marriage is traced from the covenantal relationship between God and Old Testament Israel. In that covenant, God entered a relationship with Abraham, Isaac, Jacob, Moses, etc. His promise to them was, "You will be my people and I will be your God" (Exod 6:7). That covenantal relationship was fulfilled in Christ in the New Testament as sign of God's fidelity to his promises. Pope Francis points out that Christ gave himself for us and continues to dwell in our midst.[12] That is the good news upon which marriage anchors.

The pope addressed the transmission of life and the rearing of children through the "intimate partnership of life and love." In marriage, sexuality "is ordered to the love of man and woman." The marriage union basically centers on the spouses. It transforms human sexuality into its divine purpose. Through their conjugal union, the couple appreciates each other. Even without children, the couple "can have a conjugal life full of meaning."[13] Meanwhile, conjugal love becomes both an expression of love and a capacity to give life thus, "Be fruitful, multiply, fill the earth and subdue it" (Gen 1:28). Andreas Kostenberger distinguishes four ways by which sex fulfills the divinely ordained purposes and plays a crucial role in marriage as follows:

1) Procreational: Procreation is part of God's creation mandate for the man and the woman. It is also the natural outflow of sexual union unless hindered by the contraceptive devices, thwarted by abortion, or prevented by infertility. Conjugal love is therefore, "sex in the service of God."

2) Relational and social: Sex is tied to the relational and social dimension of the husband-wife relationship. Conjugal love serves to

10. Francis, *Amoris Laetitia*, 71.

11. Sheen, *Three to Get Married*, 106.

12. Francis, *Amoris Laetitia*, 59.

13. Francis, *Amoris Laetitia*, 80.

alleviate the man's aloneness and provides companionship, resulting in the man and the woman becoming "one flesh" (Gen 2:24).

3) "Public good": The author represents the opinion of Christopher Ash who sees marriage as "encompassing the benefits of ordered and regulated sexual relationships in human society." Kostenberger maintains that anyone who wants to engage in pure sex needs his heart cleansed in order to experience God's creation ideal for the first human couple thus, "And the man and his wife were both naked and were not ashamed" (Gen 2:25; see Ps 51:10).

4) Marital pleasure: Sex, when enjoyed between a husband and a wife in the context of a faithful, lifelong marital union, gives great pleasure. Sexual stimulation, sexual climax, and sexual fulfilment are God's gracious gift for humanity, to be gratefully enjoyed without shame, guilt or fear.[14]

We must note that through conjugal love, marriage realizes its divine intention and orientation. And as Pope Paul VI taught in *Humanae Vitae*, love should be made fecund in marriage and not confined wholly to the loving interchange of husband and wife. Thus, "Marriage and conjugal love are by their nature ordained toward transmission of life and the rearing of children . . . the supreme gift of marriage and contribute in the highest degree to their parents' welfare."[15]

The gift of family comes from the gift of marriage. In the family, God gave man and woman the capacity to set up "a complex of interpersonal relationships, a fatherhood and motherhood, filiation and fraternity."[16] Christ took flesh in the family, and by his divine incarnation, set the Holy Family of Nazareth as model of Christian family. According to Pope John Paul II, "In this regard the Holy Family, which according to the gospel (cf. Matt 2:14–15) lived for a time in Africa, is the 'prototype and example for all Christian families' and the model and spiritual source for every Christian family."[17]

In Africa, marriage and family is believed to be gift from the divine. During my research work on this topic, I interacted with diverse cultures

---

14. Kostenberger and Jones, *God, Marriage, Family*, 81–82.

15. Paul VI, *Humanae Vitae*, 9.

16. *Familiaris Consortio*, 15.

17. *Ecclesia in Africa*, 81.

in the African continent to depict this representation. Let us see how these cultures regard marriage and family as God's gift to the community.

The Gurunsi of Upper Volta Ghana

The Gurune-speaking people originate from Upper East Region of Ghana and belong to the clan called Gurunsi. Culturally, the Gurunsi belief and lived experience of marriage and family is consistent with their world view that life originates from the almighty God and returns to him in the end. Thus, marriage is understood to be social and divine institution. Through the union of the man and woman, God enables the perpetuation of family by procreation. The Gurunsi people believe that the choice of a marriage partner should receive the blessing of God to succeed. This begins already from courtship which involves seeking the blessings of their ancestors whom they believe are custodians of sacred traditions. The ancestors mediate the will of God for the family. Hence, sacrificial offerings to the ancestors often form the foundation for courtship.

In the Gurunsi culture, the most important ritual which conveys the sanctity and inviolability of the marriage covenant is called "Nu'si gnwe'a" literally meaning the "beating or clapping of hands" during which a cock is offered in an attitude of supplication. Hence a rite of supplication is that the almighty God would accept and bless the marriage with fertility, and that new life through child bearing is the primary reason for marriage. For the Gurunsi people, children are gifts from God. Every newborn child is considered a visitor named "Asampana": "Saana, paa na" meaning a visitor has arrived.[18]

The Akans of Ghana

The concept of marriage as gift is mostly implied in the Akans community of Eastern Ghana as essential to the development and engagement of kinship ties. For the Kwahu clan of Akan community, marriage is traditionally tied to the family because it brings basically two families together. The Kwahu believe that marriage is a blessing from God, and from this blessing come children. The child born into the family is well cherished. The newborn child receives a name at birth because the Kwahu believe that the individual acquires personal and corporal identity through the

18. George Asigre is from Bomatanga of Upper Volta Ghana.

family. The individual is integrated into the community through the various rites of passage—puberty, marriage, funeral and widowhood—all in a family-oriented manner.[19]

The Yaamba of Yaana in Burkina Faso

Located in the Central Eastern part of Burkina Faso, the Yaamba believe that marriage is a gift from God through the blessings of their forefathers. The word "helper" describes the wife which is possible through the intercession of their forefathers. The Yaamba also believe that marriage is a gift from the community. Therefore, marriage cannot take place in Yaamba without the approval of the community. For the Yaamba, marriage is defined as a union of four parties: God, the community and the two spouses. Each of the components is deeply respected. The idea of gift reflects strongly in the naming of newborn child in Yaamba and communicates belief in God as the giver of children. "God" means "Wend" or "Wendnam." Some popular names in Yaana are, "Wendensong" meaning "God's Help," "Wendkouni" meaning "God's Gift," "Ninbnoma" literally meaning "Having people is good" or "Community is a good thing."[20]

The Esu of Cameroon

For the Esu clan in the northwest province of Cameroon, marriage is closely tied to the idea of having children. Marriage for the Esu, is a gift from God which everyone should embrace. For this reason, a non-married adult in Esu is not taken seriously. Parents wish that their children get married and start a family as soon as possible. The family can only be whole in Esu with addition of children. Hence parents do everything possible to have children including offering special prayers to God because of the strong belief that children are gifts from God. Marriage makes man and woman responsible in Esu land.[21]

19. Florence Ansong is from Kwahu in the eastern part of Ghana.
20. Alexis Zabsonri is a Yaana in Burkina Faso.
21. Veronica Zeh is from Esu in Northwest Province of Cameroon.

The Teso of Uganda

Georgina told a story of her grandfather from the Teso tribe in the northern part of Uganda. He was the chief of the clan and a wealthy man.
He was married to a dozen wives at a time, because of his wealth and
influence in the community. Some of the wives were given to him as
compensation from those he assisted financially. The community usually
sent their daughters to work for him because they believed he could take
care of them in marriage. Teso people believe that marriage can only take
place with the approval of both the spouses and the community. Since
God gave a man wealth, his richness should be used to support others
through marriage and the family.[22]

The Yoruba of Nigeria

The Yoruba culture permits a man to marry more than one wife only if he
has the resources to make them happy or happier than they (wives) were
in their fathers' houses. It also permits in case of death, that a man can
marry his brother's wife and inherit all that is his (brother's). A typical
Yoruba man will be permitted to see his woman publicly only if the man's
family has gone to perform the rites of "MOMIMO" meaning formal introduction of the marriage rites. Families of both parents usually waited
outside to witness the outcome of the couple's first sexual intercourse.
This is because the Yoruba culture places great importance on the family
and community. The couple is expected to be source of pride to their
families, and that way, pride to the entire community to which they belong. Marriage in Yoruba land is to maintain purity because it originates
from God.[23]

The Igbo of Nigeria

The Igbo of Nigeria celebrate marriage in numerous ways. Marriage is
usually preceded by various traditional rites to usher in the new couple
into the community. Igbos believe that their ancestors take part in the
marriage ceremony, for that reason, they carry out pre-nuptial investigations to prove the suitability of the couple for marriage. The community

22. Georgina Omuse is from Kenya but his father was Ugandan.
23. Femi Agbona is from Ibadan, western Nigeria.

participates actively in the entire marriage ceremonies in deep appreciation to God. Igbos see marriage as a means of continuing their cultural values, and are grateful to God for such gift. They accord great celebration to the arrival of the newborn with chants, songs, gun salutes accompanied with cultural dances. They reflect their belief in naming their children. Thus, "Onyinyechi," "Chinenye," "Chinyere," "Chukwuebuka," etc., are some of the names signifying God as the giver of children in Igboland.[24]

Cardinal Onaiyekan describes the entire idea of marriage in African culture thus, "It is believed that God must be consulted to sanction the intention of a young man and woman to marry. There is also the belief that, along with God himself, the ancestors are involved in the process. All this stresses the fact that marriage is a sacred institution. Our people are therefore not surprised at the Christian doctrine of marriage as a sacrament, which they take squarely in their stride."[25]

The Family and the Church

Trinitarian Image

The Synod of Bishops on the Family recognized that the Trinity images the human family, enlightened by Christ. According to the Synod, from Christ, "through the Church, marriage and the family receive the grace of the Holy Spirit, so as to bear witness to the Gospel of God's love until the fulfillment of the Covenant on the last day at the Wedding Feast of the Lamb (cf. Rev. 19:9; John Paul II, *Catechesis on Human Love*)."[26]

The image of the Trinity in the family can be seen from the Old Testament creationist account when God uttered those words, "Let us make man in our image and likeness" (Gen 1:26). God guided the Israelites in a loving relationship. He was to them a father. His relationship with Israel also captures a husband-wife image that draws Israel back from their straying paths, "For your creator is your husband . . ." (Isa 54:5); "As a young man marries a virgin, so will your sons marry you, and as a bridegroom rejoices over his bride, so will your God rejoice over you" (Isa 62:5). This love is manifested in a definitive way in Christ in the New

---

24. Anthony Ebo is from Anambra state in Igboland of southeast Nigeria.
25. Aymans, *Eleven Cardinals Speak*, 67.
26. Synod of Bishops, *Final Report of the Ordinary General Assembly*, 38.

Testament (see 1 John 4:8). Through baptism, humanity is initiated into this divine image, "In the name of the Father, and of the Son and of the Holy Spirit," and becomes adopted into God's love.

In marriage, couples become bound by this bond of love. Couples say to each other at the exchange of marriage consent, "Take this ring as a sign of my love and fidelity; In the name of the Father and of the Son and of the Holy Spirit." While addressing the National Catholic Prayer Breakfast in Washington, DC, on May 17, 2016, Robert Cardinal Sarah maintained that the generous and responsible love of spouses, made visible through the self-giving of parents, who welcome and nurture children as a gift of God, makes love visible in our generation, and makes present the perfect charity of the Trinity. The divine image thus manifests in an authentic love for children who are products of married life between a man and a woman.[27] Thus, "male and female he created them." Cardinal Sarah echoes Archbishop Fulton Sheen in his theology of the Trinity in the family thus:

> Because Spirit impregnates marriage, there is first seen in it the reflection of the mystery of the Trinity. As the Father knows Himself in His Wisdom, or Word, or Son, Who is distinct but not separate, so the husband discovers opposite to himself one in flesh with him. As the Father knows Himself in His Son, so man knows himself through the person opposite. He is present to himself in her for, thanks to sex, two persons are merged and revealed, one to the other. As the Father and Son are one in nature through the Spirit of Love that binds them, so the husband and wife find unity in sex, despite their differences, through the bond of love that makes them one. The descent of the Holy Spirit upon the Apostles not only made them one but also apostolic and fruitful in the development of the Mystical Body of Christ. So, too, husband and wife, through the deepening of their unifying love, become fruitful unto new life, thanks to an earthly Pentecost that begets raw material for the Kingdom of God.[28]

God is a communion of persons—Father, Son and Holy Spirit—three distinct persons, yet one. Cardinal Sarah stressed that the triune God dwells within each of us and imbues our whole being: God's own image and likeness. He insists that the trinitarian image of family is reflected in so many ways in Africa thus, "In the continent of my origin,

27. Harmon, "Full text: Cardinal Sarah at the National Catholic Prayer Breakfast."

28. Sheen, *Three to Get Married*, 106–7.

Africa, we declare: 'Man is nothing without woman, woman is nothing without man, and the two are nothing without a third element, which is the child.'"[29]

Let us illustrate the trinitarian image that the family orchestrates, and as Pope Francis states, "Even though the analogy between the human couple of husband and wife, and that of Christ and his church, is 'imperfect,' it inspires us to beg the Lord to bestow on every married couple an outpouring of his divine love."[30] The dad, in that human sense, can be said to be the pillar that strengthens the home. The mom complements dad's love, both uniting in a conjugal manner to recreate love in their children. Children give life and vigor to the love of their parents. In that sense, I can propose loosely a family creed that runs thus, "I believe in dad, the pillar of the family. I believe in mom, the heartbeat of the family. I believe in the children who proceed from the dad and the mom, who together with the dad and the mom are united in God's Love as one happy home." This is the image of God's love epitomized in the family.

How then can we address infertility in a typical African Christian family? According to Philippe Cardinal Ouedraogo of Ouagadougou, marriage is, "not only an alliance between a man and a woman, but also and above all an alliance between two families." Procreation is therefore seen from two perspectives: a means to perpetuate posterity and a gift from God. The African Christian views infertility as threatening his spiritual and cultural roots. Ouedraogo opines, "Procreation is so important in marriage that for some people it is the principal objective of the marital union, which viewed from the social perspective, is not only a means of cohesion through the interplay of alliances, but also a means of increasing and perpetuating one's posterity."[31]

In some cases, infertility creates pastoral problems. It affects the teaching on indissolubility of marriage in a complex way. Meanwhile, Cardinal Ouedraogo reiterates the position of the church that sterility does not diminish the indissolubility of the marital bond. In traditional African marriage, the husband, in such case, is bound to keep and to care for his sterile wife, even though that husband can take a second wife to secure the permanence of the family.[32] That may degenerate to another

---

29. Harmon, "Full text: Cardinal Sarah at the National Catholic Prayer Breakfast."

30. Francis, *Amoris Laetitia*, 73.

31. Miller, *Christ's New Homeland*, 74.

32. Miller, *Christ's New Homeland*, 75.

crisis in relation to the faith of the couple. Pastors of churches need to take into consideration the family structure and the place of children in marriage within the African context. One-on-one catechesis is necessary to deal with families facing the challenges of infertility. Such couples should be accompanied compassionately for them to understand that the family can be sustained if only couples see their union as representing the image of God. As Pope Francis remarks, "It is particularly helpful to understand in a christocentric key . . . the good of the spouses (*bonum coniugnum*), which includes unity, openness to life, fidelity, indissolubility and, within Christian marriage, mutual support on the path towards complete friendship with the Lord," and that ". . . only in contemplating Christ does a person come to know the deepest truth about human relationships."[33] Thus the church's teaching stresses that, "spouses to whom God has not granted children can have a conjugal life full of meaning, in both human and Christian terms."[34] God still loves and blesses their union, since, "marriage was not instituted solely for the procreation of children . . . Even in cases where, despite the intense desire of the spouses, there are no children, marriage still retains its character of being a whole manner and communion of life, and preserves its value and indissolubility."[35] In such circumstance, Pope Francis maintains, "I encourage those who cannot have children to expand their marital love to embrace those who lack a proper family situation . . . adopting and accepting someone unconditionally and gratuitously, they become channels of God's love."[36]

Ecclesiological Image

The fathers of the Second Vatican Council stated that the family is the domestic church, and that parents should, by their example, be the first preachers of the faith to their children.[37] The family becomes a means to promote and uphold the Christian community in the marriage covenant. Pope Francis describes the church as "a family of families, constantly enriched by the lives of those domestic churches."[38] This relationship

---

33. Francis, *Amoris Laetitia*, 77.

34. Catholic Church, *Catechism of the Catholic Church*, 1654.

35. Vatican II, *Gaudium et Spes*, 50.

36. Francis, *Amoris Laetitia*, 179.

37. See Vatican II, *Lumen Gentium*, 11.

38. Francis, *Amoris Laetitia*, no. 87.

between the church and the family is captured in terms of reciprocity in the words of the Synod Fathers, "The Church is a source of good for the family, and the family a source of good for the Church."[39]

The ecclesiological image of the family enables couples to recognize the missionary nature of marriage. Couples support each other and as well to educate and train the children in the proper way of the church. The Council Fathers describe the apostolate of the family this way:

> The mission of being the primary vital cell of society has been given to the family by God. This mission will be accomplished if the family, by the mutual affection of its members and by family prayer, presents itself as a domestic sanctuary of the church; if the whole family takes its part in the church's liturgical worship; if, finally it offers active hospitality, and practices justice and other good works for the benefit of all its sisters and brothers who suffer from want.[40]

Catholic parents have enormous responsibility in this regard. They are "cooperators in grace and witnesses of faith for each other, their children, and all others in their household; the first to communicate the faith to their children; to educate them by word and example for the Christian and apostolic life; to prudently help them in the choice of their vocation and carefully promote any sacred vocation which they may discern in them."[41] To be the primary vital cell of the society implies playing an active role in shaping the spiritual and social life of their children. Children look up to parents to guide them in their growth and to imbibe the faith tradition. Cardinal Kasper opines, "In Catholic families, there were and still are little house altars (domestic shrines), at which the family gathers for common prayer in the evening or at special times (Advent, Christmas Eve, situations of need or misfortune, etc.). Such customs of popular piety deserve a renewal. One thinks perhaps of customs like the parents' blessing of their children, religious images, above all a cross in the residence, holy water as a reminder of baptismal water, among others."[42]

Young African parents still believe in this image of the family as domestic church in the modern times. In my interaction with about two hundred African couples who have been married between five to fifteen

---

39. Synod of Bishops, *Final Report of the XIV Ordinary General Assembly*, 52.

40. Vatican II, *Apostolicam Actuositatem*, 11.

41. Vatican II, *Apostolicam Actuositatem*.

42. Kasper, *The Gospel of the Family*, 21.

years, there was unanimity in affirming the family's role as the ecclesial image for children. These are some excerpts from the conversation:

> We were lucky to have grown in an environment where we do communal activities. The way we were raised is what has made us the Christians we are today, and it is because of those church activities we did in our neighborhood like Sunday School, Block Rosary, Holy Communion classes, and so on. That exposure is what we now tap into as parents. The issue is how do we maintain that for the next generation, our kids will lose that if we don't teach them or expose them to such environment. If they are not armed with a strong spiritual knowledge that fear of God will not be there and they won't have anything to offer to the generation after them.[43]

The conversation is whether the ecclesial image of family should be inculcated in early childhood or later in life to enable a good spiritual foundation.

> Grace is very critical. God shows it to whom he wills. Some people are just unlucky while some, as bad as they are, are blessed with marriage. I strongly believe it is not something you start praying for when it is time to marry. My mother taught us to pray for marriage partner ever since we were children. Without God, it is tough to make it even with the widest experience in life. Family prayer helps keep the bond of the family. You can't underestimate that, period.[44]

These views corroborate the message of Pope Benedict XVI to Latin American and Caribbean bishops in 2011, "No effort is therefore wasted in promoting anything that can help to ensure that each family, founded on the indissoluble union between a man and a woman, accomplishes its mission of being a living cell of society, a nursery of virtues, a school of constructive and peaceful coexistence, an instrument of harmony and a privileged environment in which human life is welcomed and protected, joyfully and responsibly, from its beginning until its natural end."[45]

African parents make efforts to make their home church-centered by directing their children in the ways of the faith early enough. They share the Scriptures and make effort to inculcate morals into them. Being

---

43. Austine has been married for ten years and has three kids.

44. Tony has been married for eight years and has two kids.

45. Catholic Church, *Compendium on the Family and Human Life*, 156.

domestic church for African parents, means instituting a tradition of prayers and exemplary life in the home.

Anthropological Image

In the introduction to the book, *Letter to Families*, Archbishop Charles Chaput of the Archdiocese of Philadelphia wrote, "When God revealed himself to man through the prophets and through his Son, he used every day human language to make the mysteries of his inner life available to us. Words like Father, Son, bridegroom, bride, spouse, and even man and woman are of inestimable mystical depth in the pages of the Bible. God knew that by using these words—words that would resonate with the deepest and most heartfelt experiences of his people—he would succeed in giving us a glimpse of the love that is the Trinity."[46] Pope John Paul II traced the origin of the family to what he called "the genealogy of the person." Per him,

> Human fatherhood and motherhood are rooted in biology, yet at the same time transcend it. The Apostle, with knees bowed "before the Father from whom all fatherhood in heaven and on earth is named," in a certain sense asks us to look at the whole world of living creatures, from the spiritual beings in heaven to the corporeal beings on earth. Every act of begetting finds its primordial model in the fatherhood of God. Nonetheless, in the case of man, this "cosmic" dimension of likeness to God is not sufficient to explain adequately the relationship of fatherhood and motherhood. When a new person is born of the conjugal union of the two, he brings into the world a particular image and likeness of God himself: the genealogy of the person is inscribed in the very biology of generation.[47]

In the family, the anthropological is connected to the theological, begetting becomes continuation of creation and continuation of community life. Africans see the image of the human person in the manner the child is welcome into the family at birth, and helped to become an integral part of the community. The newborn baby is celebrated. The Igbo community, for instance, welcomes the child with celebratory gunshots for a boy and chants of songs for a girl.

46. John Paul II, *Letter to Families*, viii.
47. John Paul II, *Letter to Families*, 24–25.

As part of the anthropological image, Africans believe in bringing up the child for the society. This means leading the child to acquire character traits from the parents and elders that help him or her to be a virtuous person in the future. Kwame Gyekye relates that the Akan community of Ghana have several maxims that stress the importance of exemplary relationship between the adults and children for proper growth and development. These include:

- "If you, an elder, say, and do not do, you will not be feared by the young."

- "It is only when the father shows respect to his children that they grow to revere him."

- "One does not send a child to go up on the roof and then remove the ladder from under his feet."

- "When you lift up a child, you bring it down gently."

- "When an adult knows how to walk with children, they (happily) carry his traveling bag for him."[48]

These are expressions that portray the image of the person in the African child. They make the family a place of human interaction between parents, elders, and children. Gyekye further interprets the above maxims thus, "The first maxim stresses the importance of sincerity in the words of adults as part of the basis of respect for the adult person. The second says that within the family there should be mutual respect—between children and their parents. The third and fourth maxims are a warning against bad treatment of children. Adults, including parents, who are able to establish good relationships with children—this is the meaning of how to 'walk' with children—are those who according to the fifth maxim, will get on with them and win their respect, obedience, and honor."[49]

Authentic Afro-Christian Faith

In treating this topic, I will draw insight mostly from Pope John Paul II's encyclical, *Ecclesia in Africa*. Efforts to propose an authentic Afro-Christian theology has been at the heart of the African church. This seemed to be the project of the Special Assembly for African Synod in

48. Gyekye, *African Cultural Values*, 88.
49. Gyekye, *African Cultural Values*, 87–88.

1989, and especially, Pope John Paul II's Post-Synodal Apostolic Exhortation *Ecclesia in Africa*. The Synod "sought to identify appropriate means of better sharing and making more effective their care for all the churches (see 2 Cor 11:28). They began to plan suitable structures at the national, regional and continental levels."[50] It was this quest for appropriate means for pastoral care of souls that gave rise to the Symposium of Episcopal Conferences of Africa and Madagascar (SECAM) in Kampala, Uganda, in 1969. While declaring open the Synod of Africa in 1989, Pope John Paul II announced that "'the hour of Africa' has come, a favorable time which urgently invites Christ's messengers to launch out into the deep and to cast their nets for the catch (cf. Luke 5:4)."[51] The phrase, "launch out into the deep" here, defines what an authentic Afro-Christian theology should look like. The Holy Father demanded that the church looks forward in hope, quicken her steps as she travels the highways of the world.[52] Hence, "It is in the local churches that the specific features of a detailed pastoral plan can be identified—goals and methods, formation and enrichment of the people involved, the search for the necessary resources—which will enable the proclamation of Christ to reach people, mold communities, and have a deep and incisive influence in bringing Gospel values to bear in society and culture."[53]

In that sense, one wonders whether the Synod of Africa achieved its goal. The Holy Father challenged the African prelates to seek "deeper understanding of what it means to be both Catholic and African." The Synod aimed at achieving two objectives: (a) That the local churches of Africa hold a rightful place in the communion of the church. (b) That they are entitled to preserve and develop their own traditions, without in any way lessening the primacy of the Chair of Peter."[54]

Being Catholic and being African is a challenge which the African church has continued to grapple with in developing contextual pastoral approaches to marriage and family life. In our context, here, being African and Catholic is an opportunity to develop a pastoral approach in Africa that is ennobled both by the rich cultural traditions of Africa about family life and the constant teachings of the church. This is also connected

50. John Paul II, *Ecclesia in Africa*, 2.

51. John Paul II, *Ecclesia in Africa*, 6.

52. John Paul II, *Novo Millennio Ineunte*, 58.

53. John Paul II, *Novo Millennio Ineunte*, 29.

54. John Paul II, *Ecclesia in Africa*, 11.

with the second objective of the Synod, to preserve and develop African traditions in the light of the church. Perhaps, these two confirm what it means to launch not only into the deep but into the African deep to catch local African fish—making the African person truly Christian and truly African. This is the kind of approach which we are seeking in the light of the publication of AL and the two synods on the family.

In this regard, we can reflect on the message of *Ecclesia in Africa* and how this continues even in our times to offer us insightful challenges and themes for properly engaging the new threats to family life in the world and particularly in Africa. The theme of the First African Synod was "The Church in Africa and her evangelizing mission towards the year 2000: You shall be my witnesses (Acts 1:8)."[55] It considered various aspects of the church in Africa with great attention on evangelization, inculturation, dialogue, justice, and peace and as well means of social communication. If the African church should launch into the deep, it must be cognizant of the cultural and spiritual needs of Africans. If it should launch in-depth, it must be able to identify means of evangelization appropriate for Africa. If it should launch into the deep, it must be futuristic; it should consider how effective or relevant the message has been since that synod and in our times. The church should speak a language that is relevant to the polygamist in the twenty-first century. The African church should recognize the influence of technology among youths and millennials and adopt a language that appeals to them in the twenty-first century. But my concern here is what the church in Africa should do for Christian family especially in the challenging context of our times. Let us X-ray what the message of hope can offer in a strategic pastoral plan for the African family.

Announcing the Message of Hope to Christian Families

The questions asked by the Synod Fathers are, "In a Continent full of bad news, how is the Christian message 'Good News' for our people? Amid an all-pervading despair, where lie the hope and optimism which the gospel brings?" "Africa," they maintained, "is full of problems—abject poverty, tragic mismanagement of available scarce resources, political instability and social disorientation resulting in misery, wars and despair."[56] In this

---

55. John Paul II, *Ecclesia in Africa*, 8.
56. John Paul II, *Ecclesia in Africa*, 40.

section, we shall be addressing the following questions: What is Christian hope? What does hope look like for families? What are the effects of lack of hope on particularly young people in Africa?

What is Christian Hope?

Hope can be said to be one of the most used words in everyday life. The poor man has hope. The sick person has hope. The student has hope. The cleaner has hope. The barren woman has hope. The unemployed has hope. Sometimes, people don't even know what the object of their hope is, yet hope seems to be the driving force for their daily living especially in most difficult circumstances. Hope for the Christian goes deeper than the physical existence; it goes beyond the "now" of his/her environment. Saint Paul linked it directly to the resurrection of Christ thus, "If our hope in Christ has been for this life only, we are the most unfortunate of all people" (1 Cor 15:19). Christian hope therefore has an eschatological dimension.

In the preface to his book, *Christ Our Hope*, Paul O'Callaghan writes, "The essence of Christian salvation is hope. The secret of Christian faith is hope. The most precious contribution Christianity makes to the world is hope. Christ, who speaks through his body, the Church, does not promise humans perfect happiness or fulfilment on earth. Christian faith does not claim to resolve and explain here and now the world's many problems and perplexities . . . Rather, Christians believe primarily that through his Son Jesus Christ God has offered humanity salvation: salvation from sin, salvation leading toward eternal, loving communion with the Trinity."[57] The Christian hope is thus intimately geared towards man's salvation. Christians hope in the power of Christ, "who came that all may be saved and reach the knowledge of the truth" (1 Tim 2:4). Christianity challenges and prepares us to hope not because we are free from trials and temptations but because we are redeemed by the precious blood of the Lamb. Anthony Kelly writes, "As the gift of the Spirit . . . from God, in God, and for God . . . It is defined only by infinities of divine wisdom and mercy."[58]

Hope can be defined as the theological virtue which guarantees future life. It makes the Christian to believe in God, take the challenges

---

57. O'Callaghan, *Christ Our Hope*, vii.
58. Kelly, *Eschatology and Hope*, 201.

of life with belief that the tough things will give way in the end to the enduring happiness of everlasting life.

What Does Hope Look Like for Families?

In relation to marriage and family, the challenges go deeper than mere economic and social constraints. Pope John Paul compared contemporary Africa with "the man who went down from Jerusalem to Jericho; fell among robbers who stripped him, beat him and departed, leaving him half dead" (Luke 10:30–37). "Africa," according to him, "is a continent where countless human beings—men and women, children and young people—are living, as it were, on the edge of the road, sick, injured, disabled, marginalized and abandoned. They are in dire need of Good Samaritans who will come to their aid."[59] Here we recognize the various wounds which families carry. What does hope mean for the barren woman? What does the future hold for families afraid of ancestral curses? How about couples going through marital infidelities? What does hope mean for families grieving the loss of their loved ones? What does hope mean for the widow subjected to the whims of negative cultural practices? What does hope offer to the young unemployed adult after several years of graduation? These are several questions which bother families.

The message of hope should intimately link family values with the values of Christianity in Africa: "love, caring, cohesion, solidarity, mutual respect, and mutual responsibility."[60] This message must be prophetic in nature,[61] in order to capture authentic emotions of family life. It must speak up in defense of human dignity because ". . . the man who is to be evangelized is not an abstract being but is subject to social and economic questions."[62]

In 2015, Pope Francis addressed families on the problems they face regarding the aftermath of death. The pope described death as "a black hole that opens in the life of a family and for which we don't know how to give any explanation. When a loved one dies, especially a child or a parent of young children, death is never able to appear as something natural. It is 'heart-rending' when a mother and father lose a child: It's

---

59. John Paul II, *Ecclesia in Africa*, 41.

60. See Gyekye, *African Cultural Values*, 90.

61. John Paul II, *Ecclesia in Africa*, 70.

62. John Paul II, *Ecclesia in Africa*, 68.

as if time has stopped. An abyss opens that swallows up the past and the future."[63] The pope explains, "Our loved ones have not disappeared into dark nothingness: Hope assures us that they are in God's good and strong hands. Love is stronger than death."[64] In that case, hope provides answer in the resurrection. The bereaved family believes that they will meet their departed family member at the resurrection of the dead.

Considering what families go through in life, it will be wrong to imagine that solutions to all problems in the world will be solved because one is a believer. When couples are barren, when they struggle with infidelities, when families are battling with ancestral curses, when widowhood practices make the woman a victim, etc., it must be stressed that life is not over. Hope looks to the future. It is good to seek solution for these problems, to try to break away from the shackles of suffering, but hope is not all about physical liberation. Hope relates to freedom for two reasons: Christ has set us free. He has freed us from the crushing effects of sin. Secondly, we must live in the hope of gaining our ultimate freedom at the end of time. Life lived with emphasis on this world lacks the promises of hope, as Saint Paul writes, "all that we suffer in the present life is nothing in comparison with the glory which is to be revealed to us in the end of time" (Rom 8:18). Kelly encourages Christians to confront the many faces of despair in themselves and others this way, "Hope must arise and grow amidst inexplicable suffering, inevitable death, humiliating failure, meaninglessness, guilt, and fear in all its forms. It is ever up against the sheer power of evil in all its virulent manifestations. Whatever the joy and peace inherent in the gospel of hope, it offers no complacent, passive preview of things. Our hope is called to share in the patience of God."[65]

Why is the Absence of Hope Affecting People, Particularly the Young People?

Lack of hope has particularly negative impact on young persons. Pope Francis recognizes "that we live in a culture which pressures young people not to start a family, because they lack possibilities for the future."[66] In the words of the pontiff, "At times families suffer terribly when faced with the illness of a loved one, they lack access to adequate health care,

63. Glatz, "Pope Francis."
64. Glatz, "Pope Francis."
65. Kelly, *Eschatology and Hope*, 13.
66. Francis, *Amoris Laetitia*, 40.

or struggle to find dignified employment. Economic constraints prohibit a family's access to education, cultural activities and involvement in the life of the society. Families in particular, suffer from problems related to work, where young people have few possibilities and job offers are very selective and insecure."[67] It is as if hope is dwindling among many families in the absence of a guaranteed future. Why?

1) Misconception of Christian faith: There is no gainsaying that many families lack the proper understanding of their faith. Ironically, people go to church, worship God, yet fear their freedom. Many preachers in Africa reduce Christianity to the level of physical prosperity, hence liberation theology is at the center of preaching in churches. There is a misconception that the individual who worships God ought to be free from all forms of suffering. This is not the image of Christ, the Lamb of God, who "though he was in the form of God did not count equality with God, something to be grasped" (Phil 2:6). The absence of hope affects people in such situation because the idea of imaginary freedom creates in them false sense of hope.

2) "Hyper-worldism": There is a growing attitude of excessive concentration on worldly and material things. Today's society is distracted to the point that values are defined by the powers of consumerism and the social media. Some couples become entrapped in the web of pornography which dwindles their marital hope. Pope Francis "expressed concern about this current spread of pornography and the commercialization of the body, fostered by a misuse of the internet, and about those reprehensible situations where people are forced into prostitution."[68] These factors drastically affect family life, lead to failures in relationships, encourage anti-life practices, and cause numerous marital problems such as infidelity, separation and divorce.

3) Economic and political problems: It remains a big concern as to how families which are constantly threatened by hunger, starvation, fear, despair and loss can confidently sustain their faith. In Africa, for instance, economic and political problems have led many families to question their hope. Some wonder whether they are still

67. Francis, *Amoris Laetitia*, 44; see Synod of Bishops, *Final Report of the XIV Ordinary General Assembly*, 14.

68. Francis, *Amoris Laetitia*, 41.

God's creatures. Young people are forced into migration while the elderly resign to despair and death. Van Nam Kim writes, "Political orders which directly cause hunger, persecution, and deprive other human rights are against hope offered to all human beings by Jesus Christ."[69] When people are hungry, they seem to be angry even with God whom they feel permit oppressive forces to threaten their lives.

Meanwhile, we wish to stress the importance of the message of hope even in situations described above. The hope which the African church conveys should be forceful enough, and detached from the socio-economic and political calamities seen in Africa. Hope should proclaim the reality of Christ. It should invite families into the safe space of their faith. According to Saint Paul, "Not only that; let us exult, too, in our hardships, understanding that hardship develops perseverance, and perseverance develops a tested character, something that gives us hope, and a hope which will not let us down, because the love of God has been poured into our hearts by the Holy Spirit which has been given to us" (Rom 5:2–5). The message of hope must connect Africans fundamentally to their Christian identity. It is in this context that we consider the Family Ministry as imperative for the African church.

What Family Ministry Should Look Like

Proposing a homogeneous pastoral plan for marriage and family in Africa is daunting task because of the diverse nature of the vast continent. So, what I offer here is a model which can be contextualized according to pastoral needs and circumstances. However, I am proposing that this is a ministry which should be central in our dioceses and parishes like the pastoral council and the finance council. The Family Ministry should be a diocesan statutory body which coordinates the parish Family Ministries. It should be headed by the diocesan bishop, and should comprise canonists, moral theologians and priests with professional experience in marriage and family life. Lay experts on marriage and Natural Family Planning, Catholic couples with at least five years of marriage experience, committed Catholics in the single life, representatives from the young adults and youth. For instance, a model of the Family Ministry can be seen in the ecclesiastical province of Bamenda in Cameroon which has about four million people, with 20 percent Catholic population. Archbishop

---

69. Kim, *A Church of Hope*, 179.

Cornelius Esua explained that Bamenda archdiocese established the Family Life Office (Family Ministry) in 1984. The Family Life Office caters for the Family Apostolate in each parish including marriage formation, formation for Natural Family Planning, spiritual and pastoral life of the family, Christian Family Movement, Marriage Encounter and family associations such as Catholic Men and Women Associations. The Family Life Office also formulates Integral Family Life including children's programs. The office is directed by couples and has been established in all parishes of the archdiocese of Bamenda.[70]

Pope Benedict XVI stated, "Family ministry has an important part to play in the evangelizing activity of each of the different particular churches, promoting a culture of life and working to ensure that the rights of families are recognized and respected."[71] Africa is undeniably rich in preserving her cultural values and beliefs regarding marriage, human life and family. This was orchestrated at the last Synod on the Family in Rome. The forty-eight prelate-representatives from Africa were all united in defense of marriage. When questioned on shared life experiences on the continent regarding family, Archbishop Thomas Msusa, Malawi representative, head of the Blantyre archdiocese and vice-chairman of east Africa's regional bishops' conference stated, "We are bringing the same message. Let us live proudly the heritage of what we have received: the Christian family."[72] Cardinal Berhaneyesus Demerew Souraphiel of Addis Ababa, Ethiopia highlighted some of those peculiarities as, "polygamy, the communitarian aspect of marriage, dowries and love for posterity."[73] Archbishop Esua corroborated that both monogamy and polygamy, for instance, are recognized as parts of the traditional marriage in Cameroon. However, he stressed that the church in Cameroon recognizes only monogamous marriage. I will go on to outline below, elements that should be part of the family ministry in the African church.

70. Oral interview with Archbishop Esua, August 8, 2016.

71. Catholic Church, *Compendium on the Family and Human Life*, 155.

72. McElwee, "Malawi archbishop: Africans at Synod sharing same message of proud heritage."

73. Njuguna, "Of African Family Values and the Synod."

Inclusive Religious Education

When I was growing up, we used to attend catechism classes. They were tagged different names, CCD, infant catechism, etc. In the native Igbo language, this was called "*nkuzi nke okwukwe*" which translates as "faith formation classes." Teachings on church doctrine began with learning basic prayers, the Creed, then the mysteries of the Trinity—God the Father, Son and Holy Spirit. The lessons introduce the child into the basics of faith. As children, we memorized those prayers. Those were major steps in the faith formation. Some Catholic communities established Block Rosary Crusade groups for children and youths. As adults, too, evening catechism lessons were organized in parishes. The priests used to teach catechism classes on Sundays. Experiences and local stories were shared. These were moments to deepen the faith of the adult Christian. Ironically, those opportunities for teaching the faith seem to be disappearing today.

We need to rediscover the importance of religious education in Africa. The Ethiopian Cardinal Souraphiel is upfront in this regard in describing the role of the church, "She (the Church) provides religious education for children grades 1–12. She makes available Catholic schools from kindergarten to the university level, where truths of the faith and moral truths are part of the learning experience. She provides classes in Natural Family Planning, family counseling, and pastoral care, especially in the sacrament of reconciliation and forgiveness. She counteracts such contemporary trends such as hedonism, abortion, euthanasia, and value-free sex education. Most importantly, she provides the sacraments, whereby every man, woman, and child can obtain the spiritual help he needs to resist temptation, to pursue virtuous living, and to grow in the worship and praise of God."[74]

The church should recognize her enormous responsibilities in the education of the family. Pope Francis argues for the church's cooperation with parents through suitable pastoral initiatives to fulfill their educational mission.[75] Initiating religious education for African families should be an inclusive agenda. It must take into consideration the mental capacity of children, the exuberance of teenagers and youths, the attractions of young adults, and the concerns of parents in planning such programs. Images, diagrams and videos should be actively inserted into religious education to tell stories in compelling manner.

74. African Pastors, *Christ's New Homeland*, 93–94.
75. See Francis, *Amoris Laetitia*, 85.

Ongoing Marriage Formation

In 1985, Pope John Paul II spoke to the Episcopal Conference of Cameroon in Yaounde, "In Africa today formation in the faith . . . too often stops at the elementary stage, and the sects easily profit from this ignorance."[76] Marriage preparation programs in most parts of Africa simply fall short of the standards. In most parishes in Nigeria, for instance, Pre-Cana classes are left in the hands of catechists and instructors some of whom are not properly trained in marriage formation. They inherit such responsibilities merely by their offices, which unfortunately, they assume with no formal qualifications. Recently, Kelechi and Ijeoma attended marriage prep classes for their wedding in a semi-urban parish in the South East of Nigeria. Kelechi narrated that the catechist would only tell him stories each time they gathered. Sometimes, the catechist would cancel classes. At other times, he would insinuate that marriage course was a mere routine, and that those who took their marriage courses still had problems after all. That implied that couples should not overemphasize marriage preparation.

On the contrary, marriage preparations in the church should be systematic and consistent. Engaged couples should have course outline to cover and a workbook to complete at the end of their classes. With the help of the Family Ministry, parishes should train educators to help prepare couples for marriage. Engaged couples should be introduced to the fact that marriage is a living sacrament and not merely the wedding event. They should be prepared to the idea of living their married life as vocation. Ongoing seminars and conferences should be organized by the Family Ministry for couples after marriage. For example, although Christian marriage is in decline in the U.S.A., efforts to give couples the best preparation program are still emphasized. The Office of Marriage and Family Life in the Catholic Archdiocese of Baltimore, for instance, uses a detailed marriage program for engaged couples based on the following sources:

a) FOCCUS pre-marriage inventory: The FOCCUS Inventory is designed to help engaged couples appreciate their unique relationship, learn more about themselves, and discuss topics important to their lifelong marriage. At FOCCUS, engaged couples are guided to discuss important topics including communication, problem-solving,

76. John Paul II, *Ecclesia in Africa*, 76.

religion, dual careers, parenting, intimacy, finances, etc. Facilitators are usually sponsor couples trained from the church community.[77]

b) Pre-Cana class: Engaged couples attend online classes and retreats to prepare for marriage. The Pre-Cana program is designed to serve the convenience of engaged couples due to work schedule, schools and other conflicting pressures. Pre-Cana questions address issues related to finances, sex, lifestyle expectations, and gender roles. Sometimes, nearby parishes join to promote Pre-Cana meetings for engaged couples in a cluster or community.[78]

c) PREPARE/ENRICH: This is an online assessment tool for both married and unmarried couples who want to understand and improve their relationship. By asking key questions in the beginning of the assessment, PREPARE/ENRICH addresses each couple's relationship stage, situation, challenges, philosophical/spiritual orientation, and personalities and tailors the inventory to assess the couple's strengths and areas of challenge where growth will be most beneficial. Each partner completes the inventory independently by answering approximately 200 questions.[79]

These systems are geared towards integral development of couples in marriage. The African church can adopt some of these programs to suit the African situation. Attention must be expanded beyond the wedding ceremony. Both engaged and married couples should be mission oriented in the marriage preparation. They should continue to receive ongoing formation in areas of communication, problem-solving, religion, equality, parenting, intimacy, finances, friendship, children, etc. The hot topics of marriage should be constantly discussed and not avoided.

The challenge of technology and social media should be acknowledged while considering these programs. A typical African will also not believe in the efficacy of online marriage preparation. Since Africans are community oriented, the communitarian dimension should be emphasized. Using PREPARE/ENRICH for example, each engaged-couple chooses a mentor-couple independently. The mentor-couple work with them throughout the six-month period of marriage preparation. Mentor couples should be adequately trained, be practicing Catholics and

77. See http://www.foccusinc.com/foccus-inventory.aspx.

78. See http://www.catholicmarriageprep.com.

79. https://www.prepare-enrich.com.

married for at least five years. They should be credible and faithful. Their role would be to facilitate discussions on various issues in marriage, not moderators who control discussions. At the end, they use the workbook to evaluate the performance of the engaged couples who would submit the workbook to the Family Ministry for their file and documentation. The practice of selecting wedding sponsors based on financial or social standing few days before wedding in Africa should be eliminated or improved. The idea of abandoning engaged couples in the hands of ignorant catechists for marriage instructions should also be a thing of the past.

Marriage and Family Programs in Catholic Schools

Pope John Paul II described Catholic schools as "places of evangelization, well-rounded education, inculturation and initiation into the dialogue of life among young people."[80] This stresses the importance of sound and integral academic programs in Catholic schools. Catholic schools need to take cognizance of the entire goals and objectives of children's upbringing in planning their academic curriculum. These should include marriage and family life. Like the priesthood, marriage is a vocation. It covers the entire gamut of a person's life. It should be given adequate preparation. Cardinal Müller remarks, "Remote preparation for marriage, that is, from childhood and adolescence on, ought to be one of the first pastoral priorities in education. A child who discovers that he is unconditionally loved as a son will recognize himself in adolescence as someone who feels impelled to love another person and, finally, in adulthood, after recognizing his spousal dimension, as someone who discovers that his love is fruitful."[81]

The question is whether Catholic education in Africa can improve pastoral care for marriage and family. The diocesan Synod of Ouagadougou, Burkina Faso, recommended taking additional measures to safeguard the faith of young Catholic believers.[82] The answer may also be partly contained in the Ethiopian Cardinal Souraphiel's explanation of the crucial role of the church in Africa thus: "She makes available

80. John Paul II, *Ecclesia in Africa*, 102.

81. Granados, *The Hope of the Family*, 19.

82. See Oedraogo, in *Christ's New Homeland*, 73.

Catholic schools from kindergarten to the university level, where truths of the faith and moral truths are part of the learning experience."[83]

How does the African church prepare her children for marriage and family life? In his address to Catholic women in 1941, Pope Pius XII said, "It is a curious circumstance and, a lamentable one, that whereas no one would dream of suddenly becoming a mechanic or an engineer, a doctor or a lawyer, without any apprenticeship or preparation, yet every day there are numbers of young men and women who marry without having given an instant's thought to preparing themselves for the arduous work of educating their children which awaits them."[84] Marriage formation and education has to be accorded greater attention in schools. Academic curriculum should include elements of married life. Malawi Archbishop Msusa stated, "What is needed for us in Malawi is catechesis—teach young people to see married life as a vocation, a call."[85]

If we compare marriage with vocation to the priesthood, then we understand how little education couples receive prior to marriage. In the seminary for instance, the entire academic, moral and intellectual formation of the student aim at his pastoral life as priest. This takes long years of preparation. To a great extent, same should apply for those seeking marriage. Dietrich von Hildebrand opines that marriage must be compared to Holy Orders "in its character as a Sacrament—a source of specific graces, a dispenser of graces."[86] Hildebrand's idea is that marriage should be appreciated because of its sacramental content. In a similar sense, preparations for marriage and family life should be introduced in Catholic schools. Issues such as health, children, religion, finance, sex, in-laws, etc., are silent until marriage preparation, and sometimes not even addressed. Couples stumble into them and work out their own formula after marriage. This should not be the case. The vocation of marriage should be a subject deliberately included in Catholic schools' curricula.

Catholic Family Tuition Support (CFTS)

There is need to introduce "Catholic Family Tuition Support" program as pastoral strategy to encourage Catholic education in Africa. This is

83. African Pastors, *Christ's New Homeland*, 93–94.

84. Pius XII, *Davanti a Questa*.

85. See McElwee, "Malawi Archbishop."

86. Hildebrand, *Marriage, The Mystery of Faithful Love*, 53.

necessary because many families are threatened by poverty and cannot satisfy the educational needs of their children. Poverty, for sure, is a major threat in Africa, and hampers the faith too. The Catholic Archdiocese of Philadelphia Schools states, on its website's "Scholarships & Financial Aid" page: "Each school in the Archdiocese sets its own tuition, but we've put together a comprehensive portfolio of need-based and merit-based opportunities available to existing or incoming AOP students. These programs, in addition to offers available from individual schools, can drastically reduce—or even eliminate—tuition costs."[87]

Unfortunately, tuition supports are very scarce in African continent already scourged by poverty. The "Catholic Family Tuition Support" fund should receive special days for donations in the church like any other appeal fund program. Bishops and archbishops also should appeal to philanthropic individuals and institutions both local and abroad to support the course of maintaining such fund. Dioceses and archdioceses should recognize the financial imbalance among parishes and provide more support to poorer parishes to promote Catholic education. Families that receive financial support from the church are usually grateful. They, in turn, render services in their capacity for the growth and sustenance of the church.

Family Apostolate: Outbound Evangelization

The Family Apostolate should be part of the Family Ministry. It is the idea of meeting individual families where they are. It is a parish apostolate of praxis that promotes traditional marriage, family life and spirituality. It recognizes that families function well "by the reception of the sacraments, prayer and thanksgiving, the witness of a holy life, and self-denial and active charity; and that the home is the first school of Christian life and a school for human enrichment."[88] In 1964, John Robinson highlighted the following as reasons to establish the Family Apostolate in Africa:

a) "The widespread abandonment of fundamental points of Christian marriage and family morality;

---

87. See the "Scholarships & Financial Aid" page of the Archdiocese of Philadelphia Schools' website, http://www.aopcatholicschools.org/financial-aid/.

88. Catholic Church, *Catechism of the Catholic Church*, 1657.

b) The emergence of women as a social, and ultimately as a political force in the service of the family;

c) The development of the spirit of partnership in the conjugal society;

d) Family movements and the rally to the aid of the family on the human plane;

e) The Christian Family Movement."[89]

Establishing a Family Apostolate in parishes would be a great avenue to improve pastoral relationships among priests and the faithful. The new evangelization calls each Christian to deepen their faith, believe in the gospel and go forth to proclaim it with their lives. Hence, the Family Apostolate should establish a connection between the church and families; and unite families as members of Christ's Body. It should dedicate itself to the spiritual welfare of families in the Catholic Church.

In contemporary business world, successful industries adopt business modules that are consumer-oriented and customer-friendly. Businesses do not sit and wait for customers to come to them any longer, rather they follow them with their products. It is called "outbound marketing." Recently, Microsoft took aggressive steps towards eradicating the Zika virus. The company announced on June 22, 2016, that it developed a trap that would identify specific breeds of mosquitoes and record when each mosquito entered the trap. The traps arc expected to speed the process of identifying mosquito borne illnesses, and provide more data about when the diseases arrived.[90] In a similar fashion, the Family Apostolate proposes a strategy of "outbound evangelization" able to identify family needs. It formulates a strategic plan to actively reach out to members of the Catholic faith and beyond—take prayers and blessings to their homes, draw vibrant spiritual exercises using the social media, design online evangelization using video, Facebook, Twitter, Instagram, etc., to engage young adults, youths and millennials. Reflections, homilies, lives of the saints, audios and videos should be the catchment technique to be posted on parish Facebook pages. Parishes should design brief prayer cards and leave contacts for families that need to pray with their pastors. Beyond setting up Christian communities, pastors should regularly visit the homes of their parishioners and connect with them through the ministry of presence.

89. Robinson, *The Family Apostolate and Africa*, 3.

90. McFarland, "Microsoft is testing a new mosquito trap to fight Zika."

Having personally tried this pastoral approach in the Catholic church of Glen Burnie, Maryland, in the U.S., the success of the Family Apostolate can be measured through the following outcomes:

- Improved prayer life among parishioners.

- Active normal relationships between pastors and the faithful.

- Increased interests in volunteer services among individual families in the church.

- Increased interests in retreats among married couples.

- A strong sense of online networking and social media following as a way of evangelization.

- Increased requests for resources that support couples such as Natural Family Planning, Natural Procreative Technology programs, spiritual direction and counseling services.

Conclusion

Three things define the life of the typical African—God, family, and community. Keeping this in view in ministering to the family in African culture is of pastoral importance. Cardinal Sarah gives us a picture of what growing up in his village community as a child in Guinea looked like: "Every evening, the Fathers of Ourous gathered the children near a large cross set up in the mission courtyard, as if to symbolize the heart and center of the village. We could see it from far away: we oriented our entire lives by it! It was around this cross that we received our cultural and spiritual education. There, as the sun slowly set, the missionaries introduced us to the Christian mysteries."[91] This was the picture that informed the cardinal from Guinea, and the image he carries to this date. The triad for him was the Holy Ghost Fathers, his family and the Ourous community. His integration of the Holy Ghost Fathers as the background of his childhood formation showed that God is the origin of family life in Africa. The community is people united by the love of God. That is why the Christian faith in Africa is presented as the faith of the community.

Africans want to feel their pastors. They love to be close to them. They love to listen to them. Africans want to worship God through their community. Family life is essentially community life. Marriage goes

91. Sarah, *God or Nothing*, 25.

through the community. Children come through the community. Names are given through the community. Hence, the various rites of passage try to integrate the individual into his/her community in Africa. Here, we recognize the words of John Paul II, "A faith that does not become culture is not fully accepted."[92] Again, he asserts, "African cultures have an acute sense of solidarity and community life. In Africa, it is unthinkable to celebrate a feast without the participation of the whole village. Indeed, community life in African societies expresses the extended family."[93]

To keep the vocation of family alive, the African faith needs to be kept local. This does not mean discarding the foreign elements of socialization and Westernization. It means sustaining the Christian faith through African culture. These include wealth of cultural values,[94] profound religious sense,[95] a sense of sin and purification,[96] love and respect for life and children,[97] love for the elderly, as well as acute sense of solidarity and communal life.[98] These are values that Christianity promotes in general. They are the values that keep the marriage institution and family vocation profoundly Christocentric.

The vocation of family in Africa accentuates the fact that the history of humanity finds its meaning in Christ, the incarnate Word of God. It is a vocation that should look to Jesus in the African way. The mission of Jesus is to restore humanity to the image of God. This is what the African church must emphasize; restoring marriage and family to that image and dignity intended by God. This involves setting marriage couples on the right path from the beginning through adequate marriage formation, proper ongoing pastoral and religious education. A family ministry should eminently unite families to the love of God in the church through adequate pastoral care. In the family vocation, couples should be made to recognize above all, that Christ makes himself present in a profound way in the sacrament of marriage.[99]

92. John Paul II, *Address to the Italian National Congress of the Ecclesial Movement for Cultural Commitment.*

93. John Paul II, *Ecclesia in Africa*, 43.

94. John Paul II, *Ecclesia in Africa*, 42.

95. John Paul II, *Ecclesia in Africa*.

96. John Paul II, *Ecclesia in Africa*.

97. John Paul II, *Ecclesia in Africa*, 43.

98. John Paul II, *Ecclesia in Africa*.

99. See Francis, *Amoris Laetitia*, 67.

Bibliography

Aymans, Winfried. *Eleven Cardinals Speak on Marriage and the Family*. San Francisco: Ignatius, 2015.

Catholic Church. *Catechism of the Catholic Church*. Washington, DC: US Catholic Conference, 1994.

Dodaro, Robert, ed. *Remaining in the Truth of Christ*. San Francisco: Ignatius, 2014.

Francis. *Amoris Laetitia: On love in the family*. Vatican City: Libreria Editrice Vaticana, 2016. http://w2.vatican.va/content/dam/francesco/pdf/apost_exhortations/documents/papa-francesco_esortazione-ap_20160319_amoris-laetitia_en.pdf.

Granados, Carlos. *The Hope of the Family: Dialogue with Gerhard Cardinal Muller*. San Francisco: Ignatius, 2014.

Gyekye, Kwame. *African Cultural Values: An Introduction*. Accra: Sankofa, 2003.

John Paul II. *Dives in Misericordia*. Washington, DC: U.S. Catholic Conference, 1981.

———. *Ecclesia in Africa*. Washington, DC: U.S. Catholic Conference, 1996.

———. *Familiaris Consortio*. Washington, DC: U.S. Catholic Conference, 1982.

———. *Novo Millennio Inuente*. Nairobi: Paulines, 2001.

Kasper, Walter. *The Gospel of the Family*. Mahwah, NJ: Paulist, 2014.

Kelly, Anthony. *Eschatology and Hope*. Maryknoll, NY: Orbis, 2006.

Kim, Van Nam. *A Church of Hope: A Study of the Eschatological Ecclesiology of Jürgen Moltmann*. Lanham, MD: University Press of America, 2005.

Kostenberger, Andreas J., and David W. Jones. *God, Marriage, Family: Rebuilding the Biblical Foundation*. Wheaton, IL: Crossway, 2010.

Mba, Cyriacus S. *A Handbook on Marriage: Some Moral, Pastoral and Canonical Reflections (Book Two)*. Owerri, Nigeria: Jeybros, 1997.

McElwee, Joshua. "Cardinals reportedly criticize synod in letter to Francis, but signatories disassociate." *National Catholic Reporter*, October 12, 2015. https://www.ncronline.org/news/vatican/cardinals-reportedly-criticize-synod-letter-francis-signatories-disassociate.

———. "Malawi archbishop: Africans at Synod sharing same message of proud heritage." *National Catholic Reporter*, October 12, 2015. https://www.ncronline.org/news/vatican/malawi-archbishop-africans-synod-sharing-same-message-proud-heritage.

McFarland, Matt. "Microsoft is testing a new mosquito trap to fight Zika." *CNN Business*, June 22, 2016. http://money.cnn.com/2016/06/21/technology/microsoft-mosquito-zika/.

Njuguna, Francis. "Of African Family Values and the Synod." *National Catholic Register*, October 6, 2015. http://www.ncregister.com/daily-news/of-african-family-values-and-the-synod.

O'Callaghan, Paul. *Christ Our Hope: An Introduction to Eschatology*. Washington, DC: Catholic University of America Press, 2011.

Paul VI. *Evangelii Nuntiandi*. Washington, DC: U.S. Catholic Conference, 1976.

———. *Humanae Vitae*. Washington, DC: U.S. Catholic Conference, 1968.

Perez-Soba, J. J., and Kampowski, S. *Going Beyond Cardinal Kasper's Proposal in the Debate on Marriage, Civil Re-Marriage, and Communion in the Church*. San Francisco: Ignatius, 2014.

Pius XII. *Davanti a Questa: The Pope Speaks to Mothers*. London: Catholic Truth Society, 1941.

Pontifical Council for the Family. *Compendium on the Family and Human Life.* Washington, DC: U.S. Conference of Catholic Bishops, 2015.

Robinson, John M. *The Family Apostolate and Africa.* Dublin: Helicon, 1964.

Sarah, Robert. *God or Nothing: A Conversation on Faith with Nicolas Diat.* San Francisco: Ignatius, 2015.

Sarah, Robert, et al. *Christ's New Homeland: Africa.* San Francisco: Ignatius, 2015.

Sheen, Fulton J. *Three to Get Married.* New York: Appleton-Century-Crofts, 1951.

———. *Letter to Families: The Saint's Reflections on the Grandeur of Marriage and Family Life.* Manchester, NH: Sophia Institute for Teachers, 2015.

United States Catholic Conference. *Putting Children and Families First: A Challenge for Our Church, Nation, and World.* Washington, D.C.: Confraternity of Christian Doctrine, 1991.

Vatican II. *Apostolicam Actuositatem: Decree on the Apostolate of the Laity.* November 18, 1965. http://www.vatican.va/archive/hist_councils/ii_vatican_council/documents/vat-ii_decree_19651118_apostolicam-actuositatem_en.html.

———. *Dei Verbum: Dogmatic Constitution on Divine Revelation.* November 18, 1965. http://www.vatican.va/archive/hist_councils/ii_vatican_council/documents/vat-ii_const_19651118_dei-verbum_en.html.

———. *Gaudium et Spes: Pastoral Constitution on the Church in the Modern World.* December 7, 1965. http://www.vatican.va/archive/hist_councils/ii_vatican_council/documents/vat-ii_const_19651207_gaudium-et-spes_en.html.

———. *Lumen Gentium: Dogmatic Constitution on the Church.* November 21, 1964. http://www.vatican.va/archive/hist_councils/ii_vatican_council/documents/vat-ii_const_19641121_lumen-gentium_en.html.

Von Hildebrand, Dietrich. *Marriage: The Mystery of Faithful Love.* Manchester, NH: Sophia Institute, 1997.

4

The Vocation of the Family
in Relation to the African Situation

BONAVENTURE UGWU

Introduction

The family is a vocation which can only be fully and clearly understood in the light of the life and teaching of Christ and of his church. Seen in this light, it becomes obvious that marriage and family is a call to communion, mutual self-giving, faithfulness, procreation,s and training of children. From the same source, one would also see that there is an inseparable connection between marriage/family and the church as well as society at large. There is also a link between the sacrament of matrimony and other sacraments. Furthermore, marriage is closely associated with the incarnation and other mysteries of salvation as revealed in Jesus Christ. Pope Francis directs our attention to these facts and thus invites all men and women of goodwill especially Christian families to focus their gaze on Jesus whose words and deeds in embracing his own mission on earth offer a model of how to embrace the vocation of the family.

This chapter seeks to highlight how the propositions of the Holy Father on the vocation of the family herein apply to and challenge the modern understanding and practice of Christian marriage and family in Africa using the Igbo cultural group as an area of particular interest. Can the African marriage and family find in the tradition of Jesus and of his church an effective model for the restoration and fulfilment of God's plan for their own life and mission? In what follows, we shall try to respond to this question and also propose some practical suggestions about what should be done to strengthen marriage and family life in African society. This project receives its impetus from the recognition of the Synod Fathers which was adopted by Pope Francis that "Every country or region, moreover, can seek solutions better suited to its culture and sensitive to its traditions and local needs."[1]

Key Themes and Teaching in Chapter 3 of *Amoris Laetitia*

This chapter develops and advances some fundamental teachings of the church on the vocation of the family. It offers a biblical foundation for the church's teaching through a Christological reflection on the meaning of vocation and how it specifies such daily practices for married couples which could help them bear authentic witness to marriage and family life in the world today. This task is accomplished under six thematic sections, namely: the teaching of Jesus on marriage, the teaching of the church on marriage, the sacramentality of marriage, some negative or imperfect elements found in marriage and family, the transmission of life and the raising of children, and finally the relationship between family-church.

The teaching of Jesus on marriage is founded on his own life and mission and it is such that by gazing on them one can readily understand God's plan and mission for marriage and family. Through the New Testament witness, Jesus offers a positive understanding of marriage; as a gift which needs to be safeguarded against all forms of challenges. The indissolubility of the marriage union, which appears to some people as a yoke, is in fact one of the divinely approved measures of protecting the gift.[2] From beginning (the Incarnation) to the end (his death on the Cross), the story of Jesus on earth was inseparably connected to the family. The covenant of marriage, which originated in creation, finds its full meaning in Christ and his church and bear witnesses to them too.[3] Thus, seeing

1. Francis, *Amoris Laetitia*, 3.
2. Francis, *Amoris Laetitia*, 62.
3. Francis, *Amoris Laetitia*, 63.

itself through the mirror of Christ and the church, the family is able to face the vicissitudes of life at all times.[4]

The church teaches that love is at the center of marriage and family and that there is an intrinsic bond between this love and the generation of life, as well as the church. Thus, being the community of life and love,[5] the family is also a form of domestic church.[6] These insights which the chapter offers on the teachings of the church on marriage are drawn from the Second Vatican Council's *Gaudium et Spes*, Pope Paul VI's *Humanae Vitae*, Pope John Paul II's *Familiaris Consortio*, and Pope Benedict XVI's *Deus Caritas Est*.

The union of two baptized, man and woman, has been raised by Christ to the dignity of a sacrament through his incarnation and Paschal Mystery.[7] This union, which is grounded on the grace of baptism, is an efficacious sign of Christ's love for the church.[8] Marked by total self-giving, faithfulness and openness to new life,[9] the sacrament of matrimony bestows on the spouses the capacity to love, to be at the service of the church, to live in hope and practice charity and to ultimately attain the joys of everlasting life. Thus, from the point of the sacramentality of marriage, Pope Francis discredits the view that marriage is a social convention, an empty ritual or the merely outward sign of a commitment and affirms that "a gift given for the sanctification and salvation of the spouses."[10]

The chapter goes further to shed light on the relationship between Christian marriage as a sacrament and natural marriage found in different religions and cultures of the world. On the basis of the fact that "the order of redemption illuminates and fulfils that of creation," it is stated that natural marriage can only be understood and fulfilled in the sacrament of matrimony. As if to provide grounds for the inculturation of the sacrament of love, the pope notes that there are some positive values of marriage which the church can learn from other cultures. Again, attention is drawn to certain imperfect situations of marriage in which some people find themselves. In keeping with the precepts of *Familiaris*

4. Francis, *Amoris Laetitia*, 66.

5. Vatican II, *Gaudium et Spes*, 48.

6. Vatican II, *Lumen Gentium*, 11.

7. Francis, *Amoris Laetitia*, 74. See also, *Code of Canon Law*, 1055.

8. Francis, *Amoris Laetitia*, 71.

9. Francis, *Amoris Laetitia*, 73.

10. Francis, *Amoris Laetitia*, 72.

Consortio,[11] the pope renews the call on pastors to discern and evaluate with sympathy such situations and to treat the persons involved with love, for example, people who are living together without marriage or are only married civilly, divorced and remarried. This could be done "while clearly stating the church's teaching" on marriage and family.[12]

In continuation of the explication of the vocation of marriage and family in the light of Christ and the church, the pope affirms that conjugal love and union are ordered to the well-being of the spouses and also to the procreation and upbringing of children. However, the full meaning of conjugal life is not diminished or destroyed by childlessness. Moreover, a couple without children of their own can also express their fruitfulness through adoption or foster parenting.[13] In all, it is against the nature and vocation of the family to reject or terminate life in all its stages since it is the sacred place or sanctuary where life is conceived, cared for and protected in all its stages.[14] Schools, the state and the church are reminded of their responsibility of cooperating with parents whose duty it is to educate children in addressing the present day challenges of raising children.

Finally, the relationship between family and the church is treated and described as an interplay. Re-echoing the teaching of the Second Vatican Council that the family is "a domestic church,"[15] the pope avows that "The Church is a family of families, constantly enriched by the lives of all those domestic churches."[16] The church is a communion of many domestic churches and the interplay between them shows that "the Church is good for the family, and the family is good for the Church."[17] Therefore, the entire Christian community has a lot to gain by safeguarding the sacrament of matrimony.

11. John Paul II, *Familiaris Consortio*, 84.

12. Francis, *Amoris Laetitia*, 79.

13. Francis, *Amoris Laetitia*, 82.

14. Francis, *Amoris Laetitia*, 83.

15. Vatican II, *Lumen Gentium*, 11.

16. Vatican II, *Lumen Gentium*, 87.

17. Francis, *Amoris Laetitia*, 87.

Theological Reflection on the Vocation
of Marriage and Family in Africa

There was a couple known to me and whose story I followed very closely. The man and wife were happily married for years but they had no child. They took so many steps to see that the problem was solved but without success. The woman suggested that they adopt children but the man was opposed to his wife's proposal. According to him, his kinsmen will not accept adopted children into their extended family. In the end, the man pulled out of the marriage and the union collapsed after over twelve years of conjugal life. He married another wife with whom he had some children. Another marriage which I was closely associated with was destroyed because there were only female children born by the couple. In theory, the man did not accuse the woman of being responsible for their plight but the cultural pressure weighed heavily upon him in seeking to end the marriage. In a patrilineal society where descent, succession and inheritance go through the male line, having no male offspring among the Igbo means having nobody to perpetuate the family line; something close to ancestral death since male generativity is understood in this culture as the route to immortality. Traditionally, some marriages are contracted by parents and a good number of women are married when they are too young to make real personal choices.

These kinds of experiences represented above give me reasons not only to appreciate the teaching of the pope about the vocation of the family but also to raise some questions regarding its implications and applicability to the African cultural context. Do Africans marry and conduct family life for the same reasons that the pope outlined in *Amoris Laetitia*, chapter 3? Are there continuities and discontinuities between the teaching of Christ and the church and the African way of marriage on this matter? Is it possible to have a model of marriage and family that is truly Christian and truly African? In this section, we would look at marriage and family life in Africa in the light of the teaching of Pope Francis. We shall consider the following: the place of love in African marriages, procreation, the education of children and the challenges of change for families in today.

Love in African Marriage and Family

Given the strong emphasis which Africans place on procreation, a casual observer can easily jump to the conclusion that love does not play a central role in marriage and family in Africa. In fact, a colleague of mine once said that couples in Africa do not show love to one another because they do not kiss, embrace, hug themselves or move about with hands held together as is the case in most places in the West. In the first place, the tendency to evaluate the way of life of Africans using the Western style of life as measure is always a temptation for many people who fail to appreciate that peoples differ and that particular cultural behavior and cultural knowledge are often incommensurate when viewed cross-culturally with other cultures.

The fact is that married couples in Africa have several ways of expressing their mutual love. Among the Igbo of southeastern Nigeria, a woman expresses love for her man through what comes out of the kitchen; the way she prepares the food, the type of dish and the time it is served all together show love. The way she addresses the husband when they are alone by themselves and when people are around speak a lot about love. She defers to him out of love. The man in turn shows her love by the way he cares for her. Their love is also seen in the context of staying together after a meal under a tree in the moonlight. The way he pats her on the back or calls her bespeak love.

The picture painted above might lead one to think that the Igbo expression of love in marriage is overly materialistic. This is not the case. The Igbo understand the body as the symbol of the person. Hence, the "body" or "*aru*" stands for the person. One common way of asking a person if he or she is fine is literally to say: Is your body present or intact? *Aru odikwa gi?* The person might respond affirmatively: "*Aru di m*" (My body is intact and present), or negatively: "*Aru adiro m*" (My body is not present or intact). This way of seeing and defining the human being agrees with Uzukwu's affirmation that for Africans, "The body is the center of the total manifestation of person in gestures."[18] Thus, the expression of love in the first instance is connected to the body.

Beyond material gestures, married couples among the Igbo express deep conjugal love towards one another in the form of patience, forbearance, forgiveness and understanding. These virtues are central to St. Paul's

---

18. Uzukwu, *Worship as Body Language*, 10.

list of the content of genuine love[19] (1 Cor 13) and they are not found in short supply in most marriages in Igboland even in this modern time. Usually, difficulties created by prolonged sickness by one of the spouses or children in the family, financial insufficiency and death pose serious challenges capable of breaking down of marital union. The low rate of divorce among the Igbo in spite of such challenges is attributable to the mutual love of spouses. The centrality of love in marriage often forms part of the homilies preached by priests at wedding celebrations.[20]

In sum, love is fundamental to the Igbo understanding and practice of marriage and the family. However, the particular ways by which spouses express their love for one another is highly influenced by the people's culture. In some ways they agree or disagree with what obtains in other cultures. Since no culture is perfect or complete in itself, the Igbo of today keep borrowing from other people some ways of expressions of love between married couples. In all, their love in marriage usually intends procreation.

Procreation and Childlessness in African Marriage and Family

It is often said that Africans have children as their primary reason for marriage. In *Ecclesia in Africa*, Pope John Paul II remarks that "in African culture and tradition, the role of the family is everywhere held to be fundamental. Open to this sense of the family, of love and respect for life, the African loves children."[21] However, the fact is that there is hardly any culture where marriage and procreation are not so closely connected. The church is not an exception to this. The ecclesiastical law stipulates that marriage "of its own very nature is ordered to 'the well-being of the spouses and to the procreation and upbringing of children.'"[22] Pope Francis reiterates this teaching using the words of Paul VI in *Humanae Vitae*, that there is an "intrinsic bond between conjugal love and the generation of life."[23] Procreation is so central to marriage that "Antecedent and

19. See 1 Cor 13.

20. In a wedding ceremony held in a church in Abuja, Nigeria, Msgr. Theopilius Okere reminded the man and the woman that "Love makes marriage" and that "Matrimonial love as all love must take a clue from Jesus's love, a love that is total self-giving, up to self-immolation and sacrifice." See Okere, *Okere in His Own Words*, 438–39.

21. John Paul II, *Ecclesia in Africa*, 80.

22. *Code of Canon Law*, 1055.

23. Francis, *Amoris Laetitia*, 68.

perpetual impotence to have sexual intercourse, whether on the part of the man or on that of the woman, whether absolute or relative, by its very nature invalidates marriage."[24]

For Africans with particular reference to the Igbo society, people are immortalized through their children. To be without children is to have one's name wiped away from the face of the earth. In addition to continuing the family tree, children are also needed because they constitute the work force in the house. Subsistent, non-mechanized farming was the mainstay of the economy of the traditional African family and the more children one has, the better placed one is in terms of workers. Again, children constitute the primary assurance for the welfare of their parents especially in their old age. The future of couples without children is often bleak and no one would usually opt for such predicament. In fact, "children constitute the prestige, security and wealth of their parents."[25] Today, with changes in the economic situation of most African societies, family sizes are beginning to dwindle but having children remain great treasures therein. It is not surprising, therefore, that "Marriage is not considered complete until there is a child/children out of the marriage."[26]

The failure to have children in marriage is a very big challenge for an African who intends to bear witness to Christ through the sacrament of marriage. In my pastoral ministry, I have met many families facing the challenge of childlessness in their marriage. The story of the couple told above is a typical case. Speaking of childlessness in respect of the Christian in Igbo land, Adibe categorically states that "The worst thing to happen to an Igbo man is not to have a child of his own named after him."[27] Childlessness in the African culture brings with it humiliation, anguish, grief and torment, especially to women who are often blamed for it. It is a cross which robs those who carry it of social status. Ugorji rightly notes that childlessness at times strikes at the unity and indissolubility of the marriage bond in favor of divorce or polygamy, since some people tend to believe that a marriage is not blessed by God when no child is born to it.[28] During traditional marriage ceremonies as well as on wedding days, prayers are repeatedly offered by different persons for the fruit of

24. *Code of Canon Law*, 1084.

25. Ezeanyino, "Childlessness and Adoption," 331.

26. Enemali, "Impotence and Sterility," 521.

27. Adibe, *The Crises of Faith and Morality*, 184.

28. Ugorji, "The Challenges of Christian Families," 127.

the womb for the couple. At the reception parties usually held by and for couples after wedding, a good number of the gifts brought by friends and relatives are things intended to be used by new born babies. Words and actions leave nobody in doubt about the expectation of the people for the newly married couples regarding procreation.

When, by the grace of God, children are born, another challenge immediately emerges, which is, their training. This is nonetheless tasking.

The Challenges of Raising Children by Families in Modern Africa

It is nearly impossible to conceive of a human being without basic education, training or socialization. Sociological studies show that "Without socialization, an individual would bear little resemblance to any human being defined as normal by the standards of his society."[29] Through education, a child learns how to speak a language, to walk, to eat, to wear clothes, to relate with others and a host of other things that differentiate human beings from animals. Generally, parents are the first educators and formators of their children. In line with this, the Second Vatican Council remarks that "As it is the parents who have given life to their children, on them lies the gravest obligation of educating their family. They must therefore be recognized as being primarily and principally responsible for their education. The role of parents in education is of such importance that it is almost impossible to provide an alternative substitute."[30]

In a typical traditional African setting, the education of children is the shared responsibility of the whole members of the extended family. Children have series of elderly men and women whom they call father or mother, uncle or aunt, brother or sister and they collaborate with parents in their training. My upbringing was a combined project done by first my parents, then my uncle and my grandmother. Such is the story of many individuals among the Igbo. In fact, from the time a woman gives birth to a child, her mother or another close relative of the same rank comes to assist her nurse the newly born baby. Among the Igbo, this visit is called *Omugo* and it is very important in the life of every newborn baby and its parents. The mother of the baby does little or nothing outside breastfeeding the child. The duration of the *Omugo* depends on a number of factors such as the skill, health and strength of the mother of the baby or the

29. Haralambos and Heald, *Sociology*, 5.
30. Vatican II, *Gravissimum Educationis*, 3.

ability of the family to cater for the visiting grandmother. Starting thus from the cradle, the collaborative system of training children among the Igbo continue till they attain maturity as adults in society.

Today, with rapid socio-economic, political, cultural and religious changes taking place in the world and Africa, the training of children is becoming more challenging in families. In times past, the man used to be the breadwinner while the woman spent most of the time at home with children. Nowadays, due to economic pressure, many parents have to engage in full time work outside their homes in order to meet up with their financial obligations in society. This implies that they have to leave their children at the mercy of others. House-helps take the place of parents while the latter become almost like strangers in the house. Often times, these house-helps are young girls with little or no experiences or skills about parenting. Moreover, by spending many hours daily without one another, the solidarity between couples as well as with their children weaken to the point where they do not need themselves to be happy and fulfilled.

The absence of parents from home for most hours of the day has led to culture of sending out children so early to school; to the crèche, kindergarten, nursery, primary school and so on. Years back, children were meant to spend at least six years with their parents before they could begin primary school. At the age of six, it was expected that a child's hand is able to cross over his or her head and touch the ear on the other side of the head. Any child who failed this test was disqualified from beginning school. By the present practice, children of barely one year old are enrolled in school where teachers practically take over the place of parents as the first educators of the children.

Some influences of the mass/social media on society constitute another big challenge for parents in educating their children. Information and communication technology makes all sorts of electronic gadgets and programs available everywhere and the young have access to them always. Often times, children are more knowledgeable about the internet and other media programs than their parents. Parents cannot control the content of what is communicated to their children. Some of the values disseminated by the media are counter to the ones which parents offer to their children. When this happens, children are left in confusion as to which values to take. Rightly so, Pope Francis, quoting the 2014 Synod Fathers, observes that "one of the fundamental challenges facing families today is undoubtedly that of raising children, made all the more difficult and complex by today's cultural reality and the powerful influence of the media."[31]

In present-day Nigeria, for instance, there is a regular production of home movies by the Nollywood video industry. Many of these movies promote fetishism, prostitution, and the desire to get rich quick. On its part, many media programs from the Western world highlight violence, horror, pornography, divorce, single parenthood and same-sex union. The importance of hard work, honesty, accountability, transparency and loyalty are scarcely promoted through the movies. Similarly, the personal, social and spiritual values which constitute the hub for authentic human development are going into extinction at a high velocity.[32]

The electronic or digital age in which we live today has made parenting more challenging than before. Iwuoha draws the attention of parents to the dangers of this reality[33] and Ugorji decries the failure of many parents to pay vigilant attention to the ideas the media carry into the private intimacy of their homes.[34]

There are other factors and changes in African societies that have significant impacts on the vocation of marriage and family institution especially by Christian couples united by the bond of the sacrament of matrimony.[35]

The emergence and continuous growth of city life in Africa have adverse effects on marriages and families. In the first place, with the shift from agriculture to crude oil as the mainstay of the Nigerian economy, life in the rural areas became less attractive. Most of the infrastructures that are associated with modernity are concentrated in the cities of Lagos, Onitsha, Aba, Port Harcourt and lately Abuja giving rise to rural-urban migration. Usually, the man leaves his family in the village and goes to the city in search of greener pastures with hope of coming back later to take them along with him. In the meantime, as he lives in the city alone and visits home once in a while, the physical unity of the family is affected. In the cities, families suffer a number of limitations. With regards to accommodation, many families are forced to live in places that less conducive fulfilled existence or for bringing up children. As people go

31. Francis, *Amoris Laetitia*, 84.

32. Obi, "Proper Child Upbringing," 54.

33. Iwuoha, "Challenges Posed by Digital Reality," 588–608.

34. Ugorji, "The Challenges of Christian Families," 131–32.

35. Nwanunobi, *African Social Institutions*, 52, makes a serious observation regarding the rapid changes which families in Africa are undergoing.

away from the rural areas (villages), they tend to leave behind some of the well-tested traditional values for which Africans are known such as the extended families relations, respect for people especially the aged, and community solidarity. These values are not readily replaced by new ones. In the end, children easily fall prey to delinquent and criminal sub-cultures that are dangerous to proper character formation.

Poverty is one of the adverse factors affecting families in Africa in realizing their vocation as a community of life and love. In the book of Proverbs, the wise one sheds light on the possible danger of poverty as he prayed: "Two things I beg of you, O God, do not deny them to me before I die: Keep lies and falsehood far away from me, give me neither poverty nor riches. Give me just as much food as I need, lest, satisfied, I deny you and say, 'who is the Lord?' Or else out of necessity, I steal and profane the name of my God."[36] Generally, many families cannot afford the basic necessities of life such as food, clothing, shelter, education, medical facilities and means of transportation. This is not to talk of other essentials as security, rest and recreation. In the long run, people who are brought up under the situation of poverty tend to feel marginalized, inferior, dependent, and helpless.[37] All these hamper the actualization of the goals of the family. In practical terms, poverty has driven a number of children from such families into prostitution, child-labor, street hawking, and other situations where they are abused and harassed.

Helping the Family in Africa to Realize Its Vocation

As ongoing efforts to strengthen the family are to be given priority in the church, the pope expresses that the church is called to cooperate with parents through suitable pastoral initiatives, assisting them in the training of their children.[38] In this section, we shall set out a few proposals, steps or pastoral approaches that could be taken by the church, married couples or individuals in order to help families actualize their vocation by responding more effectively to the challenges highlighted above.

36. Prov 30:7–9.
37. Haralambos and Heald, *Sociology*, 154.
38. Francis, *Amoris Laetitia*, 85.

Institute Marriage Schools

The first step to take to help Christian families—particularly in Africa—to actualize their vocation is that the church should institute marriage schools at parish or diocesan levels. In these schools, those who are unmarried but intend to marry would be trained on how best to embrace the family vocation. Provisions would be made in the school for continuous education for the already married on the most excellent ways to face the challenges of their chosen vocation. The church has many documents and teachings on marriage and family which could be used together with the Scripture to create the curriculum of the school. In the same way as the church has established structures and programs of formation for those who aspire to the consecrated and priestly vocation, it should have for marriage. There should be the equivalents of seminaries and formation houses for aspirants to family life. The customary marriage courses organized for men and women about to marry in the church hardly meets the need of providing the basic requirement for formation of people for marriage and family life.

Establish Schemes and Programs of Ongoing Formation

In the absence of marriage school or in addition to it, schemes and programs of ongoing pastoral formation on the vocation of Christian family should be established in every parish. The content and methodology of this program is to be carefully worked out to meet the needs of spouses in their contexts. Seminars, sharing of experiences and quizzes could be built into the scheme. The movement of couples from one stage of formation to another is recognized and rewarded by some awards or positions of leadership in the Christian community.

Strengthen and Revitalize the Process and Rites of Christian Initiation

Initiation has got to do with how people are inducted or integrated into society as a whole or a group within it.[39] Usually, "in traditional Africa, initiatory passage rites formed the bedrock for socialization, entrenching personal identity in a world of interrelationship, and consequently,

---

39. I use initiation here in a wider sense to include what may be generally understood as Christian formation.

determining the assumption of social and religious roles."[40] Secularization, modernity and Christianity have not succeeded in annihilating this bedrock of African socialization. So far, "the heart and mind of the African hold fast to initiation as a veritable means of socialization and identity in society."[41] The goal of every initiation is the transformation of those who go through the process. This should be the goal of Christian education and faith formation.

Uzukwu observes that among some African Christians there is certain disquiet about the effectiveness of the present practice of Christian initiation. These concerned Africans' "wish for and propose a Christian initiation whose pedagogy is not 'purely intellectual' but must include 'emotional (affective) elements' that would give a greater human density to the truth being communicated."[42] One of the ways of addressing this problem is to expand the content and method of catechesis and faith formation including the rites of celebrating the Christian mysteries in order that they bring about real conversion of those who go through them.

With regard to marriage and family, this expansion can be achieved, first, by including issues pertaining to the vocation of family in the content of the deposit handed over to catechumens preparing for baptism, confirmation, and First Holy Communion. Secondly, some traditional ways of initiating men and women into adulthood ready for marriage may be explored and integrated into the rites of preparing Christians for family life.[43] For instance, in times past, women intending to marry were first made to undergo training in another family with a woman to mentor her. This could be improved upon; since the present historical situation may not allow a prolonged living experience in another family, a three weekend of insertion in designated families by the man and woman is possible. At the end of the three weekends, another final weekend like in a forest of initiation would be organized for final preparation. By combining learning in theory and practice in the training of men and women for marriage, they will be better prepared to take up and live their call.

---

40. Uzukwu, *Worship as Body Language*, 229.

41. Ugwu, "Christian Initiation and Formation," 157.

42. Uzukwu, *Worship as Body Language*, 244.

43. The Second Vatican Council directs that "In mission countries, in addition to what is furnished by the Christian tradition, those elements of initiation rites may be admitted which are already in use among some people insofar as they can be adapted to the Christian ritual..." See Vatican II, *Sacrosanctum Concilium*, 65.

Adoption as Family Apostolate

Teach Christians about the significance of adoption in the mystery of our salvation. The option of adoption which the pope offers childless married couples is not favorably considered by many Africans. Even when the spouses concerned accept it, there is usually serious pressure and opposition from the extended families against adoption. To help couples on this matter, the church needs to do more in terms of preaching, teaching and seminars to create greater awareness among Christians about the import of adoption in the history of salvation. It should be made clear that adoption in Christian families is not measure taken by couples when all human efforts to have children have failed.[44] It should be made clear to every believer that Christianity is a religion in which adoption forms a principal part of the good news. Adoption is the established way through which human beings gain entrance into the family of God.[45] We are children of God only by adoption. Adoption should be an option for every Christian family and not only for those who have no biological children of their own. Thus, the Fathers of the Second Vatican Council aptly stated that adopting abandoned children is first among the various works of the family apostolate.[46] This truth of our religion needs to be communicated to Christians even before they get married.

Emphasize Faith and Make Use of Science

Furthermore, childless marriages should be approached with faith and scientific data. A number of factors which obstruct a man or a woman from procreating can be medically cured. Unfortunately, many people quickly jump into conclusions and resort to spiritual and sometimes superstitious measures as solutions. Childless couples should be assisted by competent ecclesiastical ministers to seek medical attention or to carry out the necessary tests and follow medical advice for the treatment of some anomalies. This may help to reverse the situation that prevents them from giving birth. A lot of the causes of childlessness in marriages are curable and some preventable if couples are exposed to the right medical institutions and personnel on time.

44. This is the idea which many people have, and it is expressed in Ezeanyino, "Childlessness and Adoption in Christian Families," 338.

45. Ugwu, *Spiritual Inferiority Complex*, 67.

46. Vatican II, *Apostolicam Actuositatem*, 11.

Prepare Couples to Cope

In all, in the education to couples before marriage, pastors should endeavor to prepare their minds on the essence of Christian marriage and how to cope in the case of childlessness. They should help them to understand that "Spouses to whom God has not granted children can nevertheless have a conjugal life full of meaning, in both human and Christian terms. Their marriage can radiate a fruitfulness of charity, of hospitality and sacrifice."[47] Again, the Fathers of the Second Vatican Council teach that ". . . even in cases where despite the intense desire of the spouses there are no children, marriage still retains its character of being a whole manner and communion of life and preserves its value and indissolubility."[48] The implication is that children are a gift from God[49] and that the "Christian marriage ideal includes a readiness to accept barrenness as well as fruitfulness from God's hands."[50] Childless couples, in that situation, could also have recourse to God in prayer because he is the author of life. They should pray for serenity and happiness in their situation.

Pastoral Accompaniment of Parents

Sometimes, parents feel a sense of being alone in their struggle to remain faithful to their vocation of companionship with one another and the service of training of children. For a closer pastoral care and to enable families attend to the problems that face them with a unity of purpose and action, and in the spirit of solidarity, it is advisable to form associations of families in parishes and church communities.[51] Pope John Paul II rightly expresses that "loving the family means being able to appreciate its values and capabilities, fostering them always. Loving the family means identifying the dangers and the evils that menace it, in order to overcome them. Loving the family means endeavoring to create for it an environment favorable for its development."[52] These tasks of love can be achieved faster and more effectively in the context of the association

---

47. *Catechism of the Catholic Church*, 1654.

48. Vatican II, *Gaudium et Spes*, 50.

49. See Ps 127:3.

50. Shorter, *African Culture and the Christian Church*, 182.

51. Ugorji, "The Challenges of Christian Families," 134.

52. John Paul II, *Familiaris Consortio*, 86.

of families. Family counseling may also be promoted as part of pastoral accompaniment.

Conclusion

In this chapter, we have reflected critically on how the teaching of Pope Francis on the vocation of the family (in chapter 3 of *Amoris Laetitia*) applies to the African marriage and family situation. From our reflection, one gathers that the teachings of Christ and the church on the vocation of the family find their home in the soil of Africa, but not without some serious challenges. The problems of childlessness in a culture where procreation is second to no other value in marriage, the difficulties associated with raising children in modern times, and the demands of rapid changes in the world today are highlighted as heavy crosses on parents and families. However, it is noted that these challenges experienced in marriages and families in Africa with regard to their call can be faced squarely by looking at Christ, trusting in the guidance of his body, the church and engaging the people's culture in dialogue. Christ redeemed marriage, made it a sacrament, and continues to assist those who are married in their marital and family situations. He never ceases to accompany "their steps in truth, patience, and mercy."[53] Therefore, the church in Africa is called upon to be at the service of the family, particularly through its pastors. They should let married couples and their families see Jesus by the special interest, care, and love it shows them. Seven proposals are made on how this could be effectively done by the church and it is strongly believed that their application would help Christian families in Africa immensely towards the realization of their vocation. In the meantime, more study may be done on these proposals to sharpen them further for maximum effectiveness.

Bibliography

Ayisi, Eric. *An Introduction to the Study of African Culture*. London: Heinemann, 1980.
Catechism of the Catholic Church.
Eminyan, Maurice. *Theology of the Family*. Malta: Jesuit Publications, 1994.
John Paul II. *Ecclesia in Africa*. Vatican City: Libreria Editrice Vaticana, 1995. http://w2.vatican.va/content/john-paul-ii/en/apost_exhortations/documents/hf_jp-ii_exh_14091995_ecclesia-in-africa.html.

53. Francis, *Amoris Laetitia*, 60.

————. *Familiaris Consortio: On the role of the Christian family in the modern world.* Vatican City: Libreria Editrice Vaticana, 1981. http://w2.vatican.va/content/john-paul-ii/en/apost_exhortations/documents/hf_jp-ii_exh_19811122_familiaris-consortio.html.

Nwanunobi, C. Onyeka. *African Social Institutions.* Nsukka, Nigeria: University of Nigeria Press, 1992.

Obi, Isidore. "Proper Child Upbringing in Niger Delta." Student paper presented for a seminar at Spiritan International School of Theology, Attakwu, Enugu, Nigeria, December, 2010.

Ugorji, I. Lucius. "The Challenges of Christian Families in our Times." *West African Journal of Ecclesial Studies* 10 (2012/2013) 127–34.

Ugwu, Bonaventure Ikenna. "Christian Initiation and Formation at the Service of Reconciliation, Justice and Peace in Africa." In *The Church in Africa: Witness to Justice, Peace and Reconciliation, A Post-Synodal Reflection and Reception,* edited by Luke E. Ijezie, et al. Abuja: Catholic Theological Assocation of Nigeria, 2013.

————. *Spiritual Inferiority Complex: How to Overcome It.* Enugu, Nigeria: SAN, 2010.

Uzukwu, E. Elochukwu. *Worship as Body Language, Introduction to Christian Worship: An African Orientation.* Collegeville, MN: Liturgical, 1997.

Vatican II. *Gaudium et Spes: Pastoral Constitution on the Church in the Modern World.* Vatican City: Libreria Editrice Vaticana, 1965. http://www.vatican.va/archive/hist_councils/ii_vatican_council/documents/vat-ii_const_19651207_gaudium-et-spes_en.html.

5

Love in Marriage

Gabriel Tata

Introduction

The theme of family, together with love and marriage, has been a recurring subject in Christian theology throughout history. The family is always understood as having an instrumental dynamic in which marriage is acknowledged as basic and necessary for such matters, as well as spiritual discipline and maturity. What one knows or thinks about marriage influences and orients how one lives the reality. But today, what is marriage? This question invites us to reflect upon the critical and invaluable reality of the marriage in a manner which is anthropological, ethical, and pastoral. This means listening to the context and challenge of the family today in its complexity.

The purpose of this contribution is to show that any serious attempt to foster marriage-love and the family in African context must pay attention to the question of its foundation. In this instance, the epistemological and moral foundation on which marriage is built is very important. The research is divided into three axes. The first, with an approach of commentary, will present and analyze love in marriage (the fourth chapter of *Amoris Laetitia*, AL). The second target will explicate the living experience of the family and marriage, its realities in the context of Africa, in particular Yoruba context. Lastly, it will re-examine the situation of family in the African context. Consequently, we shall suggest pastoral solution and try to reconstruct a model of family which can respond to the salvific plan of God through the paradigm of African conception of marriage and family.

In these three axes, the main attention will be directed towards the theological and moral argumentation which is present in the text of reference. The reference to other magisterial documents and pertinent contributions of selected theologians, especially from the area of moral theology, will serve as support for our presentation.

A Textual Commentary Approach

The fourth chapter, "Love in Marriage," which starts with a phenomenology of love by a collection of brief passages carefully and tenderly describing human love in absolutely concrete terms, grasps the quality of psychological introspection that enters into the behavior of the spouses (positive and negative) and the erotic dimension of love.[1] We can say this is an extremely rich and valuable contribution to Christian married life, unprecedented in previous papal documents.

In effect, it is about rediscovering the beauty and the dignity of the marriage-love, together with its light and shadows. Such an approach allowed the bishops to point out some challenges, mainly a lack of a greater freedom of expression and a better recognition of the rights of spouses, the growth of individualism which deforms couples bonds which ends up considering each component of family as an isolated unit.

Here, the project is a modest attempt to pursue the same purpose of *Gaudium et Spes* in the area of marriage and family.[2] So, married life is a status, a state of life constituted by marriage and animated by married love. It is the modality through which married people live their calling to holiness and to perfection. It is a life lived with and for one another. The husband lives for the wife and the wife lives for the husband. To live with each other is to be united in communion of their whole person in a close union of spirit. This communion of persons disposes them to share their joys and hopes, grief and anxieties. It entails being by and with one

---

1. Francis, *Amoris Laetitia*, 90–164. It is from a painstaking, focused, inspired and poetic exegesis of the Pauline Hymn to Love (1 Cor 13:4–7).

2. See Vatican II, *Gaudium et Spes*, 47–52; or Chiavacci. *Gaudium et Spes*, 202.

another through the thick and thin of life. This is well expressed by the couples when they declare their matrimonial consent.

Growing together graciously means that marriage is founded on authentic reciprocal love. It is in this communion that each and every member of the family finds happiness. And when there is happiness and satisfaction in marriage and family their stability is guaranteed. In living with one another, the couples live by dedicating themselves and their resources, talents, time and treasures to the spiritual, emotional and physical good of one another. From these semantic and contextual analyses, marriage understood as intimate partnership of married life and love can be seen as a state of life animated by reciprocal love and therefore characterized by a close, personal and friendly relationship between a man and a woman. It is a relationship which derives from personal friendship. This friendship is built on the foundation of reciprocal love and it is animated, sustained by the same reciprocal love. As such, each person desires, seeks and does all in his/her power to help the other become a better version of himself and herself.

Love, as has been said repeatedly, is the foundation of fulfilling and lasting marriage. It is likewise its sustenance. Love sustains marriage through the reciprocal commitments of the partners. While writing on the commitment of love, John Powell affirms: "Love is a commitment to the satisfaction, security, and development of the one loved. In loving you I am committed to the fulfillment of your needs, whatever they may be."[3]

Given this fact, the responsibility to be assumed in marriage becomes a challenge of love and commitment for love. Genuine love is active, its dynamism undiminished by the passing of years or the shifting of circumstances. Of its essence, such love is creative; it generates and sustains life. It craves being out in the open where it can grow and spread to others. When the spouses love each other with deep responsibility, they touch the ways and destinies of each other, of their children and of the human family. Responsibility is intrinsic to love.

The term service summarizes all that love entails. One who loves serves. To serve is to be of help to the other. Husbands and wives are helpmates. Every decision has a series of corresponding responsibilities. One of the responsibilities of marital love or rather, the responsibility of marital love is mutual service. The duty to honor, to protect and to be

3. Powell, *The Secret of Staying in Love*, 44.

faithful is the concrete manifestation of the service which the lover renders to the beloved. The generation and education of children is likewise an expression of the reciprocal love of the spouses. To serve is to seek and promote the good of the beloved, the partner in this communion of life and love, and the children that will be born of their union.

Nevertheless, marriage in the context of modernity brings with it new challenges at a time of unprecedented social and theological change.[4] This change in patterns of Christian marriage has become a focus of controversy, a subject of redefinition. Married love encompasses all that love entails. It is a reciprocal love between a man and a woman who mutually bestow and accept one another as husband and wife. For this very reason, it is also "the love that is expressed through the proper acts of marriage."[5] This definition affirms that marriage is a common life of love between persons of different sex, and that this community of life is born with a free and irrevocable act, *quo coniuges sese mutuo tradunt atque accipiunt*. Chiavacci affirms that this mutual bestowal and acceptance has to do with the total gift of themselves, that is, of their very life. So, sexual intercourse, with the physical gift of self that it entails, is rather a sign, an expressive and favorable instrument of this irrevocable gift.

When love is reciprocal, when there is self-giving by both partners in marriage, regardless of the challenges that may arise in the day to day life of couples, they will always find reason and strength to hold on to their marriage because married love is a decision and a commitment to the good of one another in good times and in bad. Therefore, the listening church, tried to rethink the theology of marriage and family in so far as it speaks positively and meaningfully to people's experience in the contemporary world.[6] Such kind of theology might have as point of departure loyalty to Jesus Christ, loyalty to the Bible, loyalty to experience, loyalty to culture, and finally, loyalty to the people of God.[7]

Conjugal love embraces the totality of the person of the wife, husband (and also children): the instinctive, affective and spiritual elements of the person. It seeks the interest of the other without any ulterior motive. It is to be of help to one another and to the children. This help consists of moral and spiritual support, economic and material sustenance and

---

4. See Thatcher, *Marriage after Modernity*.

5. Chiavacci, *Gaudium et Spes*, 202.

6. See Uzukwu, *A Listening Church*, 1996.

7. Thatcher, *Marriage after Modernity*, 30.

physical presence.[8] In building a successful marriage, couples will need to always remember that both of them have equal dignity as husband and wife.[9] No one is superior to the other. As equals no one should try to dominate the other or feel more important, rather, each should strive to outdo the other in service.[10]

No one should try to be better than the other. In the relationship of marriage, there is no need of any room for competition. AL follows the thoughts of Pope John Paul II in his apostolic exhortation, *Familiaris Consortio*: "The family in the modern world, as much as and perhaps more than any other institution, has been beset by the many profound and rapid changes that have affected society and culture."[11]

We can also observe that being both a social and Christian structure, the family continues to face new changes, both positive and negative. These mutations are due to economic progress, sexual-moral revolution, techno-scientific development, and cultural ideologies. They are reinforcing individualism and killing the spiritual meaning of love and partnership. Thus, they are increasing in the society the monadic tendency as well as the egocentric bent instead of sharing life. Indeed, bonds are replaced by boundaries.[12]

The "transformation of love" that concludes the chapter shows that loving attraction does not lessen but changes as sexual desire can be transformed over time into the desire for togetherness and mutuality. Those who love really leave an indelible mark in the life of those that they love. When I think about my own life, I am always full of gratitude to my parents, siblings, family, friends, acquaintances and a whole lot of unknown benefactors who have been good to me. I am led to the conclusion that my life, like the lives of all those who are loved, is a mosaic realized with beautiful stones made out of the love, care, and concern of these persons who beautify our lives with their presence, tenderness, affection, and friendship.

The aspiration of each should be how to help the other (and one another) to become a better version of him/herself (and of themselves). Love requires nearness and it grows in and through nearness. So, couples

8. Tata, *Vivere-insieme*, 124.

9. See Miser, *The Partnership Marriage*.

10. See Francis, *Amoris Laetitia*, 97–98.

11. John Paul II, *Familiaris Consortio*, Introduction.

12. Anderson and Cotton Fite, *Becoming Married*, 74.

should enjoy being together and always make time to be together. Above all, couples should learn to appreciate the fact that, as human beings, each of them is unique. It is an existential error to want to be like the other or to want the other to be like you. It is important to recognize and appreciate the uniqueness, peculiarities and singleness of each person, his/her strengths and weaknesses inclusive and try to live or cope with them.

Contextual Reflection of Marriage and Love

This part would like to grasp many elements of the situation of the African family. Our reflections on this do not give a full picture of the continent. Therefore, we would like to share few things about the Yoruba family today. This methodological choice seems necessary because Africa is a continent with enormous and diversified rich cultures and lifestyles.[13] For a theology in African context it is unconceivable to discuss marriage patterns without assessing the issue of family. That is why our main interest is to portray the changes which are taking place in marriage from which information can be derived on the changes that have so far been encountered.

Communitarian Life as Foundation of Marriage

All about marriage in the African context starts with the worldview of communitarian anthropology in which life is perceived as something that embraces and includes ancestors, the living and those yet to be born, the whole of creation and all beings: those that speak and those that are mute, those that think and those lacking thought.[14] The visible and invisible universe is regarded as a living-space for human beings, but also as a space of communion where past generations invisibly flank present generations, themselves, and mothers of future generations.[15]

According to Bujo, "*Cognatus sum, ergo sum*" (I am, because we are) means that life of the individual is abundantly lived when it is shared and

---

13. See Idowu, *Olodumare*; Mbiti, *Concepts of God in Africa*; Mbiti, *African Religions and Philosophy*.

14. We quote one of the best researchers about this anthropological vision: Bujo, *Foundations of an African Ethic*.

15. Tata, *Anthropologie Communautaire Africaine*.

hidden in the life of his/her community.[16] This great openness of heart and spirit in the African tradition predisposes us to hear and to understand the notion of family, to appreciate the mystery of the marriage, and thus to value human love to the full, along with the conditions in which the spouses are living. In this sense, family in the Yoruba context is not only constituted by the man, his wife and children, it is about local unity which involves a multitude of patterns and relationships, something which implies the union and the community with the whole society, the ancestors and the dead of the clan.[17]

There is a kind of socialization (which does not go without conflicts) among the kids who most of the times end up calling any of their uncles "my father" and vice versa. Such kind of family becomes nuclear community which other relatives of the head of the family afterwards join.[18] One who breaks this relationship by divorce or physical separation breaks, at the same time, the vital union with the whole community. For this reason, family is protected by something more than a simple passionate love of spouses, whose living together is protected by the vital union among parents, children, elders, ancestors, and goods.

In this sense, many words and spellings have been used by African researchers—*ubuntu, harambee*—to refer to a supreme moral value, protector of harmony within the society.[19] The ethics of *Ubuntu* and *Harambee* stand on the evidence that in African cultures there is respect for life.[20] This ethics tells us that a man is a true husband only with other members of family, the woman is a true wife when she tries to establish relationships with others in a family setting, which accomplishes the humanness of any humanity. For this reason, the other members of the extended family are not banished or marginalized from the spouses. On the contrary, they are esteemed and perfectly integrated within their families, of which they are indeed the pinnacle. The sacredness of human life is protected by taboos and rituals. There is respect for the dignity of the human being. Other values like faithfulness, solidarity, hospitality, moderation are sacred. These values shape the moral demands and any attempt of division is perceived in personal and communal dimensions

16. Bujo, *Foundations of an African Ethic*, 4.

17. Bujo, *Plea for Change of Models of Marriage*, 19–33.

18. Richards, "Bemba Marriage and Present Economic Conditions," 30.

19. Ki-Zerbo, *Repères pour l'Afrique*, 114; Oxford Living English Dictionary, "In the Spirit of Harambee."

20. In fact, if children are treasured, abortion is an abomination.

as a sickness which needs healing.[21] Therefore, forgiveness through the palaver is a process of healing of both husband and wife in order to keep the matrimonial bond. In fact, the palaver is a communication, another very important factor in the building of a successful marriage. The palaver not only serves to solve problems, it is also a sharing of life, is a great necessity in building happy homes.[22]

This moral behavior allows Laurenti Magesa to say that in Africa the family life inherently is bound together with human life to form a natural harmony.[23] Every day is an occasion of encountering God or the ancestors through piety and worship, giving to the whole African life a sacredness dimension. So, marriage and family are also sacred and should be protected against any evil which might create division and separation.

The appreciation of relatives inspires the Africans to treat the elderly with greater dignity, because of their wisdom, sometimes obtained at a high price, that the elderly can influence the family in a variety of ways. Their experience naturally leads them not only to bridge the generation gap, but also to affirm the need for mutual support. They are an enrichment for all members of the family, especially for young couples and for children who find in them understanding and love.

Marriage between Relationality and Humanity

The perspective here wants to put in interaction anthropology and ethics. The main reason is to identify the key distinguishing quality of what marriage-love means in African context: it deals with relationality and humanity. In effect, if we agree that one of the fundamental characteristics of the African communitarian anthropology is relationality, it is because, in accordance with their structural dimension, the Africans are constituted for the whole of their life by relational bonds.[24] The need to relate with one another is not negotiable because no one is self-sufficient.

---

21. In case this harmony is broken due to hatred, jealously, selfishness, anger, pride, genocide, there is a need of a spiritual healing both as individuals and as a community, a role played by diviners.

22. Powell, *The Secret of Staying in Love*, 59–60.

23. Magesa, *What is Not Sacred*, 59.

24. Tata, *Vivere-insieme*, 124.

This is why relationship is likewise an ethical necessity in the life of spouses.[25] Because they can give and find meaning in their relationships through the logic with which they relate with one another as persons, moral subjects gifted with intelligence and free will and so capable of knowing and willing the good. Therefore, only relationships and humanity can make marriage and love fount of joy, happiness and peace. But this demands that we share with one another what they are and have.[26]

The common being has to prevail over self-interest, namely, must prevail on having more. In fact, if the spouses try to reproduce in their own existence the divine way of being, the way of relational life, their love becomes the vitalizing force of an authentic life of love.[27] For this reason, we say that love arouses that particular joy which is experienced in giving rather than in receiving; each of the spouses desires primarily the good of the other and in this finds true happiness. At the very foundation of relationship lies therefore this reciprocal gift of self which is the expression of the unconditional openness to the other.[28]

That means marriage in Africa "is a social act because of the presence of the spouses' families. It involves the whole community and invites it (the community) to the awareness of a common cause."[29] Thus, a good marriage is not only defined by the high points, it is also defined by how the spouses and their relatives handle the low points. It is how they survive conflict and struggle in an equitable progressive way. It is the marriage and relationship that had the weight of challenges bearing down upon them and resolved through mutual growth in everything. That is a real marriage. It is like a body that has an immune system for future challenges.

Naturally, to promote relationality and humanity there is need of the responsibility. In effect, husband and wife are endowed with the agency to be responsible. Said another way, living together makes them to become responsible to community's ethos and be accountable for their responses and/or actions towards community, others, and creation. This notion may be more appropriately understood when viewed through the worldview of a clear instruction of responsibility: living together implies

25. Tata, *Vivere-insieme*, 124–25.

26. Tata, *Vivere-insieme*, 124.

27. Faggioni, *Sessualità, Matrimonio, Famiglia*, 137.

28. Balcius, *L'agire*, 62.

29. Tata, *Vivere-insieme*, 83.

that husband and wife have to keep in mind the necessary will, even if it is not always exercised in a positive manner, to exercise responsibility in relationships with others that are affirming, life-giving, and supportive.

Vitality: Marriage for Life

This paragraph looks at the phenomenology of life as the starting point of African communitarian anthropology, from the understanding of how familial life constitutes a fundamental dimension of marriage-love.[30] In Africa, it is through marriage and love that the mystery of life is propagated and handed down. Marriage-love allows procreation and makes humankind to be co-creator with God. It is "social hunger" which drives people to create family bonds, to live together so that they can provide to each other with companionship.

The sense of familial life puts the spouses in a situation where they start to develop consciousness initially directed toward a partner but afterwards include parents, children, brothers, sisters, cousins, uncles, neighbors and other relatives and eventually the whole community, in favor of protecting of life.[31] In this line, the dominant feature of African families is its ability to "make new things out of old," and to draw forth new solutions from the traditional resources of family institutions by creating a large horizon of interrelationship.[32]

With John Mbiti we can say that "married life has its problems but, in spite of them all, it is an infinitely rich and beautiful mystery which cannot be exhausted even by happiest marriages. It is only love in marriage which unfolds the riches and beauty of that mystery. Having unfolded them, love goes on to sustain and crow them."[33] It is this love which helps married people to overcome their marital problems but also multiplies the joy and happiness of living together as a family. According to Lucy Mair, this type of family, that is open to life, could be theologically also considered domestic church. In effect, one of the main features that distinguish married love from love in the general sense is the fact that it is open to the generation of life.[34]

---

30. See Nkafu Nkemnkia, *Il pensare africano come vitalogia.*
31. Mbiti, *Love and Marriage in Africa,* 109.
32. Bujo, *Plea for Change of Models of Marriage,* 98.
33. Mbiti, *Love and Marriage in Africa,* 221.
34. See Mair, "African Marriage and Social Change," 1–177.

The Yoruba speaking peoples depict their high regard for fertility and displeasure infertility in names like: *Omon lade ori* (children are crowns), or *Omon l'owo* (children are money). This is made possible because conjugal love is also lived and expressed in the union of bodies between the husband and the wife. This union manifests the fullness of married love. Married love in addition to the unitive dimension also has a procreative dimension which is inseparably connected to the unitive. And so, it is open to the generation of life which would be a concrete fruit of conjugal love lived in truth and in its fullness.

In sum, African families have rich and noble cultural values where families help each other, live together and take part in all social, political and economic affairs in times of difficulties and joys. Families have a significant role in the life of the church and society. It is clear that good families build strong community where people love each other and live together in harmony. This anthropological approach is contextual in the sense of inter-cultural theology in dialogue between the universal message of the gospel regarding family, and the contemporary situation about family and African culture as a response to AL. Because, in the name of solidarity, Africa will continue to render its service to the Catholic Church and help the needy, poor, widows, orphans and elders who are without any help. Only, communitarian solidarity can help young people to understand the meaning of marriage and help married couples with problems.

Nevertheless, today, the young Africans meet problems to preserve the noble family life, traditions and cultures that they inherited from their forefathers. They are imitating the culture and living style of others, instead of exercising theirs and living it for themselves. How should each African look at his own inner richness, keep it and make it grow?

Pastoral Application

Here, we would like to bring pastoral caregivers together from Yoruba (Nigeria, Benin, and Togo) for a discourse on new ways of care and counseling. There is the need to promote the intercultural exchange, to learn more and more about care and counseling in different contexts of our continent and to become aware of common spiritual backgrounds and cultural differences. Though distinguishable, politics, economics, ethics, marriage and family life are inseparable from one another and each is an integrated part of communitarian realities. Every event have a spiritual dimension.

Personal Experience as a Catholic Couple in Yoruba Context

When the spouses pass years without getting a child, there are often many pressures from their families: what's the matter with her (the wife)? If on the one hand, their families were worried about the wife, on the other hand, the concrete proposals are made to the husband in order to fill the void in the event of irreversible infertility.

We can say that the importance of offspring is noteworthy in the vision of African communitarian marriage. If marriage is meant especially for the continuation of the human species, namely for extension of life, the love of offspring in marriage is so strong that children are almost considered a necessary condition for the validity of marriage.

What often happens, when a marriage is childless, the man invariably seeks a second wife from whom he hopes to have children.[35] Sometimes, because of barrenness, some women leave their husbands to try their luck with another man from whom they hope to have children. Sometimes also, they do begin to have children with another man. A possible scientific explanation for this could be that the one of two spouses is genetically incompatible.

In addition, when there is repeated infant mortality, very often a woman leaves her husband for another man, and the children begin to survive. Today we may suspect that these are cases involving genotype incompatibility, a problem that is removed with a change of spouse. The same can happen when in a family the children are all girls and the man urgently needs a male heir who will take over the name of the family. Oftentimes the man will marry another woman simply for this reason. Because of all these cases that underscore the importance of offspring in African communitarian life, there are many and varied ways to describe the aims and activities of the theological discipline of pastoral theology. Each description undoubtedly will have its high points and points of difference, but at bottom, pastoral theology could maintain an underlying conviction that God intends for spouses to flourish and live positively.

---

35. Although a marriage without children is difficult to sustain, strictly speaking, it is not true to say that in African tradition, marriage without children is considered invalid.

Therefore, pastoral care must lead to the understanding of marriage and family life.

Anthropology of Misfortune as a Pastoral Hermeneutic

At the theoretical and practical levels, the Yoruba, in most cases, established a correlation between relationship, health and sickness. Infertility and sterility are associated with personal or group badness: anonymous wickedness, malediction, evil practices.[36] On a worldview which assumes the effective presence of numberless spirits, and regards all life as one, with no clear distinctions between the material and the non-material, the natural and the supernatural let alone the superstitious mentality, the solution to all problems of ill-health, as of concern or anxiety generally has been sought squarely within the framework of religion, magic or witchcraft. The brief or long time of infertility of a couple is often considered as a disaster and explained in terms of the result of an offense against the ancestors, violation of social taboos, or an attack by deities and evil spirits.

This situation leads us to consider the relationship between childlessness, illness, and misfortune in the Yoruba traditional spirituality. Due to their despair, the childless Christian couple search for meaning and solutions beyond the ambit of their Christian faith. The search for drastic solution could lead them into going from churches to churches seeking signs and wonders, the conjuring of spirit, consulting of the *Babalawo* (*Ifa* priest), combating with witches and wizards.

Therefore, the fundamental theological element underlying the Yoruba tradition is the archetypal value of life that comes from and finds its origin in *Olodumare* (God) and must be preserved by all means. Thus, the affirmation, the preservation and reinforcement of life dominate the religious thinking, social thoughts and health systems of the African traditional people. To live in the Yoruba context is to participate in the protection of life, the survival of the family and the continuity of the community. One is called to share in the life-giving processes through ways of living in the community and one's capacity to transmit life to the next generation.

36. Tata, *L'anthropologie de l'infortune*.

Infertility and Christian Ethics of Procreation

Infertility becomes a crucial problem of marriage; the inability to conceive a child after a whole year of non-contracepted sexual rapport between a couple is a complex problem. The impossibility to have a child is often due to some particular physical defect either in the husband or in the wife. Such defects could include physiological dysfunction as well as anatomical, genetic, and endocrine and immunological problems.

The most frequently mentioned serious consequences of being childless are in the realm of community effects, in-law effects, and effects on marriage. These severe effects concern almost exclusively women. This might be partly caused by still prevailing ideas that infertility is a woman's fault or the denial of the existence of male infertility. This situation creates an extremely difficult life for childless women, especially in communities in which people are well-known to each other. In this sense, being marginalized makes life very difficult in a village or quarter in which community life is the center of most human interactions. The reactions of in-laws, and especially the mother-in-law, also make childlessness difficult to bear. In this sense, what's the spirituality in a life threatened by illness?

The pastoral theology in the African context has to conscientize that, as a matter of fact, infertility is not a "woman's thing" or a "woman's disease"; it could very well be due to some anomaly in the man. Therefore, the aim of a good pastoral approach will be to examine the concept of infertility particularly as it affects the Yoruba Christian couple, the several solutions often proffered as a way out of infertility, and particularly, the ethical challenges connected with a number of these proffered solutions.

It is important to represent the church's vision here. We have perused the challenges, principally ethical in nature, which infertile couples, particularly Yoruba Christian couples face in their quest to circumvent the problem of infertility in their marriage. Even just a few of these challenges have demonstrated the difficult situation these couples have to deal with. The troubles that they face are not in any way light for the church. So, their problems in the world are the existential problems of the church. The alternatives given to the Christian couple as a means of combating infertility are often plagued with several ethical predicaments.

Conclusion

Love is the foundation of any and of every authentic relationship where the one wishes and does all that is necessary to promote the good of the other. It is in the nature of the human person to love and to seek the good. Relationships make us what we are. As human beings, we are always in relationship with one another. Our relationships with parents, siblings, friends, colleagues, and a host of other persons are constitutive of our being. These are relationships founded (on) and animated by love, and as such, given the transforming capacity and dimension of love, they beautify our life filling it with meaning and laughter.[37]

Thus, the virtue of love represents, in a certain sense, one of the specificities of Christian life. A fundamental pastoral question: how must Africa go? What must Africa do between tradition and modernity? We say that Africa must change. But even if, more and more, the traditional worldview is being abandoned by Africans themselves, we have to pay attention to, not Westernize, the African communities. Letting our culture assume the Western worldview could be the source of much sorrow and even psychological illness for those who try to live and work in a different ideological climate.

Here again, the church is called to recognize and articulate an authentic African Christian theology that is integrative, pastoral, and therapeutic. It goes without saying that African pastoral healing has to develop what appears to it as a reasonable explanation; not to provide such an explanatory model would result in an intolerable existence. This means that the pastoral healing practices will be often culturally congruent and internally consistent within the Christian worldview and frame of reference.

Bibliography

Anderson, Herbert, and Robert Cotton Fite. *Becoming Married: Family Living in Pastoral Perspective*. Louisville, KY: Westminster/John Knox, 1993.
Balcius, Vidas. *L'agire: Tra Virtù e Opzione Fondamentale*. Rome: Urbaniana University Press, 2016.
Bujo, Benezet. *Foundations of an African Ethic: Beyond the Universal Claims of Western Morality*. Nairobi: Paulines Africa, 2001.
———. *Plea for Change of Models of Marriage*. Nairobi: Paulines Africa, 2009.

37. See Jeanrond, *A Theology of Love*.

Chiavacci, Enrico. *Gaudium et Spes: Testo Latino e Italiano con Comment e Note*. Rome: Editrice Studium, 1967.

Faggioni, M. Pietro. *Sessualità, Matrimonio, Famiglia*. Bologna: EDB, 2011.

Francis. *Amoris Laetitia: On Love in the Family*. Vatican City: Libreria Editrice Vaticana, 2016. http://w2.vatican.va/content/dam/francesco/pdf/apost_exhortations/documents/papa-francesco_esortazione-ap_20160319_amoris-laetitia_en.pdf.

Idowu, E. Bolaji. *Olodumare: God in Yoruba Belief*. London: Longman, 1969.

Jeanrond, Werner G. *A Theology of Love*. New York: T and T Clark, 2010.

John Paul II. *Familiaris Consortio: On the Role of the Christian Family in the Modern World*. Vatican City: Libreria Editrice Vaticana, 1981. http://w2.vatican.va/content/john-paul-ii/en/apost_exhortations/documents/hf_jp-ii_exh_19811122_familiaris-consortio.html.

Ki-Zerbo, Joseph. *Repères pour l'Afrique*. Dakar: Panafrika, 2007.

Mair, Lucy P. "African Marriage and Social Change." In *Survey of African Marriage and Family Life*, edited by Arthur Phillips, 1–177. London: Oxford University Press, 1953.

Mbiti, John S. *African Religions and Philosophy*. London: Heinemann, 1990.

———. *Concepts of God in Africa*. London: SPCK, 1970.

———. *Love and Marriage in Africa*. London: Longman, 1973.

Miser, Andrew L. *The Partnership Marriage. Creating the Life You Love . . . Together*. Wroclaw: Create Space, 2004.

Nkafu Nkemnkia, Martin. *Il Pensare Africano come Vitalogia*. Rome: Citta Nuova, 1995.

Oxford Living English Dictionary. "Harambee." *Oxford English Dictionary*. Oxford University Press. https://en.oxforddictionaries.com/definition/harambee.

Powell, J. Joseph. *The Secret of Staying in Love*. Cincinnati: RCL Benziger, 2012.

Tardits, Claude and Audrey I. Richards. "A Propos du Mariage Bemba." *L'Homme* 14:3 (1974) 111–118.

Tata, Gabriel. *Anthropologie Communautaire Africaine: Solidarité Dynamique ou Tragique? Essai d'une Herméneutique Morale Chrétienne*. Rome: PUU, 2012.

———. *L'Anthropologie de l'Infortune: La Maladie et l'Autre. Essai d'une Herméneutique du Modèle Yoruba*. Berlin: PAF, 2015.

———. *Vivere-insieme: Aspetti Etico-sociali dell'Antropologia Africana*. Rome: Urbaniana University Press, 2014.

Thatcher, Adrian. *Marriage after Modernity*. New York: Universal, 1993.

Uzukwu, Elochukwu E. *A Listening Church: Autonomy and Communion in African Churches*. Maryknoll, NY: Orbis, 1996.

Vatican II. *Gaudium et Spes: Pastoral Constitution on the Church in the Modern World*. Vatican City: Libreria Editrice Vaticana, 1965. http://www.vatican.va/archive/hist_councils/ii_vatican_council/documents/vat-ii_const_19651207_gaudium-et-spes_en.html.

6

Love Made Fruitful

BARNABAS SHABAYANG

Introduction

Love made fruitful in Christian marriage is manifest in the gift of children. John Cardinal Onaiyekan of Abuja, Nigeria asserted strongly that as Africans: "our concept of marriage is the importance of offspring. Marriage is meant especially for the continuation of the human species. The love of offspring in marriage is so strong that children are almost considered a necessary condition for the validity of marriage."[1] We know already that Christian Scriptures as well as the Magisterium uphold that the origin of love itself is God, thus, "Love is always a gift of God" (*Amoris Laetitia* [AL] 228). It causes us to state that in the general sense; love is the focal language of God, of angels, and of human beings. Even as conjugal love generates, sustains and grows human life; as AL vividly teaches that: "Love always gives life. Conjugal love 'does not end with the couple... The couple, in giving themselves to one another . . . a permanent sign of their conjugal unity and a living and inseparable synthesis of their being a father and a mother.'"(AL 165). In the church through sacramental participation, it is expected that the couple through love made fruitful in child

---

1. Onaiyekan, "Marriage in the Contemporary World." See also, Ziegler, "Protectionism and Poverty."

136

bearing, "give not just themselves but also the reality of children, who are a living reflection of their love" (AL 165). Thus, within the context of religious metaphor, it can be said that we Africans value the seed of this fruitful union of a man and a woman that yields life. In a metaphorical way, this can be expressed as a mustard seed which blossoms in God's creative love through their offspring, the gift of children.

In the Judeo-Christian tradition, love communicates fruitfulness, multiplication of being, and promotes mutual fraternity (AL 123). The abiding presence of God is love, love made fruitful in marriage, which is the signature of God at creation (Gen 3:1–6). More so, St. John poignantly teaches: "God is love" (1 John 4:16). The evergreen nature of the generative love of God is centered on the Holy Trinity *(AL 29)*, even as Christian teaching on the dogma of the Trinity is the message of divine love that multiplies salvific resources by connecting it to the redemptive salvation of human beings bequeathed by the Christ-centered event—the Paschal Mystery. In a more interactive engagement, connecting divine love to human generative love in marriage, AL richly affirms: "After the love that unites us to God (via the sacraments and faith expressions), conjugal love is the 'greatest form of friendship'" (AL 123).[2] Thus, as Africans, we believe that life is transmitted by marriage, engaged by mutual friendship between consenting male and female adults and families in respect and dignity. In the African worldview, there is no isolation of an orphan[3] or a widow, because as soon as the head of the family in the person of the father is dead, the extended family or the community— *Umunna* (Igbo), *Iyali* (Hausa), *Tsut* (Bajju)—takes over the immediate socio-economic needs of the person(s) and provides for the basic needs of the person(s). As Africans, we do have a traditional way of handling these emergencies as these basic needs can neither cause hunger nor lack of shelter, etc.; thus, it behooves us to put a stop to these dangers that are posing a threat to the survival of the person. Before the advent of Christianity and Islam in Africa, it was unheard of for a poor person to retire or go to bed on an empty stomach. In fact, "it was inconceivable to find in a traditional African society with its communalism and extended family system, a person languishing in poverty."[4] Again this vivid account

2. Aquinas, *Summa Contra Gentiles* III, 123; cf. Aristotle, *Nicomachean Ethics*, 8, 12, 174.

3. Shorter, *Religious Poverty in Africa*, 11.

4. Nwaoru, "Poverty Eradication: A Divine Mandate," 204.

confirms the solidarity that Africans give to those who are disadvantaged in life so that they are not alone:

> Both the rich and the poor individuals were completely secure in African society. Natural causes brought famine, but they brought famine to everybody—"poor" or "rich." No one starved, either for food or for human dignity, because he lacked personal wealth; he could depend on the wealth possessed by the community of which he was a member.[5]

In view of the above assertion, a strong point not mentioned in the document is specifically that we, the Africa church, welcome warmly this rich post-synodal document that emphasized the unique role of love in the family; being a believing community of faith and witness. Africans know consciously within our DNA that an elder in faith and morals in the person of Pope Francis teaches with clear discipline. In African cosmology, it is explicit that when an elder speaks "within traditional African culture, leadership is moral leadership,"[6] hence the wise application of this rich document to daily life in our African continent. As it will be applied by the fruitful work and the pastoral initiatives of the hierarchy, the pastors of souls and seasoned theologians in this process are under review. Therefore, we assert that we know as Africans that the moral leadership of the pope is exemplary because "who one is, speaks louder than what one has." Moral character defines power,[7] as this power has been exercised by the pope, based on salvific value.

We intend below to take a cursory view of AL, analyzing its rich content in the light of other magisterial documents with the same focus; while finally applying its content and "spirit" to the socio-cultural world view of the African Catholic clergy and the faithful in the light of appreciating the holistic value of the Christian family.

Commentary on the Text of Chapter 5—Love Made Fruitful

This section critically discusses and examines three key issues in text, context, and spirit as they relate to the African soul—the family. These include the celebration of the sacredness of human life in the womb and promoting its dignity; the indispensable and unique role of biological

5. Nyerere, *Ujamaa*, 3–4.
6. South African Catholic Bishops' Conference, *Integrity in Ministry*, iii.
7. Catholic Bishops' Conference of Nigeria, *Called to Love*, 7.

parents for their offspring; and respect and care for the elderly until natural death in the family. This will further be cast in the light of some magisterial documents that treated similar or related issues, juxtaposing these and contextualizing these terms to demonstrate the relevance of AL to the African subregion. The purpose is clear: to underscore the import of the document we shall interrogate by a cursory analytical discourse the concepts of the attractiveness of the Afro-socio-cultural milieu of enrichment by marriage and birth; the unique and fruitful love of a mother and a father; and the need of recognizing the bestowal of spiritual fraternity amongst people through the Eucharist which enhances family ties.

The Attractiveness of the Afro-Socio-Cultural Milieu of Enrichment by Marriage/Birth

The document discusses the beginning of human life located in the womb of a woman receiving and bringing forth new life within the institution of marriage. It upholds: "Each new life allows us to appreciate the utterly gratuitous dimension of love which never ceases to amaze us. It is the beauty of being loved first: children are loved even before they arrive" (AL 166). It presents love as the focus of parenting, as maintained by Pope Francis in his catechesis earlier about the value of healthy family life.[8] The pope teaches that a new child, arriving as the fruit of conjugal love, is a huge blessing, not self-achievement. Thus he writes: "The gift of a new child, entrusted by the Lord to a father and a mother, begins with acceptance, continues with lifelong protection and has as its final goal the joy of eternal life" (AL 166). It clearly shows then that the gift of children in Christian marriage is a divine blessing that comes directly from God to a particular family in the church.

Africans celebrate the bond of fruitful love in a large family in varied shades and colors; these may be in their social engagements like the birth of new babies, marriages, title-taking, or even the burial of the elderly. This presently has a deep connotation of sacramental presence as it is understood in terms of physical intimacy and deep ecclesial communion. This is well expressed in the universal character of the Church, which promotes support, bigger interactions, charity, and love as found in big African circles; and by virtue of baptismal character, Christians receive the gift of being adopted children of God (Rom 6:3–11) and becoming

8. See Francis, "Catechesis," 8.

members of the Church (AL 167). Thus, cautioned in the exercise of "responsible parenthood" as taught by Pope Paul VI—"[r]esponsible parenthood is exercised by those who prudently and generously decide to have more children"[9]—the church encourages parents to train them responsibly.

Africans celebrate in unique ways the early signs of a woman's pregnancy and ensure her well-being and care until the arrival of the child. We revere and uphold the woman's womb to be sacred and a blessing of the ancestors and the gods. In African cosmology, the woman's womb is likened to the earth; it brings forth abundant, rich fruits. Thus, AL 168 teaches: "Each woman shares in 'the mystery of creation, which is renewed with each birth.'" Love and fruitfulness thus become the gain of the family and the church in the increase of membership through baptism. Therefore, AL warns against using the rich fruit of the womb—pregnancy—for scientific verification (AL 169); the caution is clear: "A child is a human being of immense worth and may never be used for one's own benefit." Pope Francis asserts authoritatively: "Children are a gift. Each one is unique and irreplaceable . . . we love our children because they are children, not because they are beautiful, or look or think as we do, or embody our dreams. We love them because they are children. A child is a child"[10] (AL 170). The pope tasks Catholic parents to welcome with love and joy the fruit of their womb: "The love of parents is the means by which God our Father shows his own love. He awaits the birth of each child, accepts that child unconditionally, and welcomes him or her freely" (AL 170).

Africans are agrarian by nature, as life is largely sustained by farming, and births of male children guarantee a larger domestic work force and a future. That is why Africans, in a unique way, celebrate the arrival of a newborn, especially a male child, as every birth adds to the high value, number, and dignity of the family. As such, the mere mention or concept of abortion is taboo and forbidden.

The Unique and Fruitful Love of a Mother and a Father

The affirmation of the generative love of both the father and the mother in marriage is rooted in cultural and religious foundations which express the arrival of a child in the family. The pope teaches that God uses the

9. Paul VI, *Humanae Vitae*, 487–89.

10. Francis, "Catechesis," 8.

parents to give life to the newborn and in being faithful to this voca-tion, parents "show their children the maternal and paternal face of the Lord" (AL 172). The pope further teaches: "Mothers are the strongest antidote to the spread of self-centered individualism . . . It is they who testify to the beauty of life" (AL 174). This emphatic statement captures the soul of the African ancestral teaching of the indispensable role of a mother in the family. It is quite true that "[w]ithout mothers, not only would there be no new faithful, but the faith itself would lose a good part of its simple and profound warmth . . ." (AL 174). Pope Francis did not just stop at that indispensable role played by mothers in our homes in Africa as elsewhere, but reverently thanked them in these words: "Dear mothers: thank you! Thank you for what you are in your family and for what you give to the Church and the world" (AL 174). On the flip side, however, he classifies the clear role that must be played by the father in each family: "Fathers who are too controlling overshadow their children, they don't let them develop" (AL 177). This offers a cautionary note to all African fathers who bully their children using the excuse of home train-ing to avoid this dangerous trend by using healthy and helpful means of correction and education in sound morals as well as by modeling the Christian life in their own daily witnessing to the Gospel.

The African spirit in the family is all-embracing; all members rise to assist all vulnerable children in the family, clan, and community. Pope Francis emphasizes the need for closer family bonds between parents and children. In this regard, he is solicitous that children in difficult situations (e.g., those who are refugees, homeless, and orphans) should be sup-ported in foster homes. He calls for married couples "to foster a culture of encounter and to fight for justice. God has given the family the job of 'domesticating' the world and helping each person to see fellow human beings as brothers and sisters" (AL 183–84). He emphasizes the need for voluntary and unconditional charity in the midst of poverty, hunger, and war that is prevalent in so many countries, especially those in Africa.

Creating Spiritual Fraternity Through the Eucharist and Family Ties

Pope Francis points out that rich families must bring up their children through faith formation and sound moral education (AL 185). Thus he teaches: "The Eucharist demands that we be members of the one body of the church. Those who approach the Body and Blood of Christ may not wound that same Body by creating scandalous distinctions and divisions among its members" (AL 186). He teaches that the celebration of the Eucharist brings about a sense of communal solidarity and social responsibility animated by love and a sense of justice. Against this backdrop, many European and American theologians and scholars who do not understand the concept of Eucharistic inculturation in Africa tend to view cultural initiatives at the celebration of the Mass as fetishes, incorrect and unwelcomed. Laurenti Magesa strongly opposes these negative biases: "they [Western writers] have come to realize that interpretations of African culture by Western scholarship were sometimes contrived and inaccurate."[11] This further points out the obvious truth in the words of Janheinz Jahn that "those who expect to see in their fellow men fools, blockheads, or devils, will find evidence to confirm their prejudices."[12] Perhaps this has been the negative storyline of Africa, even though *Ecclesia in Africa* (1994) and *Africae Munus* (2011) have tried to correct the wrong interpretation of the Eucharistic celebration in Africa using drums and African metaphors and folklore. But AL does not address the African perception of Eucharist.

Nevertheless, based on the ecclesial universal connection to God through the spiritual nourishment in the Eucharist, basic interconnectedness and relationship will develop, not only by blood, but by faith and morals. Social responsibility creates a wealth of faith which is Christ-centered. As Pope Francis says, "We are all sons and daughters. And this always brings us back to the fact that we did not give ourselves life but that we received it. The great gift of life is the first gift that we received" (AL 187–88). He therefore calls for mutual respect for one another, especially on the basis of giving due honor to parents in the family as required by the Fourth Commandment of God. That is why he insistently urges: "parents must not be abandoned or ignored, but marriage itself demands that they be 'left,' so that the new home will be a true hearth, a place of security, hope and future plans, and the couple can truly become 'one flesh' (Gen 2:24)" (AL 190). He concludes that section by inviting married couples to be simple sons and daughters of God: "Marriage challenges husbands and wives to find new ways of being sons and daughters" (AL 190).

Since the Eucharist as spiritual food strengthens Christians, it ought to lead them to have compassion for the elderly. On this the pope begins

11. Magesa, *African Religion*, 30.

12. Jahn, *An Outline of the New African Culture*, 20.

with the poignant invitation: "Do not cast me off in the time of old age, forsake me not when my strength is spent" (Ps 71:9). AL raises important questions about how parents are treated by their children as they grow old and invites young couples, and society in general, to pay adequate attention to the aging among us: "attention to the elderly makes the difference in a society. Does it make room for the elderly? Such a society will move forward if it respects the wisdom of the elderly" (AL 192). African authenticity and genuine fruitfulness emerge from the abundant blessings that come from proper care of the elderly in each family, clan, and community. They in turn bestow and bequeath ancestral blessing and invoke divine blessings on their children and grandchildren, and this will reap great fruitfulness for the caregivers. Thus, care for the elderly persons in our families and communities is a mission of love. It is a domestic religion, an expression of natural love given willingly and freely without expecting payback by government agencies or insurance companies. These elderly parents bequeath reverential blessings to their children and grandchildren for the care given to them until death; hereby it is expected to bear an inherent everlasting fruitfulness on the caregiver. This discussion, however, was omitted in *Amoris Laetitia*.

From the foregoing, Pope Francis further engenders the spirit of creating the bond of social responsibility amongst brothers and sisters. In his words, this bond will bequeath a lasting and enduring legacy of fruitfulness and love in the family. He writes: "Growing up with brothers and sisters makes for a beautiful experience of caring for and helping one another" (AL 195). It is not just a common relationship, but a fruitful one; thus,"It must be acknowledged that 'having a brother or a sister who loves you is a profound, precious and unique experience'" (AL 195). He further emphasizes the genuine love that needs to be given by the larger family; for us in Africa, this occurs in the well-knit, community-oriented life in the extended family, clan, and community where life is lived and shared (AL 197–98). This expedient and expressive life already is a religion in most African communities; we need to guard against its corruption.

Contextual Reflection and the Analysis of AL

The thrust of the contextual reading and moreso the theological analysis that reflects on the application of key terms, locating its relevance within the *sitz-im-liben* of the African worldview, is an obligation. The mission of this section is to juxtapose the rich ecclesio-cultural terms that could be applied to AL like interrogating and examining the African consciousness on the socio-cultural assimilation of the uniqueness of a child's birth as a gift of God, accompanied by the type of name given; the Eucharist as a divine meal of community sharing and the African value of the sacredness of the meal as the apex of union; the union of a man and a woman in marriage as the bestowal of divine and ancestral blessings leading to love made fruitful in childbearing. This great task lies before the African Catholic priest as elder, mediator, and reconciler[13] who needs to exercise his scholarly role as pastor of souls, as an educator and a theologian in the twenty-first century. AL presents specific challenges to African theologians and pastors as well as to all those involved in family life ministry. Among the numerous tasks and responsibilities mentioned above, located in the reading, re-reading, interpreting, and contextual application of AL, we need to point to the direction of both pastoral life challenges and exigencies. In the rest of this chapter, I would like to point out ways in which African Catholics can embrace the message of AL as a Gospel to the family.

African Reception of AL

In African cosmology, generative, positive words are transmitted by the mouth of the elder[14] in the family, clan, or community, drawn from long-standing relationships with the ancestors,[15] bequeathed by the Supreme Being—God. Thus, transmission of enviable rich tradition is communicated by oral media.[16] When it comes to the institution of marriage, elders believe that, through spoken words, marriage brings love made fruitful in bearing children. Thus, life is often interpreted as a cycle of love that hibernates, procreates, multiplies, and bears rich fruit as much as it is supremely connected to the Ultimate Being—God. Pope Francis, as an elder of faith and morals, has spoken universally in the rich and resourceful document of AL. Many of the issues addressed are cases that directly affect Europe and America—acceptance of the homosexual

---

13. Shabayang, *African Catholic Priest as Elder, Mediator, and Reconciler*, 7.

14. See Catholic Bishops' Conference of Nigeria, *Ratio Fundamentalis Institutionis Sacerdotalis*, 7–8.

15. See Mbiti, *African Religions and Philosophy*, 133 and 126.

16. Bujo, *Foundations of an African Ethic*, 57.

lifestyle or same-sex unions; the deliberate choice of single parenthood; government-approved abortion; the gross neglect of the elderly and parents in isolated homes. However, these excessively negative issues (AL 19-21, 28, 34, 176–78, 190, 192) are also beginning to rear their ugly heads on the African continent among the literate and educated working-class in major cities. Thus, our discourse in this volume hopes to be an enrichment that will help curb the progression of these negative trends.

The post-synodal document of AL is warmly received by the African hierarchy, theologians, and the laity. It unveils the mystery of the orthodoxy that accompanies the Catholic interpretation of love from inside marital vows to the outside implications it poses. It also, perhaps, reinterprets the actions of love and service needed for re-engineering our focus and emphasis on the continent from now to the future (AL 7, 13, 39, 68, 80, 87). It is a document that contains factual biblical (AL 8, 21–28) and experiential orthodox statements on the Christian meaning of marriage, pinpointing the mystery of God's design for married life (AL 7, 38, 40, 68, 80, 87).Yet we affirm that, for us Africans, "Marriage is one of the fundamental elements which strengthen and reestablish the community; it signifies an anamnetic solidarity with one's ancestors. Moreover, it is a *communio* with one's ancestors which ultimately achieves a communicative fellowship that transcends death."[17] It is obvious that an African reception of AL must engage some of the proposals creatively and critically in order to develop relevant pastoral approaches which respect the doctrinal and universal message of this important magisterial document.

The obvious must be pointed out clearly, that the composition of the character of marriage (as discussed in AL), seen in the womb of faith, is an enigma to persons outside the Catholic culture of doctrine and sacramental faith expression. To calibrate its rich , holistic content is attractive because it is a document that handles the nexus and the heart of the human person: the family. By its issuance, the church serves as both a wise teacher and a loving mother; thus Pope Francis started the document with these words: "The Joy of Love experienced by families is also the joy of the Church" (AL 1).

---

17. Bujo, *Foundations of an African Ethic*, 57.

The Anthropology of Marriage and the Arrival of a
Child as a Mustard Seed of Love

The Afro-cultural world celebrates love as fruitfulness; once our being is
in consonance with the Supreme Deity (God) and Mother Earth, all the
natural and supernatural elements most not only comply, but serve to
bring forth the fruitfulness of their beauty in creating harmony, in promoting peaceful coexistence and bequeathing abundance. According to
Magesa, "Marriage and other forms of legal sexual unions are meant to
ensure procreation and the preservation of life and the life-force through
sexuality and its physical expression in sexual intercourse."[18] *Ad initio*,
recognition of the power of procreation that will later be celebrated in
marriage begins in the process of initiation ceremonies of young boys
into the cultural milieu of a given tribal group in Africa. This becomes
even more evident as Africans are well-known to celebrate the four elements of Earth, Fire, Wind, and Water[19] as gifts that not only promote
fruitfulness but generate and bring forth the love of God to human beings; in extension, this equally develops and propels deep family love
among human beings in expressing their cultural heritage. Thus, it is natural to Africans to celebrate the beginning of human life through and by
means of the institution of marriage of a young, hard-working man and a
charming female maiden. According to Magesa, "marriage is understood
universally in African Religion to be the institution that makes possible
the practical expression of the cherished fecundity. It is the acceptable
social structure for transmitting life, the life that preserves the vital force
of humans, families and clans."[20] In favor of such a position then, such
union is blessed by the parents, elders of the community, the ancestors,
and God, in the hope that the marriage will be blessed with children who
will carry on the traditions of the family and the church.

Against the backdrop of Pope Francis's discussion of the European
concept of a larger family tie, in the African worldview, marriage is more
extensive as it has a deep communal character beyond just the two persons involved. It implies giving much accorded respect to the in-laws
on both sides of the divide. Huber wrote: "In many cases, the bride and
groom are not even allowed to speak the proper names of their in-laws."[21]

18. Magesa, *African Religion: The Moral Traditions of Abundant Life*, 133.

19. See Shabayang, *The Importance of Sacramentals in the Catholic Church*, 15–18.

20. Magesa, *African Religion: The Moral Traditions of Abundant Life*, 110.

21. Huber, *Marriage and the Family in Rural Bukwaya*, 158–63.

They address them only as "father or mother, which they now become, other than simply on account of age alone."[22] The account below of the Luo people is a clear example of the extensive respect accorded to in-laws:

> If a man meets either of his parents-in-law on a path he makes a detour, and if he has to speak to them he does so with his back turned to them, especially when he speaks to his mother-in-law, who also turns her back to him . . . A man who neglects these rules is said to be *wangatek*, to have strong eyes, and he makes a gift in compensation for his negligence. A man respects the whole lineage into which he has married. He can face the younger people but not their elders. He respects also the older people of the lineage of his wife's maternal uncle, for they are also his ore, his in-laws.[23]

From the foregoing, it is clear that varied African people and cultural ties are held in high esteem, as people are far closer to each other, and relationships that exist between persons are deeply rooted in family ties. That is why one is expected to respect, honor, and dignify the elders, older persons, and the clan one is marrying from as well as the entire community. Young people preparing for marriage need to know each person's family background, whether the family of the young man are great farmers, fishermen, or hunters, and whether the young man is a warrior, brave and courageous. Magesa once again asserts: "Young people desire and pray for fertility and virility. A woman will want to select a virile young man for a husband to 'give her children,' and a young man will pray for a wife to bear him many children."[24] Even so, Bujo further reiterates that, in traditional African societies, "[m]arriage is one of the fundamental elements which strengthen and reestablish the community; it signifies an anamnetic solidarity with one's ancestors."[25] This cosmic reality confirms that marriage enhances population growth and community development.

22. Magesa, *African Religion*, 116.

23. Evans, *The Position of Women in Primitive Societies*, 242–43.

24. Magesa, *African Religion: The Moral Traditions of Abundant Life*, 133.

25. Bujo, *Foundations of an African Ethic*, 57.

The Choice of a Special Name at Birth is a Gift of Parenthood

In African cosmology, love is the natural gift of person-to-person in practical things that add value to life: the supply of food to stop hunger; water to quench thirst; the gift of marriage to procreate; land to produce food. For us in Africa, the cosmic world order is often seen as a harmonious flourishing of all realities especially characterized by procreation, abundant life, wealth, and human and cosmic flourishing. Magesa correctly teaches that, "[f]or Africans, conception and birth in the human species correspond very closely to the same activities in the plant and animal species. They correspond also to human contact with the soil and its fertility, that is, cultivation, planting and harvesting."[26] The joy that greets the arrival of a new life in the family of a newly married couple has no bounds. It is obvious that "[t]he moment of conception is therefore a time of great joy for husband and wife, but also for the whole clan. Conception indicates and assures that the universe is in good order and that the ancestors are happy. It is a very significant step not only for the validity of the marriage contract but also for its consolidation."[27] This further confirms that the signature of a good marriage hinges on the immediate arrival of a new child. Thus it is very important to know that the birth of children is not the result of a married man and woman's active sexual life but rather comes about as a precious gift of God, the ancestors, and the blessings of the elders in the family and clan. As Magesa powerfully puts it: "Conception is not seen as merely a result of man and woman coming together in the act of sexual intercourse. It is most basically understood as the result of a blessing from God and the ancestors. Without divine and ancestral blessing, conception may well not be possible."[28] Therefore, there is no gainsaying that the three super elements responsible for the coming forth of a new life in a legal, traditional family in Africa are God, the ancestors, and the married couple. For example, amongst the Dinka people of South Sudan, it is believed that "God, ancestors, mother, and father must all cooperate for conception to take place. Mother and father 'copulate to beget jointly and give birth, while God intercedes to create' and the ancestors assist in protecting the creation from the malevolent powers of destruction. Every individual is therefore the outcome of

26. Magesa, *African Religion*, 83.

27. Magesa, *African Religion*, 82.

28. Magesa, *African Religion*, 83.

human act, God's creation, and ancestral blessings."[29] Expressly observed then, children bring eternal and ancestral wealth, as they constitute the full properties of marriage.

A woman's fertility is a clear precondition for the validity of a marriage in the African socio-cultural world. This issue is central and non-negotiable for the preservation of traditional marriage in almost every African tribal group; thus, Cardinal Onaiyekan writes:

> A marriage without children is difficult to sustain. However, strictly speaking, it is not true to say that in African tradition, marriage without children is considered invalid. There are therefore no grounds for trying to promote any theological hypothesis aimed at making barrenness a ground for dissolution of a Catholic marriage in Africa, as some people have tried to suggest. But what often happens is that when a marriage is childless, the man invariably seeks a second wife from whom he hopes to have children.[30]

Invariably, the absence of childbearing and offspring does not constitute grounds for divorce, but in traditional African society, every effort is made prior to marriage to eliminate any factors or problems which will make procreation impossible.[31]

The choice of a befitting name for the newborn child is part of the grander exercise of welcoming the child into the family, clan, and community. One can say, from the point of view of African theology, that the aspect of love made fruitful in marriage in AL reflects clearly the African traditions of abundant life through procreation and ancestral communion. We Africans celebrate in a unique way the new arrival of a child. It is traditionally believed, amongst Africans, that every new child has a trademark of the ancestral prodigy: "a newborn child is often thought to be the reincarnation of some ancestor who is seeking to return to this life, or at least part of his spiritual influence returns."[32] This cardinal belief is held to maintain affinity with the immediate past good elders, now become ancestors. Most often, the type of name given reflects the heroic acts once performed by these mediate or immediate deceased elders, now

29. Deng, *The Dinka of the Sudan*, 30.

30. Onaiyekan, "Marriage in the Contemporary World." See also Ziegler, "Protectionism and Poverty."

31. See Magesa, *African Religion*, 84–86.

32. Parrinder, *West African Religion*, 95; see also Parrinder, *West African Psychology*, 57–68 and 115–31.

become ancestors. Magesa once again writes on the importance of this exercise: "Naming involves the incarnation or actualization of a person (an ancestor), a certain desired moral quality or value, a physical trait or power, or an occasion or event."[33] This socio-cultural duty is usually carried out by the elderly man or woman in the family, clan, or community, using cultural metaphors, employing native proverbs, incantations, and songs of praise, and it usually involves the sharing of free food and drinks. In fact, as Charles Nyamiti vividly puts it, "To confer a name is therefore to confer personality, status, destiny, or express a wish or circumstances in which the bearer of the name was born."[34] That is why, in African cosmology, we hold strongly that the name given to a child indicates history, love, wealth, profession of faith, and hope for the future. Some names are unisex, while others are by gender. The few examples below illustrate the type of quality names given to children amongst some of the major tribes in Nigeria—within the Igbo tribe, Chinonso ("God is near"); among the Yoruba people, Oyeku ("fully blessed"); and within the Hausa tribe, the name Balarabe ("born on Wednesday" or "middle of the family"). Other tribes may name a child after an immediate past ancestor; for example, the Bajju of Kaduna may name a child Kazzahchiang ("God sees everything"); Zigwai ("We thank God"); or Katung ("community of God's people"). The naming ceremony offers one the opportunity to appreciate the rich theological hermeneutics in Africa. It equally redirects the intellectual quest by African theologians to retrieve the values of these names, by positioning the child in the African worldview as a person that is priceless; thus, it is an opening for an inculturation theology, to indicate how the child is a gift to the community and the church, even in the choice of baptismal names.

The Unity of Ritual Meals/Eucharist

Eating communal meals has both domestic and cult functions in African cosmology. In each African family, marriages are purely contracted by observing traditional rites, and so too the naming ceremonies for a new child during which food/drinks are served, shared, and provided communally. In these ceremonies of joy, sharing meals involves providing the best choice of food and drink; these are paramount to adding value to

33. Magesa, *African Religion*, 87.
34. Nyamiti, "The Naming Ceremony in the Trinity," 42.

and enhancing the richness of the ceremonies. An African does not eat alone; it is forbidden, taboo. Food is central, cultic, and sacred, and it cements communal engagement. The Kenyan priest-anthropologist, John Mutiso-Mbinda, emphasizes the important symbolism of the meal:

> A meal is perhaps the most basic and most ancient symbol of friendship, love, and unity. Food and drink taken in common are obvious signs that life is shared. In our [African] context, it is unusual for people to eat alone. Only a witch or wizard would do that. A meal is always a communal affair. The family normally eats together. Eating together is a sign of being accepted to share life and equality.[35]

Thus, after pronouncing the oath of consent to confirm the marriage, the couple will then provide the prescribed choice food—*pounded yam/foo-foo/tuwo; egusi, owedu, krakashi; brukutu/palm wine/moiz*—to the elders to prove willingness to contract the union of marriage. Then, following the traditional rites is the ecclesial, matrimonial Eucharist.

In the case of naming ceremonies, the eldest male or female in the family receives the child, performs a particular rite of spoken words and symbolic gestures, and dedicates the child to the ancestral lineage; this is followed by the joyful pronouncement that this child in now a member of the family. All others are called to eat, drink, and make merriment to wish the child long life and prosperity. All invited guests bless themselves with white chalk, signifying purity and taking the unique blessing of the child back home. For the special meal at a naming ceremony, Africans slaughter choice animals/birds and serve specially brewed wine to entertain their guests.

Pastoral Recommendation

It could certainly be said that Pope Francis's AL does not address deep issues that concern African existential life situations: polygamy/polyandry, barrenness/childlessness in marriage, the girl-child mother palaver, the exorbitant bride price of some tribes. But Western issues, were indeed categorically captured, like the scientific examination of the embryo to determine the type of genetic illness a child could face later in life: "A child is a human being of immense worth and may never be used for

---

35. Mutiso-Mbinda, "The Eucharist and the Family," 2.

one's own benefit."[36] And perhaps due to isolated cases in Europe and America of parents leaving children to themselves at home with toys, Francis also emphasizes parental availability to the newborn child, maintaining that the love made fruitful in matrimonial union must be duly given by both parents: "They show their children the maternal and paternal face of the Lord."[37] As for Africans, this affectionate presence and availability is in our DNA, duly given by parents, uncles, aunties, and most of all by grandparents, who are always available to introduce the child to the golden cultural heritage of the African people. Grandparents teach children, *ad initio*, the beauty of practicing the Christian religious faith in God and the essential needs to respect their parents, elders, and teachers in life. The children, at a tender age, are taught the totems of the community as well.

The particular domestic family problem most common on the African continent and mentioned in AL is infertility, which could often lead to divorce, presented vaguely in AL 246. However, Francis also handles very well some critical, perennial issues affecting African families, such as marriages involving disparity of cult, which represent a privileged place for interreligious dialogue in everyday life (AL 248). He mentions clearly and calls for sympathy and compassion as regards those struggling with single parenthood (AL 252) and worse, the death of a spouse (AL 253–54). He finally invites parish communities to provide financial assistance to children who are orphans and to assist widows who do not have employment. We, therefore, make some useful recommendations to accommodate and warmly receive AL in Africa's fifty-four countries and four islands:

1) *Pastoral Formation on Marriage as Covenant:* Marriage is a beautiful occasion of joy, unity and promotes universal and ecclesial love. We recommend that both traditional (bridal price and native custom associated with completing union in marriage) and sacramental celebration of marriage in the church be carried in one single ceremony. This will enhance the quality of life; proof of maturity of reception of faith and blend of rich African cultural values.

2) *Growing/Nurturing Marriage:* Married life is not just a joy for the entire family, clan, and community; it is most fully seen to be the mutual love, acceptance, and personal growth of the man and

36. Francis, *Amoris Laetitia*, 170.
37. Francis, *Amoris Laetitia*, 172.

woman involved. Newly married African couples must be allowed to grow and flourish without unnecessary family interference, such as a heavy financial burden placed on them by parents, in-laws, or siblings. These are trends which challenge young families in contemporary Africa.

3) *Education of Children in Christian Families*: The consciousness of cultural formation must be imprinted *ad initio* in the young life of children. Stating clearly the benefits and richness of their culture adds value to the quality of their upbringing. In educating children in their sociocultural world, it enriches them to know and understand the type of name they have been given, the names of native foods, songs, folklore or dance. This is particularly important because many young African families in big cities like Nairobi, Accra, Lagos, Abuja, Kampala, and Johannesburg do not speak the native language with their children, but rather English, French, or Portuguese. It is also important for the children to visit their grandparents in the ancestral home, rather than grandma and grandpa traveling always to the city to see them. Visits to the ancestral home may spark nostalgic recollections of a deceased relative, for example, and will offer the children the opportunity to share in the oral history as well as native food and drink. Grandparents have a magnificent way of ensuring that both cultural and ecclesial rituals of prayers are sustained.

Conclusion

In the current world structure, it must be known that concrete expressions of orthodoxy of the Christian faith have existed over two millennia, yet continuously, life is fully lived in the dynamics of worship, cultic rituals, liturgical expressions, and the pragmatic sacramental witnessing of the Church's clergy and the laity. This trinitarian faith is sealed by its baptismal character; nurtured by the salvific character of the Christ-event, the Paschal Mystery; propagated by Apostolic Tradition; and sustained by courageous martyrdom and missionary enterprise. And it is best maintained through the ongoing human procreation in the act of sacramental marriage. The crux of the matter is well handled by Pope Francis, who X-rays the dynamics of Christian family life from the cradle to the grave, underscoring the essentials of marriage as unity and indissolubility.

Christian marriage, therefore, is a covenant, a sacrament, and a precious gift of God to humanity.

Bibliography

Bujo, Bénézet. *Foundations of an African Ethic: Beyond the Universal Claims of Western Morality*. Translated by Brian McNeil. Nairobi: Paulines Africa, 2003.

Catholic Bishops' Conference of Nigeria. *Called to Love: Ethical Standards for Clergy and Seminarians in Nigeria*. Lagos: Catholic Secretariat of Nigeria, 2006.

————. *Ratio Fundamentalis Institutionis Sacerdotalis for the Catholic Church in Nigeria*. Lagos: Catholic Secretariat of Nigeria, 2005.

Deng, F. M. *The Dinka of the Sudan*. New York: Holt, Rinehart, and Winston, 1972.

Evans-Pritchard, E. E. *The Position of Women in Primitive Societies and Other Essays in Social Anthropology*. New York: Free Press, 1965.

Francis. "Catechesis (11 February 2015)." *L'Osservatore Romano*, February 12, 2015.

————. *Amoris Laetitia: On Love in the Family*. Vatican City: Libreria Editrice Vaticana, 2016. http://w2.vatican.va/content/dam/francesco/pdf/apost_exhortations/documents/papa-francesco_esortazione-ap_20160319_amoris-laetitia_en.pdf.

Huber, Hugo. *Marriage and the Family in Rural Bukwaya, Tanzania*. Fribourg, Switzerland: Fribourg University Press, 1973.

Jahn, Janheinz. *Muntu: An Outline of the New African Culture*. Translated by M. Grene. New York: Grove, 1961.

Magesa, Laurenti. *African Religion: The Moral Traditions of Abundant Life*. Nairobi: Paulines Africa, 1997.

Mbiti, John S. *African Religions and Philosophy*. London: Heinemann, 1988.

Mutiso-Mbinda, John. "The Eucharist and the Family—In an African Setting." *AMECEA Documentation Service* 282 (April 4, 1984) 1–5.

Nwaoru, Emmanuel O. "Poverty Eradication: A Divine Mandate." *AFER* 46:3 (2004) 198–214.

Nyamiti, Charles. "The Naming Ceremony in the Trinity: An African Onomastic Approach to the Trinity." *CHIEA African Christian Studies* 4:1 (1988) 41–73.

Nyerere, Julius K. *Ujamaa—Essays on Socialism*. Dar es Salaam: Oxford University Press, 1968.

Onaiyekan, John Cardinal. "Marriage in the Contemporary World: Pastoral Observations from an African Perspective." In *Eleven Cardinals Speak on Marriage and the Family: Essays from a Pastoral Viewpoint* edited by Winfried Aymans, 63–72. New York: Ignatius, 2016.

Parrinder, Geoffrey. *West African Psychology: A Comparative Study and Religious Thought*. London: Lutterworth, 1951.

————. *West African Religion: A Study of the Beliefs and Practices of Akan, Ewe, Yoruba, Igbo, and Kindred Peoples*. London: Epworth, 1961.

Paul VI. *Humanae Vitae: On the Regulation of Birth*. Vatican City: Libreria Editrice Vaticana, 1968. http://w2.vatican.va/content/paul-vi/en/encyclicals/documents/hf_p-vi_enc_25071968_humanae-vitae.html.

Shabayang, Barnabas Samaila. *African Catholic Priest as Elder, Mediator, and Reconciler: A Reflection of Christ's Kenosis in the Teachings of St. Pope John Paul II and the African Bishops*. Kaduna: Benwood Graphics, 2017.

———. *The Importance of Sacramentals in the Catholic Church*. Kaduna: Umbrella, 2015.

Shorter, Aylward. *Religious Poverty in Africa*. Nairobi: Paulines Africa, 1999.

South African Catholic Bishops' Conference. *Integrity in Ministry*. Johannesburg: SACBC Professional Conduct Committee, 2001.

7

Amoris Laetitia and the Pastoral Challenge Facing the Family in Africa Today[1]

Emily Kerama
and Eunice Kamaara

Introduction

The family in the contemporary world is in crisis: a myriad of pastoral challenges afflicts this basic social unit. The church has a mandate to respond to these challenges. In *Amoris Laetitia* (AL), Pope Francis leads to address the challenges faced through the entire spectrum of life, from upbringing through courtship, preparation for marriage, and marriage life right up to the death of a spouse. But is AL relevant to Africa, or does it answer questions that Africans have not asked? In this chapter, we respond to this question by offering a critical reading of chapter 6 of this papal exhortation on the pastoral challenges of the family from the perspectives of the family in contemporary Africa. We begin by presenting the situation of the family in Africa before commenting on the chapter to show that Pope Francis is often spot-on. However, his silence

1. This publication was made possible through the support of a grant from Templeton World Charity Foundation, Inc. The opinions expressed in this publication are those of the author(s) and do not necessarily reflect the views of Templeton World Charity Foundation, Inc.

on pertinent issues of concern to Africa—including but not limited to condom use, especially in the context of HIV/AIDS, polygamy, celibacy of priests, corruption, youth unemployment, and radicalization, among others—is worrying. Yet, we concur with the pope on the way forward: for an effective family apostolate, the church has to meticulously plan and implement concrete pastoral actions which appeal to specific cultural contexts and values. For the African context, we propose a move beyond theoretical discussions on inculturation to practical integration of African traditional values with Christian values. In this chapter, we share a model from Kenya: the African Christian Initiation Program (ACIP). ACIP is a pastoral formation and care program that supports adolescents to effectively transition into responsible adult members of the society. It is a practical reconstruction of traditional rites and rituals through which the values of relationships and community are inculcated to integrate them with Christian values.

Throughout the ages, through her ecclesial structures and more specifically her teaching authority or magisterium, the Catholic Church has emphasized the central role of the family as the basic unit of evangelization: the basic church. Therefore, the church through various avenues creates opportunities not only for reflection but also for sharing on individual and familial experiences towards appropriate pastoral care. After Vatican II, Pope Paul VI established the Synod of Bishops to interrogate the signs of the times and to provide a deeper interpretation of divine designs and the constitution of the Catholic Church, in order to foster the unity and cooperation of bishops around the world with the Holy See. It does this by means of a common study concerning the conditions of the church and a joint solution on matters concerning her mission.[2]

Drawing from the Third Extraordinary General Assembly of the Synod of Bishops and the Synod of the Family held October 4–25, 2015, Pope Francis released AL (*The Joy of Love*), an apostolic exhortation addressed to "bishops, priests, and deacons, consecrated persons, Christian married couples, and all the lay faithful on love in the family." In this chapter, we offer a critical reading of the presentation of pastoral challenges to the family in the Holy Father's exhortation, from the perspectives of the family in contemporary Africa, with illustrations from Kenya. The aim is to show how Pope Francis speaks to Africans in this exhortation and to share a pastoral care model which we hope will offer

2. Holy See Press Office, "Synod of Bishops."

what the pope calls "the art of accompaniment" in the pastoral care for families in Africa.

A Reading of AL, Chapter 6: Pastoral Challenges of the Family

It has already been mentioned that AL addresses not only the clergy but also Christian married couples, and all the lay faithful across the world, on love in the family. Does Pope Francis's chapter on pastoral challenges of the family have any relevance for contemporary Africa? In this section, we critically comment on chapter 6 (some pastoral perspectives), showing how this relates or does not relate to the contemporary situation in Africa. But first, we offer a summary on the family in contemporary Africa suffices.

The Family in Contemporary Africa

Clearly, Africa is not homogeneous so there is no such thing as the "African family." However, traditional Africans[3] share a common worldview, and the values governing the diverse customs are the same. The African traditional family is an extended family where up to three or more generations live in many households within one homestead. Each household is made up of a nuclear family. So, within one homestead, there are households of grandparents, a household for each of the sons and their families of procreation, and a household for each of the grandsons and their families of procreation. Within each homestead, therefore, there will be people who are related to each other in different ways and at different levels: grandparents and grandchildren; parents and children; brothers and sisters; stepbrothers and stepsisters; co-wives and co-husbands; mothers and stepmothers; aunties and uncles; nephews and nieces; cousins and more. Food is normally cooked and shared within households, but there are no strict arrangements on this. Members of the homestead, especially children, eat in whichever household they find food ready or whichever household mealtime finds them in or near. This serves to buttress the value of relationships and community.

---

3. Throughout this section, we deliberately use the present tense to show that traditional families and the family values associated with these exist to date even as others have been eroded by modernity.

There are no single parents in traditional African societies, because there is no divorce and in the case of death, the spouse of the deceased remarries soon after; the man marries another woman, and the woman would be "inherited" by a brother or close relative to her deceased husband. Among the Luo of Kenya, for example, "wife inheritance"[4] is a common practice to date in spite of its association with the spread of HIV.[5] There are no orphans, as children belong to the community. If both parents die suddenly, the children are absorbed into another nuclear family within their homestead. Many children are considered a blessing, and there are no families without children—a barren woman, for example, would actually marry another woman who already had children or who would have children on her behalf, and an impotent man does not "exist," because there are similar social systems in place to address this.[6] If a man dies without having had his own children, another man (usually his brother) would have children on his behalf, as occurred in the Old Testament levirate marriages.

While many traditional families continue to exist in Africa (hence the use of present tense in this section), immense social and cultural changes associated with modernization and urbanization have seen emerging forms of family; we have nuclear families (made up of a father, mother, and children) but also child-headed households, street families, single parent families, and polygamous families. Recently, the phenomenon of mistresses, otherwise known in Kenya as *mpango wa kando*,[7] has

4. The term "wife inheritance" is used here, but it is not appropriate. For a detailed description of why such a woman may not be described as a "wife" to the husband's relative and why the practice is not "inheritance," please see Agot, *Wife Inheritance*, 83.

5. Perry et al., "Widow Cleansing and Inheritance."

6 Among many African communities, the practice of woman-to-woman marriage is common. This refers to a practice in which a married woman who is barren and cannot have children of her own would, with her husband's consent, invite another woman to come and live with them. This woman would be considered a "husband" for the barren woman and would be under her care and authority, and she would have children with the barren woman's husband on her behalf. Children resulting from this relationship would belong to the barren woman.

Another social norm common across indigenous communities in Africa is the sharing of wives among male peers, with consent from the wives. Every woman is required to have at least one child with one of her husband's peers. This is desirable so as to counter the reproduction of genetic diseases associated with a couple. It also makes it difficult to identify any impotent men within that community.

7. This is a Kiswahili word which literally translates into "side arrangement"—in this case, a "side relationship." A mistress is jokingly referred to as a side plate.

become common. This renders attempts to define the family in Africa today difficult. Still, African societies find significant meaning in Christian values. However, various threats are emerging and without the buffer zone that was provided by extended families, the family in Africa faces many life challenges. Against this background, there is need to reflect on the pastoral challenges facing the family in Africa today. We will show that, just like in other parts of the world, new practical and effective pastoral responses can be proposed for Africa to create opportunities for the family to grow together. Pope Francis initiates a response to these needs in his teaching on what he considers the major pastoral challenges of the family in Africa through the entire spectrum of human life. In the following paragraphs, we comment on these challenges from an African perspective and experience.

On Preparing for Marriage

The pope focuses on premarital counseling—especially as regards passing on to young or new couples the virtues of chastity and genuine love—as a pastoral challenge all over the world today. He notes that there is need for adequate preparation for marriage and that "[t]hose best prepared for marriage are probably those who learned what Christian marriage is from their own parents" (AL 208). He refers to parents as family formators. In addition to the family preparing the individual for marriage, the pope emphasizes the need for long and open courting between fiancés and fiancées. This allows the two to know each other well enough to make an informed choice to enter into a marriage relationship. However, Francis is quick to point out that this does not guarantee that the lovers actually do know each other enough. Therefore, beyond family upbringing and long courting, he emphasizes the role of pastoral agents. He decries that pre-marriage counseling is often left to priests, who are poorly trained, implying that such pre-marriage counseling is neither appropriate nor effective. He exhorts other members of the community—including other couples and teachers—to provide realistic pre-marriage counseling to young people intending to receive the sacrament. Such counseling includes providing information and skills for "detecting danger signals before marriage" (AL 210), in order to address them or at least beware of them in marriage.

Analyses of the traditional societies in Africa suggest that preparation for marriage at the family level was effectively done through an intensive and complex system of education marked by elaborate initiation rites throughout various stages of life—from the moment of birth to life after death.[8] Each of the rites builds on the values inculcated in the previous rite. Within this system boys and girls received knowledge and skills that prepared them for marriage. However, with modernization and Christianization, this system has been largely eroded especially as children pursue education away from home. For example, the modern formal educational system in Kenya literally takes the individual away from family and community and does not pay attention to preparation for life in the family. Children in Kenya barely spend time with their family: they are in school for ten months and only at home for two months each year. But even the two months at home are barely spent with family and community as the parents are away at work for much of the time. Besides, the children spend most of the time studying to prepare for national examinations which puts anxiety and pressure on them to attain the best grades possible. The system prepares them for professional life as doctors, engineers, teachers, and lawyers with no regard for various aspects of family life. In this situation, parents look to teachers and religious leaders to provide information, for example on sexuality, but teachers have no time for this as they work to cover school curricula, and religious leaders are ill-trained to talk about sexuality. Eventually, young people rely on their peers and the public media, including social media and the internet, for this information. Various studies suggest that, while parents and religious leaders are the most trusted and the most preferred by young people to provide information on sexuality, they are not the actual sources of information.[9]

This state of affairs is complicated by the short courting periods that young people in Africa experience before they decide to marry. In Kenya, courting is generally short and uncommon. As for pre-marriage counseling, training sessions are often nonexistent or compressed into a few hours just before the wedding day. Often, the emphasis in the few premarital counseling sessions is cosmetic, addressing only the expected joys of marriage without bringing up major sacrifices that couples are called to make for a successful and fruitful marriage. The sessions are

8. Kyalo, "Initiation Rites and Rituals," 34–46; Mbiti, *African Religions and Philosophy*.

9. Kamaara, *Gender Relations*.

often led by the priest that the betrothed chose to celebrate their marriage—who is sometimes not their parish priest. Sometimes, the priest chosen to celebrate the marriage does not know the betrothed at all. As unmarried men, priests within the Catholic Church may have little knowledge about and little experience with marriage and may, therefore, be ill-equipped to offer this counseling singlehandedly.

Clearly, preparing for marriage is a major pastoral challenge in contemporary Africa. Pope Francis, therefore, speaks appropriately and directly to the family in contemporary Africa when he appeals to the great need to prepare for marriage in a realistic manner—preparing for the joys and beauty of lifelong marriage as well as for self-sacrifice, tolerance, and understanding.

On the Wedding Event

Effectively and rightfully so, Pope Francis indicates that weddings have become viewed as an event rather than part of a process in family life. Rather than focus on weddings as moments of grace and reflection towards lifelong commitments, weddings have been glamorized; they have become materialistic at the expense of future needs and love. This is evident across the world. With wedding ceremonies costing millions of dollars in certain parts of the world, the pope could not have been truer, even for Africa.

Africa has quickly copied from other parts of the world to make the wedding celebration a show and a most extravagant event, with the classiest car, the most expensive dresses and cakes, the most posh reception. There is even "The Wedding Show" as in America! Lately in Kenya, there are Toyota VX stretch wedding limousines for hire at USD 480 for four hours, not to mention choppers for hire on wedding days at USD 2,000 per hour![10] Even church weddings have become prohibitively costly as individuals "shop" for the most aristocratic church building. There is so much pomp and display with the focus increasingly placed more on the day than on the marriage itself. Sadly, many who don't have money to show off or to pay for glamorous weddings are increasingly opting for "come-we-stay unions," thereby missing the sacrament of marriage.

Africans need to hear the pope's words of caution, that "the wedding ceremony [is not] the end of the road, but instead [marriage is] a lifelong

10. "Chopper for Hire Kenya."

calling based on a firm and realistic decision to face all trials and difficult moments together" (AL 211). The pope appropriately dares young people in Africa to be different. He makes this personal challenge which will go well if young people in Africa can heed it: "Have the courage to be different. You are capable of opting for a more modest and simple celebration in which loves takes precedence over everything" (AL 215). This is a most-needed gift from the pope to young people.

On Married Life

Speaking like someone who is effectively experienced, the pope gives attention to the turbulence that couples experience as they get to know each other uninhibitedly. With little or no preparation for marriage, courting periods getting shorter and shorter, and betrotheds presenting their best to each other during courtship, within the first few years of marriage, couples realize how little they know of each other. To complicate this, the young people have a host of challenges to grapple with after the wedding: relations with in-laws, financial management, sexual intimacy, and sustaining the relationships and friendships they had in place before the marriage. When the pope refers to the challenges of inter-tribal marriages, he speaks directly to Africa. In Kenya, for example, tribalism is among the major challenges, especially to political development. It doesn't help that political parties are largely created on tribal lines. The tensions and anxieties of a mixed marriage can never be overestimated. To address all these challenges, the pope emphasizes the need for mentor couples and other pastoral agents to support young couples through these difficult early years of marriage. He notes that these young couples need to be encouraged to grow in faith and especially through shared rituals like prayer, giving weight to the well-known adage, "the family that prays together stays together."

Another major challenge facing families in Africa concerns family planning. Pope Francis affirms the natural method of family planning. As though addressing the African family specifically, the pope indicates that couples have a responsibility to themselves but also to others, to their extended family and to the wider community—both temporal and church. In traditional Africa, children belonged to the community for perpetuation of family, clan, tribe, and nation, and various systems were in place to buttress this. For example, among the Kikuyu of central

Kenya, children are named after parents, brothers, and sisters, while among the Luo of western Kenya, they are named after societal models, both in and outside Kenya. The naming systems serve to emphasize the obligation that individual couples have to the wider family, community, and humanity in general. However, with the breakdown of the extended family, within which families shared resources so that nobody lacked, poverty is increasingly becoming a reality that presses families in Africa to limit the number of their children. The difficulties of doing this within the Catholic anti-contraception law pose a major challenge.

We must note also the increasing prevalence and intensity of gender-based violence at home. The *New York Times* describes wife-beating in Africa as an entrenched epidemic.[11]

Though he mentions it in passing, the Holy Father refers to intolerable suffering which necessitates separation in certain situations today. This is a most progressive statement especially in the context of the Catholic position on marriage as lifelong commitment. The pope emphasizes the need for couples to read the danger signs and separate for the better good and to protect the vulnerable—especially children. The Holy Father is spot-on. Incidences of extreme cases of domestic violence are reported in both print and social media daily. Kimuna and Djamba explored factors associated with physical and sexual wife abuse among 4,876 married women between the ages of fifteen and forty-nine.[12] Their findings suggest that 40 percent of all married women in Kenya experience domestic violence of one kind or another; 36 percent experience physical violence and 13 percent sexual. Sadly, multivariate analysis shows that being a Christian significantly increased the risk of physical and sexual abuse. The Gender Violence Recovery Center at the Nairobi Women's Hospital estimates the prevalence of domestic violence against women of the same age to be at 45 percent. More recent findings present a worrying magnitude of gender-based violence: the 2014 Kenya Domestic Household Survey (KDHS) reveals that 38 percent of women aged fifteen to forty-nine reported experience of physical violence and 14 percent reported experience of sexual violence. And men, too, are victims of domestic violence in Kenya. The Maendeleo ya Wanaume Organization, a lobby group championing men's rights, carried out a survey in forty

---

11. "In Africa, Wife-Beatings an Entrenched Epidemic."
12. Kimuna and Djamba, "Gender Based Violence," 333–42.

selected districts in Kenya in August 2008 and found that between 1 and 1.5 million men are domestically abused by women daily.[13]

Despite the 2015 legislation in Kenya that outlaws domestic violence and provides for restraining orders in cases of marital violence, the vice remains unabated. In July 2016, Stephen Ngila made international news when he reportedly cut up the face and hacked off the hands of his wife, Jackline Mwende, with a machete, blaming her for childlessness during their seven-year old marriage.[14] Mwende, 27, described herself and her husband as "good Christians." Reports suggest that, before the tragic event, Ngila had taken to threatening Mwende, but when she reported this to her pastor, the pastor counseled her and urged her to stay and save her marriage since marriage is "lifelong." This incident brought fresh memories of a primary school teacher, Piah Njoki, whose husband, Jackson Kagwai, used the jagged edge of a broken beer bottle to gouge out her eyes because she had not borne him a son—only daughters. At the time of the incident in 1983, Kagwai and Njoki had lived together for fifteen years.[15] The old Kenyan adage of *mama ni kuvumilia* (a woman is long-suffering) is encouraged even when there are no systems and structures to control domestic violence from escalating to such magnitude—tragically, this adage is encouraged even by the church as was the case with Mwende. But men, too, are at risk. As we write this, the news in today's *Daily Nation* (the most widely distributed daily in Kenya) is of a woman, Jane Mbuthia, who has been seized by the police because she is suspected to have been involved in the murder of her husband, Solomon Mwangi.[16]

The words of Pope Francis ring in any reader's ears, about the need to detect danger signals in marriage and the need for the church to read the signs of the times and know when not to encourage couples to remain together. However, Pope Francis reaffirms, in no uncertain terms, that divorce is evil. He emphasizes the need for married couples to be patient and understanding to each other because "neither spouse can expect the other to be perfect. Each must set aside all illusions and accept the other as he or she actually is: an unfinished product, needing to grow, a work in progress" (AL 218). Individual couples, therefore, should always work to support each other, helping each other mature until perfect love

13. Muindi, "1.5m men are victims of domestic violence."
14. Muktar, "Husband hacks off wife's hands."
15. Ngige and Kamau, "I regret gouging out my wife's eyes."
16. Gikandi, "Murang'a principal's wife."

is achieved through God's grace and prayer and reconciliation. Francis rightly observes the need to protect children who are the most affected by divorce; he challenges parishes to create infrastructures for addressing these pastoral challenges and to accept and embrace the divorced.

Divorce was unknown in traditional African societies, but now, it is increasingly common. As a young Kenyan father who has been married for slightly less than five years decried to one of this chapter's authors: "I don't know what is happening. Most of my friends and age mates are facing divorce. I hope that it doesn't happen to me." One wonders what is causing the increasing frequency of divorce in the modern setting, something that was so uncommon in the African traditional setting. We would like to suggest that the answer lies in the lack of preparation for marriage and the inadequate support in acquiring the skills for partnership in marriage and for parenting; that was the strength of the traditional African family. It was done through the rites of passage and rituals that ran through the life course of an individual. With the loosening of these bonds and no adequate alternatives put in place by the church to meet this need, it is not surprising that young families are facing divorce and even life-threatening challenges. Against this backdrop, the church in Africa is grappling with an increasing number of children being abandoned and many turning to the streets for refuge.

On Single Families and on Homosexual Families

The pope isn't blind to the reality of single-parent families. This phenomenon is increasingly common in contemporary Africa. As the pope rightly observes, this happens when an individual man or woman fails to take responsibility for his or her actions. But it is becoming increasingly normal for women and men to choose single parenthood, sometimes because of their frustrations with married life. Many young people may be skeptical about marriage after what they have experienced in their family of upbringing or seen other families close to them. A young 15-year-old indicated to one of this chapter's authors that she will not get married but would like to have children. Some probing indicated that she had continuously observed her parents' unhealthy relationship and concluded that it is not desirable to get married. Pope Francis exhorts the church to be sensitive to such situations and to embrace single parents by involving them in the work of the church. This is real in Africa where pregnancy outside marriage is condemned and heavily stigmatized. Francis urges society not to excommunicate single parents and urges the church to offer pastoral care to them.

Regarding homosexuality, the pope reaffirms that it is against God's plan but that respect and dignity for all must be upheld. Homosexuality is increasingly occurring and becoming acceptable, particularly in urban Africa, albeit slowly. While Pope Francis upholds the teaching of the church on homosexual relations, he also calls on everyone to treat the homosexual person with compassion and care.

On Death

When the betrotheds take the marriage vows:, "til death do us part," little do they appreciate that death will indeed part them. The pope puts this fact straight before couples: one of you will die before the other. Therefore, grieving a spouse should not be an unexpected reality. Consequently, the church should always be prepared to offer relevant and effective pastoral care to support grieving spouses. The Holy Father gives a comforting message on Christian hope that allows a spouse to let go of the deceased partner, knowing that though no longer physically present, the loved one is not lost. He cites the Preface of the Liturgy of the Dead thus: "Although the certainty of death saddens us, we are consoled by the promise of future immortality. For the life of those who believe in you, Lord, is not ended but changed . . . our loved ones are not lost in the shades of nothingness; hope assures us that they are in the good strong hands of God."[17]

The extended traditional family in Africa was strong in supporting grieving couples. Whenever people were widowed, their entire community was obligated to care for them, with clear-cut practices for their protection and provision. But with the breakdown of these systems, widows especially are now facing many forms of injustice. In this era of AIDS, some atrocious stories are told of what happens to a widow suspected of causing her husband's death—to prove her innocence, she is told to drink the water used to cleanse the corpse of the husband.[18]

17. Francis, "Catechesis (June 17, 2015)," 8.
18. Kerama, "Ruth," 323.

What Else?

Beyond the family pastoral challenges that the Holy Father presents are many others that are pertinent in contemporary Africa. While the pope refers to family planning, he does not speak about the use of condoms which is a thorny issue, especially in the context of HIV/AIDS in Africa. In spite of the scientific evidence of the positive relationship between condom use and HIV prevention, and in spite of HIV's high prevalence in Africa, condom use remains low especially in marriage relationships. The 2012 Kenya AIDS Indicator Survey, for example, suggests that married women are more at risk of HIV infection than unmarried women, thanks to the idea of *mpango wa kando* mentioned earlier in the introduction.[19] Yet, generally, married women in Africa are unable to negotiate the use of condoms even in high-risk HIV infection situations because of unequal gender relations.[20] Against this backdrop, the pope would be seen to affirm his critics' opinion that he is not concerned about contraception in general, and more specifically, not concerned about HIV/AIDS, and by extension, not concerned about women in Africa.[21] Upon returning to Rome from his visit to Kenya, Uganda, and the Democratic Republic of Congo, Francis was asked by a journalist if the church should reconsider its position on condom use in the context of HIV/AIDS. While we appreciate his response that "the problem is bigger," his dismissive attitude then, and in this context, his silence on the issue in this exhortation addressed to the family seems insensitive to the deadly challenge facing millions of Africans within the family. We wish that Pope Francis, at minimum, affirmed Pope Benedict's position that condom use could present a step in the right direction as far as showing concern for the other person, or better still, that he had taken time to emphasize why the condom is not necessarily an effective solution to HIV/AIDS. He could have cited scientific evidence to counteract the seemingly theoretical evidence that condom use is positively related to HIV/AIDS prevention and control.[22] We appreciate the pope's cautious way of dealing with so complex an issue. Nevertheless, he would have done well to indicate

---

19. NASCOP, *Kenya AIDS Indicator Survey.*

20. Tenkorang, "Negotiating safer sex among married women in Ghana," 1353–62; Atteraya, et al. "Women's autonomy in negotiating safer sex to prevent HIV," 1–12.

21. See, for example, Associated Press, "Pope Francis indicates little concern."

22. Cf. Rezac, "Pope Francis was right about condoms and HIV."

awareness of isolated situations where condom use may be a necessary evil—for example, among discordant couples where the threat of HIV infection is real.

With the AIDS scourge and the resultant death of parents, Africa has witnessed the emergence of child-headed households and increasing populations of street families in all major towns, with all the implications of these. Closely associated with this is polygamy which is still prevalent in Africa. In Kenya, the continued recognition by the Kenya Constitution of customary marriages which allow for polygamy alongside civil marriages, keeps the phenomenon popular among some communities. In the context of HIV/AIDS, this, too, poses major challenges to the family in contemporary Africa.

For more than a thousand years, the Roman Catholic Church has taught that celibacy is required of its clergy. But the vow of celibacy puts many African priests in awkward situations as they seek to perpetuate their lineage as expected by their cultures and, at the same time, be in public Catholic Church ministry. This leads to immense tensions between being African and being Roman Catholic. For some African priests, the solution to these tensions lies in living double lives—that of a celibate priest and that of an African who values progeny and community living and is, therefore, secretly married. Fr. John Karimi of the Ecumenical Catholic Church of Christ—made up of priests who broke away from the Catholic Church to get married—observes, "Ninety-seven percent of priests live a hypocritical life. They should be allowed to maintain their sex life."[23] Further, Fr. Karimi argues that the anti-celibacy rule is not only unacceptable in Africa but also in all other parts of the world, because sex is a basic human need—sex is indispensable. Along with Fr. Karimi, many of the priests in the Reformed Catholic Church wonder: why does the Catholic Church insist on such an unnatural practice as celibacy when its entire morality is based on natural law? The pope remains silent on this. He is also silent about what happens to the children fathered by the priests.

Indeed, there are many pastoral challenges for the family in Africa; polygamy, youth unemployment, radicalization, corruption, alcoholism and drug abuse—the list is endless. How are these challenges to be prevented and addressed, or mitigated once they have happened? Fortunately, the church is not only the most widespread institution in Africa,

23. Catholic News Agency, "Anti-celibacy sect attracts Catholic priests."

but it also remains credible and influential from the grassroots level right up to the national level. The pope's suggestion for interreligious dialogue is appropriate towards multi-religious and multicultural responses as the problem affects families from all cultural and religious backgrounds in Africa.

From a contemporary African perspective, the pope appropriately and accurately presents some of the pastoral challenges for the family. One cannot help but admire his passion for the family as he appeals for strategic pastoral plans to address these challenges. Indeed, the pope is on-target when he says that pastoral care including character formation should be offered by the "parish" as the "family of families." Indeed, some African theologians have termed the church the "extended family."[24] Certainly, this "family of families" would be resourceful in providing moral formation and mentorship for the young in the face of the weakening extended family system. But the pope only touches on this crucial element of the traditional African extended family without expounding on how this may be practically and effectively reconstructed in the context of Christian pastoral care. An observation by Glen H. Stassen and David P. Gushee is relevant here, even though the two were commenting on the situation in Europe: this pastoral care will not be effective if the Mass is only once a week on Sunday morning or one hour long, as is becoming increasingly common in urban areas in Africa.[25] Churches should not be "preaching stations" but places where values are transmitted and character formed.[26] The challenge for churches is to stem the tide of secularization that has diminished the growth of the church in the West and is now moving with great speed to Africa. The evidence of this influence is that, in Kenya this year, the Atheist Association of Kenya was registered. The Association is now petitioning the Kenyan Parliament to remove the words "O God of all creation" from the national anthem. With secularization, the traditional African values of community and relationships are increasingly being replaced by the values of neoliberal capitalism: individualism, consumerism, and materialism.

We aver that the most important strategy that the pope did not refer to but which probably holds the key to addressing most of the pastoral challenges for the family in Africa is the need to integrate traditional African values with Christian values. This is critical towards making the

24. See, for example: Chukwu, *The Church as the Extended Family of God*.

25. Stassen and Gushee, *Kingdom Ethics*.

26. Stassen and Gushee, *Kingdom Ethics*.

parish a "family of families" that is relevant and appealing to the African family. The centrality of the African values of community and relationships could be emphasized through Christian values. As one of this chapter's writers has argued elsewhere, there is no contradiction between African values and Christian values; indeed, there is unity.[27] While the traditional rites and rituals through which these values were inculcated have been eroded by modernity, those rites and rituals could be reconstructed, integrated, and animated in Christian practices and rites. We will illustrate this in the next section.

We appreciate that the global Catholic Church as well as local African churches have given considerable attention to the challenges of the family apostolate. More specifically, although Pope Francis did not address all concerns of families in AL, he may not be accused of answering questions that African Christian families do not ask. However, there is more to evangelization than talking; more than teaching in seminars and training in workshops; more than commenting in public print and electronic media; and more than preaching from the pulpit. Actions and concrete pastoral solutions that address the challenges of the family apostolate by integrating traditional African values with Christian values have not been commensurate with the effort that has been put into words. Yet, we are not lacking in models of a better world. The traditional African family affords us the practicability of a non-materialistic, communal worldview and so does Pope Francis. The time for social action is now.

Addressing the Challenges of the Family in Africa: The Need for Effective and Relevant Pastoral Action for Adolescents

Africa is at a crossroads. It is on the verge of completely losing its traditional worldview which is characterized by the values of communalism and relationships associated with respect for the earth and for all creation.[28] In place of traditional African communalism within which the African way of life is lived, modernization has led individuals to appropriate values of materialism, individualism, and consumerism, all of which leave the family in crisis.

---

27. Kamaara, "No Longer Truly African, but Not Fully Christian," 90–91.

28. See Obioha, "Globalization and the Future of African Culture" and alsoKyalo, "Reflection on the African Traditional Values," 211–19.

It is against this backdrop of a confusing value system that young adolescents in contemporary Kenya are born and live, with all the pastoral challenges that face their families. On the level of lived experience, young people are a neglected lot; their experience is of a confused and confusing system of education which is neither based on the traditional worldview nor on any one, consistent modern worldview. A culture's worldview consists of acquired knowledge that people use to interpret experience and generate behavior. In the absence of a systematic process of education on responsible living, people will generate knowledge from the environment that they interact most with and choose what they consider appropriate for specific situations. In this regard, young people experience, through the adults in their families, a worldview that favors materialism and individualism at the expense of healthy relationships and as values to be pursued even at the expense of human life. The focus is on independence rather than mutual dependence; on individualism and consumerism as opposed to sharing; on ownership of created reality including fellow human persons rather than trusteeship and stewardship. This is best illustrated by the perceived objective of formal education: to access formal employment. Courses that train for high-paying jobs in fields such as law, medicine, and technology attract the best students, not because of interest or calling but because of the material and monetary value of such jobs. Thus, self-fulfillment and self-realization is measured by material acquisition and consumerism at the level of the individual. Hence, success is measured by individual acquisition of material things for individual consumption such as land, cars, houses, clothes, and furniture.

The 2016 Kenya Youth Survey report suggests that 47 percent of all Kenyan youth admire people who have made money by "hook or crook"; 50 percent would have no problem evading taxes or paying a bribe as long as they are not jailed, and about 50 percent say that it doesn't matter how one makes money.[29] The ink on the Kenya Youth Survey Report had barely dried before Well Told Story released another report.[30] The study is dubbed #SexMoneyFun because as it suggests, for fourteen- to twenty-year-old Kenyans, these three things are so complicatedly interrelated "that they deserve to be connected not just into a single concept, but into a single word. And not just any word but a digitally interactive hashtag word at that: #SexMoneyFun." According to #SexMoneyFun, 65 percent of Kenyan youth consider it okay to have a "sponsor" even when in a

29. Okeyo and Merab, "Kenyan youth have no qualms about corruption."
30. Kubania, "What the youth really think about dating and sugar daddies."

relationship, and 33 percent of all youth interviewed indicate that they do have a "sponsor." For the stranger in Jerusalem, the term "sponsor" is a colloquialism for sugar mommies and sugar daddies—that is, older and rich ("happily married"?) men and women with whom young people have sexual relationships in exchange for financial support. HIV statistics indicate that its prevalence is not only high among young people but also among married people, thanks to "sponsors" and their *mpango wa kando*.

In their thirst for #SexMoneyFun, young people engage in violent crime, murder included. Print and electronic media report, almost on a daily basis, that hard-core teenage criminals are targeted by dragnets, shot dead by the police, or lynched by mobs. Data from the Kenya prison department suggest that over 50 percent of all convicted prisoners are under twenty-five years old. Closely related to this are drug abuse and the continuing radicalization of youths and their subsequent recruitment into terrorist gangs.

Such a perverted worldview is endorsed by a system of schooling that makes no reference to human service to other persons and to other elements of the created order. Instead, the focus is on how much the individual can acquire for the self, even at the expense of human life. Such a situation is characterized by corruption, greed, selfishness, and irresponsible behavior in all aspects of life, with serious implications for the family. Worse still, the adult population, rather than recognize that it has abdicated its responsibility to young people, constantly condemns the youth as a "lost generation." However, the youth can't hold all the blame for having lost themselves, since in no human society are youth expected to guide themselves.

Despite being so deeply caught up in this development crisis, young people can change the future of this continent. Indeed, there is evidence to support our audacity to hope in African youth. Whether young people thrive or become lost depends largely on the adult population. According to Bill Gates, the future of Africa

> . . . depends on whether Africa's young people—all of Africa's young people—are given the opportunity to thrive . . . if we invest in the right things, if we make sure the basic needs of Africa's young people are taken care of, then they will have the physical, cognitive, and emotional resources they need to change the future. Life on this continent will improve faster than it ever has.[31]

31. Gates, "Giving the Mandela Lecture."

The philosophy behind the foundation of the ACIP agrees with Gates. Reference to young people as a "lost generation" is not only inaccurate but also a manifestation of adults' attempt to abdicate their familial responsibility. This labeling of the youth as irresponsible is imperialistic as it has the tendency to promote discrimination, domination, stereotyping, and escapism while spreading hopelessness and doom. One need only analyze messages and conversations among youths in such social networks as Twitter and Facebook to appreciate the creativity and hope in young people.

This two-sided picture of Kenyan youth indicates the competing forces of good and evil within human persons. More importantly, it implies that these forces may be successfully manipulated toward good. We concur with Sir John Templeton, a globally renowned philanthropist, that human beings have the power to master their character through self-control and courage for effective service to the self and to humankind: "When you rule your mind, you rule your world." The sustainable solution to youth challenges in Kenya lies not in reactionary, interventionist, short-term, and compartmentalized responses but in a proactive, long-term, holistic response.

In the absence of traditional systems and structures that support early adolescents to transition into responsible adulthood, we propose a pastoral model that borrows from traditional African values as well as from Christianity to create a system of support for early adolescents to successfully become responsible heads of families. In this, we acknowledge, like traditional Africans, that adolescence is the critical point during which men and women are made or destroyed. Hence, a national initiation rite, flexible enough to accommodate our diverse cultures, religions, and localities, would be a great investment and foundation on which Kenya could sustainably lay its social and economic development.

In the following section, we share the experience of the ACIP model which we propose as a response to Pope Francis's call for practical and effective pastoral efforts that support families in making love fruitful. ACIP seeks to complement pastoral care for families in Africa and help stem the tide of destruction that is engulfing the continent by facilitating the successful transition of adolescents to responsible adulthood. The model integrates traditional African values, rites, and rituals with Christian values.

ACIP's Integrative Strategy in Addressing the Pastoral Challenges of the Family in Africa

Out of concern over youth neglect and the confusing contemporary situation within which they grow up, some lecturers from the School of Arts and Social Sciences at Moi University initiated the African Christian Initiation Process (ACIP) as part of extension work guided by research. ACIP is guided by the understanding that the youth are not a lost generation but rather the hope for Africa's future. In recognition that initiation from childhood into adulthood is the specific moment within which men and women are made out of boys and girls—and that, therefore, intervention at this point largely determines whether the girls and boys will be made into responsible family women and men—ACIP was founded as a community-based development project.

The Mission of ACIP

ACIP's mission is to support young people through the transition from childhood to adulthood to empower them physically, mentally, and spiritually to successfully become responsible adults.

The specific objectives of ACIP are

1) Provide a modern initiation rite to support young adolescents to transit into responsible adults in their families.

2) Instill confidence and self-esteem in boys and girls.

3) Provide information and education for life.

4) Train participants in life skills: negotiation skills, conflict management, study skills, etc.

5) Provide parents' workshops—like Pope Francis, ACIP recognizes parents as "family formators" and therefore focuses on providing them with knowledge and skills to support their adolescent children into responsible adult family life.

Towards these goals, ACIP adopts an integrative strategy as follows:

1) It has a multiethnic and multireligious dimension—ACIP is an interethnic and interreligious program that encourages all communities to participate.

2) It is multidisciplinary—information, education, and training are offered from a multidisciplinary approach. ACIP has thirteen modules covering the areas of responsible time management; hygiene habits; relationships; secrets to success; gender issues; responsible sexual behavior to avoid unwanted pregnancies, sex-related stress, and sexually-transmitted infections including HIV; conflict management and peace building; and skills to avoid drug abuse and negative peer pressure. Teaching and training are done by professionals from all disciplines—medicine, psychology, sociology, religion, philosophy, public health, etc.

3) It is multisectoral—In recognition of the many stakeholders involved in youth formation, ACIP networks with various sectors of society: parents (parents' workshops), teachers, religious leaders, youth, and professionals among others. Some of the organizations that ACIP partners with are Moi University, I Choose Life, churches around Eldoret, Partners in Prevention, the UG Children's Forum, Testimony Homes, Family Impact, Strategies for Hope-London, Ministry of Youth and Sports (MOYAS) and AMPATH. It continues to seek more partners.

4) It is gender-integrative: Recognizing that society is necessarily made up of both men and women and that the genders complement one another, ACIP integrates boys and girls so they learn together in mutual trust and mutual respect for mutual benefit.

5) It has three tiers of education and skills building (negotiation, conflict management, self-esteem and confidence building skills) to support the physical, mental, and spiritual development of the youths.

6) It has practical modeling—ACIP brings in real professionals, community members, and fellow youth (like university students) who are identified as good role models, as well as persons rehabilitating from drugs, to share from their experience how to avoid such vices.

7) It adopts a fun-filled approach to learning through visits/excursions to various places and insists on relaxed learning methodologies and environments.

8) It has structures for learning across generations (the strength of traditional African socialization).

The Vision of ACIP

ACIP envisions a national program that supports all young people to transition from childhood into a responsible adulthood characterized by sexual responsibility, peaceful coexistence in the community, and morality in the family and workplace by the year 2030.

ACIP is working towards scaling-up its program to the national level through Trainer of Trainers workshops. Towards this end, in partnership with Strategies for Hope, ACIP developed a trainers' manual, *My Life—Starting Now*, published in 2010. The manual "is designed to help strengthen the capacity of churches, faith-based organizations, community groups, and individuals to respond to the 'call to care' for young people especially in early years of adolescence (11–15 years)."[32] In the immediate, the ACIP team is engaged in an assessment of the program, ten years after it was founded, to establish what has worked well and what has not, thanks to generous funding by the Templeton World Charity Foundation, Inc. As part of the assessment project, one of the questions that we have posed to the alumni of the program through anonymous questionnaires is:

"To what extent has ACIP influenced you in making your day-to-day choices?

a) To a great extent

b) To a little extent

c) To no extent at all"

None of the alumni interviewed responded "not at all" and over 95 percent said ACIP influences them.

The follow-up question is: "State one decision that you have made influenced by ACIP." The following responses have been received:

1) ACIP has helped me avoid drug abuse.

2) ACIP guides me to be responsible in sexual behavior.

3) I choose my friends well to avoid negative peer pressure.

4) I studied very hard through high school because of ACIP.

5) ACIP taught me how to relate well with people of the opposite sex.

32. Steinitz and Kamaara, *My Life—Starting Now*, 8. (This manual is available online at http://www.stratshope.org/images/resources_files/eCC8_Eng.pdf. It may be used freely as long as the authors are duly acknowledged.)

6) I am what I am because of ACIP. I don't touch (sic) drugs and I don't engage in violence.

7) I keep my body clean as I was told in ACIP.

8) ACIP helps me use my leisure time well.

9) I can say no to negative peer pressure.

10) I love working. The value of work is something I learned from ACIP.

We are still working on the assessment project. We plan to integrate the lessons learned over the years as we upscale ACIP.

Conclusion

As mentioned above, Pope Francis's teaching on the challenges of the family in the contemporary world could not have come at a better time in Africa, where many challenges are facing the family. The extended family system with its values of community and relationships is rapidly being replaced by the values of neoliberal capitalism: individualism, materialism, and consumerism. This has exposed the family institution to all kinds of evils such as gender-based domestic violence, single-parent families, homosexuality, HIV/AIDS, divorce, and even death leading to orphans, abandoned children, and households headed by children.

In this context, both community and church are challenged to respond to these pastoral challenges. In AL, Pope Francis leads the way to responding by spelling out the challenges faced through the entire spectrum of life, from upbringing through courtship; preparation for marriage and early marriage life; the challenges in marriage including gender-based violence, family planning, separation, and divorce, or the challenge of single-parent families; and the challenge of the death of a spouse. These are issues that are real to the African family.

Nobody would expect the pope, in one document, to be exhaustive in his presentation of the pastoral challenges of the family throughout the world. There are other issues challenging the family in Africa that the pope mentions in passing or does not mention; these include contraception in general, condom use especially in the context of HIV and AIDS, priestly celibacy, polygamy, youth unemployment, radicalization, alcoholism, and drug abuse

Decrying inadequate, inappropriate, and ineffective responses to these challenges, Pope Francis calls individual Christians as well as the church to meticulously plan and implement programs and structures that effectively respond to them. However, in so doing, the pope does not address the erosion of traditional African values which protected and provided effective responses to family challenges. Indeed, for Africa, we cannot overestimate the need to reconstruct these traditional values and to integrate them into whatever responses are developed. To illustrate this, we share the model of ACIP, a pastoral formation and care program that supports adolescents' transition into becoming responsible adult members of society. The program draws on the traditional African re-sources of the practice and value of rites of passage, partnering with the church to transmit holistic values for the family in Africa.

Bibliography

Agot, Evelynes Kawango. "Widow Inheritance and HIV/AIDS Interventions in Sub-Saharan Africa: Contrasting Conceptualizations of 'Risk' and 'Spaces of Vulnerability.'" PhD diss., University of Washington, 2001. https://digital.lib.washington.edu/researchworks/handle/1773/5660.

"Anti-Celibacy Sect Attracts Catholic Priests, Ex-Seminarians in Kenya." Catholic News Agency, November 21, 2006. http://www.catholicnewsagency.com/news/anticelibacy_sect_attracts_catholic_priests_exseminarians_in_kenya.

Associated Press. "Pope Francis Indicates Little Concern over Condom Use in Fight against AIDS." The Guardian, November 30, 2015.https://www.theguardian.com/world/2015/nov/30/pope-francis-condoms-aids-hiv-africa.

Atteraya, M. S., et al. "Women's Autonomy in Negotiating Safer Sex to Prevent HIV: Findings from the 2011 Nepal Demographic and Health Survey." AIDS Education and Prevention 26:1 (2014) 1–12.

"Chopper for Hire Kenya." Ngatia Executive website. http://executivecarhirekenya.com/chopper-for-hire-wilson-airport-nairobi.html.

Chukwu, Domatus Oluwa. The Church as the Extended Family of God: Toward a New Direction for African Ecclesiology. Bloomington, IN: Xlibris, 2011.

Francis, Pope. "Catechesis (11 February 2015)." L'Osservatore Romano, February 12, 2015.

Gates, Bill. "Giving the Mandela Lecture." GatesNotes (blog). July 17, 2016. https://www.gatesnotes.com/Development/Nelson-Mandela-Annual-Lecture.

Gikandi, Boniface. "Murang'a Principal's Wife Held after Body Found in Coffee Farm." Standard Media, November 15, 2016. http://www.standardmedia.co.ke/article/2000223434/murang-a-principal-s-wife-held-after-body-found-in-coffee-farm.

Holy See Press Office. "Synods of Bishops." http://www.vatican.va/news_services/press/documentazione/documents/sinodo_indice_en.html.

"In Africa, Wife-Beatings an Entrenched Epidemic." The Crime Report, August 11, 2005. http://thecrimereport.org/2005/08/11/in-africa-wife-beatings-an-entrenched-epidemic/.

Kamaara, Eunice Karanja. *Gender Relations, Youth Sexual Activity, and HIV/AIDS: A Kenyan Experience*. Eldoret, Kenya: AMECEA Gaba, 2005.

———. "No Longer Truly African, but Not Fully Christian: In Search of a New African Spirituality and Religious Synthesis." In *Theological Reimagination: Conversations on Church, Religion, and Society in Africa*, edited by Agbonkhiangemeghe E. Orobator. Nairobi: Paulines, 2014.

Kenya National Bureau of Statistics (KNBS). *Kenya Demographic and Health Survey*. Nairobi: Government Printers, 2014.

Kerama, Emily J Choge. "Ruth." *In NIV, God's Justice: The Holy Bible*, edited by Tim Stafford. Grand Rapids, MI: Zondervan, 2016.

Kimuna, Sitawa R. and Yanyi K. Djamba. "Gender Based Violence: Correlates of Physical and Sexual Wife Abuse in Kenya." *Journal of Family Violence* 23:5 (2008) 333–42.

Kubania, Jacqueline. "What the Youth Really Think about Dating and Sugar Daddies." *Daily Nation*, May, 19, 2016. http://www.nation.co.ke/news/What-the-youth-really-think-about-dating-and-sugar-daddies/-/1056/3209388/-/uh5wu7z/-/index.html.

Kyalo, Paul. "Initiation Rites and Rituals in African Cosmology." *International Journal of Philosophy and Theology* 1:1 (June 2013) 34–46.

Mbiti, J. S. *African Religions and Philosophy*. Nairobi: Heinemann, 1969.

Muindi, Benjamin. "1.5m Men are Victims of Domestic Violence: Report." Daily Nation, May 24, 2009.http://www.nation.co.ke/News/-/1056/602368/-/ujogrt/-/.

Muktar, Idris. "Husband Hacks Off Wife's Hands After Saying She Failed to Have Children." CNN, August 5, 2016. http://www.cnn.com/2016/08/04/africa/kenya-jackline-mwende-hands/index.html.

NASCOP (National AIDS and STI Control Programme). *Kenya AIDS Indicator Survey 2012: Final Report*. Nairobi: NASCOP, 2012.

Ngige, Francis and Munene Kamau. "I Regret Gouging Out My Wife's Eyes."Standard Digital, November 17, 2009. http://www.standardmedia.co.ke/business/article/1144028558/i-regret-gouging-out-my-wife-s-eyes.

Obioha, Precious Uwaezuoke. "Globalization and the Future of African Culture." *Philosophical Papers and Reviews* 2:1 (April 2010) 1–8.

Okeyo, Verah and Elizabeth Merab. "Kenyan Youth Have No Qualms about Corruption, Survey Shows." *Daily Nation*, January 19, 2016.

Perry, Brian, et al. "Widow Cleansing and Inheritance among the Luo in Kenya: The Need for Additional Women-centred HIV Prevention Options." *Journal of International AIDS Society* 17:19010 (June 2014). doi: 10.7448/IAS.17.1.19010.

Rezac, Mary. "Pope Francis was Right about Condoms and HIV." Catholic News Agency, December 13, 2015. http://www.catholicnewsagency.com/news/the-pope-was-right-about-condoms-and-hiv-49253/.

Stassen, Glen H. and David P. Gushee. *Kingdom Ethics: Following Jesus in Contemporary Context*. Downers Grove, IL: Intervarsity, 2003.

Steinitz, Lucy and Eunice Kamaara. *My Life—Starting Now: Knowledge and Skills for Young Adolescents*. Oxford: Strategies for Hope, 2010.

Synod of Bishops, Third Extraordinary General Assembly of the Synod of Bishops. *The Pastoral Challenge of the Family in the Context of Evangelization: Relatio Synodi*. Vatican City: Vatican, 2014. http://www.vatican.va/roman_curia/synod/documents/rc_synod_doc_20141018_relatio-synodi-familia_en.html.

Synod of Bishops, XIV Ordinary General Assembly, *The Vocation and Mission of the Family in the Church and in the Contemporary World: The Final Report of the Synod of Bishops to the Holy Father, Pope Francis*. Vatican City: Vatican, 2015. http://www.vatican.va/roman_curia/synod/documents/rc_synod_doc_20151026_relazione-finale-xiv-assemblea_en.html.

Tenkorang, E. Y. "Negotiating Safer Sex among Married Women in Ghana." *Archives of Sexual Behavior* 41:6 (December 2012) 1353–62.

8

Towards a Better Education of Children

RICHARD RWIZA

Introduction

The joy experienced by children is also the joy of the family. The aspiration to have children in African families is very strong. However, this natural desire to have children is facing notable challenges in the uncertain world of today. As infertility rates among couples shoot up, so do the lengths to which people go to have children, and there is a need to explore the effects of current treatments on the couple and the child. Another challenge is that of the inner lives of children of the divorced. Divorce is a serious problem. Children not living with their married parents are at greater risk of suffering child abuse. There is also the crucial issue of children born out of wedlock. These are some of the ethical challenges that ought to be taken into account in searching for strategies for the moral formation and education of the African child.

There is a need for better education of children, and we must reconsider the quality of education provided to them in the modern world. The search for quality demands being realistic in the sense of being in touch with the actual challenges facing the African child and what ought to be a more helpful response by the church. We need new pastoral strategies which take into account current scientific research on the moral development of children. The central purpose of this chapter is to provide commentaries and reflections on chapter 7 of Pope Francis's *Amoris Laetitia* (AL). I will then offer some theological and pastoral strategies for better education and faith formation of children in Africa in the context of apostolic exhortation.

Commentary: The Education of Children According to AL

The educational role of families is important. As Pope Francis points out, "Parents always influence the moral development of their children, for better or for worse."[1] In promoting a better education of children, families ought to be spheres of support and guidance. While it is not possible to control every situation that a child may experience, parents have the obligation to help prepare children and adolescents to face the risk, for example, of aggression, abuse and drug addiction.[2] There is also a deeper challenge that needs to be realistically faced: "The real question, then, is not where our children are physically, or whom they are with at any given time, but rather where they are existentially, where they stand in terms of their convictions, goals, desires, and dreams."[3] Education ought to promote responsible freedom to face challenging issues with good sense and intelligence.

Children's education has to take into account the ethical dimension. This is what leads to the moral formation of children. This dimension brings in the central role of schools. As Pope Francis notes: "Parents rely on schools to ensure the basic instruction of their children, but can never completely delegate the moral formation of their children to others."[4] The fact that it is parents who have given life to their children implies that the grave duty of educating their children belongs to them. They must be acknowledged as the primary persons responsible for their children's education. "The role of the parents in education is of such importance that it is almost impossible to provide an adequate substitute."[5] This important obligation of parents is also noted in the Code of Canon Law which states: "Before all others, parents are bound to form their children,

---

1. Francis, *Amoris Laetitia*, 259.

2. Francis, *Amoris Laetitia*, 260.

3. Francis, *Amoris Laetitia*, 261.

4. Francis, *Amoris Laetitia*, 263.

5. Vatican II, *Gravissimum Educationis*, 3.

by word and example, in faith and Christian living. The same obligation binds sponsors and those who take the place of parents."[6]

The significance of school education, however, must be acknowledged. In nurturing the pupils' intellectual capacities, which is its unique mission, it develops their capacity for sound judgment and introduces them to the cultural heritage bequeathed to them by former generations. It promotes a sense of values and prepares them for professional life. Basically, "[e]ffective schools are not measured merely in terms of their academic or intellectual performance as demonstrated in written examinations."[7] The issue of effectiveness should take into consideration the satisfaction gained as a result of schooling, the social concerns developed and expressed to one's neighbor, the ethical values one respects and practices, and the full physical, emotional, and moral growth that is promoted. In this context, the role of parents cannot be excluded: "Parents are also responsible for shaping the will of their children, fostering good habits and a natural inclination to goodness."[8]

A sound ethical education involves showing a person that it is in his or her own interest to do what is right.[9] Moral education has to deal with promoting freedom through ideas, incentives, practical appreciations, stimuli, and rewards. These are motivations for doing well in one's choices and decisions. Such motivations can help develop those proper interior norms which lead us spontaneously to do good. There is much value, for example, in using correction as an incentive to motivate ethical actions. There are parents who are busy chasing money and spending very little time with their children. For those who are not busy, there is the challenge of spending quality time together as electronic gadgets have more and more invaded people's family time. Quality time with the children is necessary so as to give them the right values, strong character, and the knowledge of the power within them as children of God. Taking them to Sunday instructions is not enough. Parents should also have time for family spirituality. In order to promote families which are "truly Christian and truly African," family catechesis must start an early age for every Christian. Even married couples need this catechesis for their ongoing formation in the vocation and mission of marriage and

6. *Code of Canon Law*, 774 par. 2.

7. Teklemariam and Akala, *Effective Schools for Twenty-First Century in Africa*, VII.

8. Francis, *Amoris Laetitia*, 264.

9. Francis, *Amoris Laetitia*, 265.

family.[10] The loving communion that is revealed and flows from every family member is the central element of family spirituality. It is expressed by caring for each other as persons created in the image of God. Pope Francis also writes about the various ways by which parents can correct their children. He proposes the following: "correction is also an incentive whenever children's efforts are appreciated and acknowledged, and they sense their parents' constant, patient trust."[11] Basically, there is a need for promoting a spirituality of family life. In this spirit, St. Paul in his letter to the Colossians (3:21) teaches: "Parents, do not provoke your children." Each member of the family structure is exhorted to play his or her proper role out of a motive of serving God.

We must also attend to the actual challenges faced in ethical formation. What many tend to forget in the face of various difficulties is that most children, most of the time, do follow the rules of their community, act fairly, treat friends normally, tell the truth, and respect their elders.[12] Anne Nasimiyu-Wasike brings up another deeper problem which has turned out to be a burning African moral question: the issue of child abuse and neglect. "Child abuse is denying children their rights to decent human life, to enjoy parental care, to receive relevant education, to inherent human culture, to acquire a name and nationality."[13] Our response to such challenges ought to be patient realism. As Pope Francis notes, "Ethical formation is at times frowned upon, due to experiences of neglect, disappointment, lack of affection, or poor models of parenting. Ethical values are associated with negative images or parental figures or the shortcomings of adults."[14]

Family life can be considered as an educational setting. According to Pope Francis, "[t]he family is the first school of human values, where we learn the wise use of freedom."[15] The importance of the family in the child's education is also pointed out by Pope John Paul II, who states: ". . . the family is the first and fundamental school of social living: as a community of love, it finds in self-giving the law that guides it and makes it grow."[16] There are, however, models of advertising that negatively

10. AMECEA, "Families Truly Christian and Truly African."

11. Francis, *Amoris Laetitia*, 269.

12. Damon, "The Moral Development of Children," 72–78.

13. Nasimiyu-Wasike, "Child Abuse and Neglect," 154.

14. Francis, *Amoris Laetitia*, 272.

15. Francis, *Amoris Laetitia*, 274.

16. John Paul II, *Familiaris Consortio*, 37.

influence and undercut the values of the family. As stated in the *Catechism of the Catholic Church*, "[p]ornography consists in removing real or simulated sexual acts from the intimacy of partners, in order to display them deliberately to third parties. It offends against chastity because it prevents the conjugal act, the intimate giving of spouses to each other. It does grave injury to the dignity of its participants (actors, vendors, and the public), since each one becomes an object of base pleasure and illicit profit for others."[17]

On a positive note, "The family is the primary setting for socialization, since it is where we first learn to relate to others, to listen and share, to be patient and show respect, to help one another and to live as one."[18] The ethical dimension of the community cannot be overlooked in the issue of family education: "The educational process that occurs between parents and children can be helped or hindered by the increasing sophistication of the communications and entertainment media."[19] This statement by Pope Francis indicates the relevance of media ethics. Christian communities are challenged to provide support for the educational mission of families. Moreover, Catholic schools have an important role assisting parents in raising their children.

There is the pressing need for sex education, which is instruction about issues relating to human sexuality, and the basic question is this: what sort of sex education is being offered?[20] According to the Pontifical Council of the Family's Charter of the Rights of the Family, "sex education is a basic right of the parents and must be carried out under their close supervision, whether at home or in educational centers chosen and controlled by them."[21] The moral framework for evaluating sexual acts and relations has been in relation to marriage—hence, a link between procreation, sexuality, and marriage—and the ideal sexual act has been considered as heterosexual. The main trend in modern Christian sexual ethics focuses more on love as a norm and less on procreation. However, it's important to remember that "[s]exuality is a fundamental component of personality, one of its modes of being, of manifestation, of communication with others, of feeling, of expressing and living human love."[22]

17. *The Catechism of the Catholic Church*, 2354.
18. Francis, *Amoris Laetitia*, 276.
19. Francis, *Amoris Laetitia*, 278.
20. Pontifical Council on the Family, *The Truth and Meaning of Human Sexuality*.
21. Pontifical Council for the Family, *Charter of the Rights of the Family*, 5, c.
22. Sacred Congregation for Catholic Education, *Educational Guidance in Human*

Parents are called not only to receive life lovingly but to nourish it humanely and to educate it in the love and service of God. They have the duty and right to provide moral formation to their children. This obligation is founded on the very nature of fatherly and motherly love.[23] Parents ought to educate their children in the sphere of human sexuality, teaching them to appreciate the beauty of their sexuality. This form of education enables a person to use one's sexual powers properly controlling oneself rather than being controlled. And the virtue of chastity enables a person to make use of the power of sexuality. Education in human sexuality is about much more than physiological changes. It ought to clarify the ethical issues involved and offer young persons clear instruction and positive approaches on how to live chaste lives.

In the context of AL, the focus is on a positive and prudent sex education given to children and adolescents as they grow older: "[t]he sexual urge can be directed through the process of growth in self-knowledge and self-control capable of nurturing valuable capacities for joy and for loving encounter."[24] Sex education should not offer explicit information at all, but rather it ought to inculcate modesty, purity, chastity, and ethical values. It should provide information while keeping in mind that children and young people have not yet attained full maturity."[25] In explaining the truth and meaning of human sexuality, "only information proportionate to each phase of their individual development should be presented to children and young people"[26]—that is, information for proportionate age. Though despised by others as a relic of a bygone era, sex education ought to foster a healthy sense of modesty. In clarifying human sexuality, the task is not merely to offer information about the nature of sex and sexuality but to help the youth integrate the provided information into their formation as mature Christians. They deserve the right information in sex education. The basic questions concern who to tell them (proper authority); where to tell them (right context); and when to tell them (convenient time).[27] This discussion is very important, because children will look for the information from other sources which may not be credible.

Love, 3.

   23. May, Marriage, 19.

   24. Francis, Amoris Laetitia, 280.

   25. Francis, Amoris Laetitia, 281.

   26. Pontifical Council on the Family, The Truth and Meaning of Human Sexuality, 124.2.

   27. Kirsch, Sex Education and Training in Chastity.

It is also important to review the types of movies and electronic content they are watching and accessing and discuss why certain content is not appropriate for them.

As Pope Francis says, "Sexual attraction creates, for the moment, the illusion of union, yet without love, this 'union' leaves strangers as far apart as they were before."[28] And so, there is a need to act fast for our youth, to help them truly and fully understand human sexuality and love. This can be initiated through open discussions to foster trust and faith in each other which would increase hope among the young. Reproductive health education is crucial and should include boy/girl relationships, self-esteem, human dignity, and communication skills.[29] Another issue is that of the absence of parental guidance, where parents have no time for their children, and as a consequence, children tend to learn about sex from outside. This vacuum exposes them to the currents of pop culture, including pornographic websites. Without parental guidance from infancy on, children have no foundation to build on for their true human growth to maturity.

Reflection: Moral Development of Children

The moral development of children has much to do with building up in them a capacity for moral reasoning, sharpening their ability to identify and appreciate moral values. It is concerned with rooting their attitudes in moral values, creating in them both an evaluative and experiential insight for practical behaviors in responding to real-life questions. On the one hand, children's conception of what ought to be done and what ought to be avoided, develops in the context of their understanding of problems to be tackled. On the other hand, that sense of right and wrong grows gradually through interpersonal relationships. And it is here that the ethical dimension of community factors in.

According to William Damon, "it is not enough for kids to tell right from wrong. They must develop a commitment to acting on their ideals. Enlightened parenting can help."[30] Motives are inner factors that move a person to act. Constance Bansikiza refers to the parental responsibility

28. Francis, *Amoris Laetitia*, 284.

29. Bahemuka, "What Hope Does the Church Offer the Young People of Africa," 103–18.

30. William Damon, "The Moral Development of Children," 72–78, 155.

in the sphere of moral conduct by noting that "children will follow suit if the parental examples in the community result in good moral living."[31] Pointing out the role of education, J. K. Nyerere states: "The child is like a tree which can have its growth stunted or twisted, or which can be fed until it grows beyond its unassisted height, or whose branches can be pruned and trained so that the maximum fruit is obtained at maturity."[32] Children are a reflection of the families they are brought up in and the society they are part of. Therefore, they need role models because they are poor at listening to what we tell them but very good at imitating our actions. For example, they won't treat others with respect and fairness if they see their parents mistreating their house helpers. In this moral growth, the environment in which the child is brought up is crucial.

Personal moral identity is also significant when people make choices. "Moral identity determines not merely what a person considers to be the right course of action but also why he or she would decide: I myself must take this course:"[33] What is basic is the resolve to act on those ideals. We tend to be aware of many moral issues but the crucial issue is that they seem to be far away from our own lives and call for responsibility. "For most children, parents are the original source of moral guidance."[34] Authoritative parenting motivates children's moral growth more surely than either "permissive" or authoritarian parenting. The authoritarian approach facilitates consistent family norms and sets limits but also leaves room for open discussion and clear communication. With the challenge of mass media posed by globalization, children are increasingly exposed to external influences outside the nuclear family. However, the parent-child link remains fundamental as long as the child is in touch with his or her home. In promoting ethical values, there is a need for parents to encourage proper peer relations. The socialization of children and adolescents is distinctively influenced by interacting in groups of others their own age. The implied peer links are basic in forging a self-identify.

A reference can be made here to James Fowler's work on faith development across the life span. He points out six stages of development of a person might pass through towards maturity, and his analysis has notable implications for religious faith. In general, it can be conceived in

---

31. Bansikiza, *Restoring Moral Formation in Africa*, 55.

32. Nyerere, *Freedom and Unity*, 226.

33. Damon, "The Moral Development of Children," 158–9.

34. Damon, "The Moral Development of Children," 159.

terms of spiritual development. Basically, it is the psychology of human development and the search for meaning.[35] Fowler's work needs to be understood contextually. In the African context, there is a need to borrow from the wisdom of *obuntu*—the manifestation of being human at one's best. As J. B. Rwelamira notes regarding Bahaya[36] traditional moral formation: "The whole approach is designed as a dialogue between the traditional model of formation that bore individuals to serve the life force of the community and contemporary system of formation."[37] Moral formation of the African child needs to be contextualized and illuminated by African humanism.

Jean Piaget's (1896–1980) painstaking observations of children have been influential in early childhood research and on school curricula and ways of teaching. "Piaget's studies of moral development are based both on children's judgments of moral sciences and on their interactions in games playing."[38] He maintained that observing children playing games and querying them about the rules offers a realistic indication of how moral principles are developed. A further technique for understanding moral development is that of narrating a short story that points out a type of misbehavior by a child or an adult. In Piaget's view, rules and respect for rules make up the foundation of morality. However, is it adequate to think of morality as consisting essentially of a certain set of rules, whatever sort of respect they might facilitate?

Known for his research in the psychology of children's moral development, Lawrence Kohlberg looked to Piaget's structuralist psychology for a scientific account or cognitive development with which moral development could be aligned. This is also important, because we know that behavior that is rewarded tends to be repeated and that which is

---

35. Fowler, *Stages of Faith*.

36. The Bahaya are a Bantu ethnic group that mainly inhabit the Kagera region of western Tanzania. Their common language, Kihaya, is a source of their solidarity, and their clan system is rooted in extended families, which are predominantly patriarchal. Their worldview is one of integrated humanism in which a person is understood in humanistic values—i.e., a person is more than matter (*ekintu*) but is also a human person (*omuntu*). In essence, a person is not an island. For the Bantu, the principle of interconnectedness is central. A life worth living is one that is lived in the community and society as a whole. From childhood to adulthood, the central aim of Bahaya moral formation was to promote the virtues, linked to humanism (*obuntu*). This is, basically, a promotion of African humanism.

37. Rwelamira, *Traditional Moral Formation*, 5.

38. Fleming, *Piaget, Kohlberg, Gilligan*, 4.

punished, discouraged. Otherwise, children would socialize themselves. "If Piaget saw children as little logicians, Kohlberg viewed them as moral philosophers."[39] Kohlberg evaluated morality by asking children to consider certain moral dilemmas, cases in which right and wrong actions are not always clear.

For inculcating moral values, there are issues on which a parent can focus. There are three common styles of parenting described by J. S. Fleming.[40] The first model of parenting is that of assertion of power, employing mainly punishment, and the second is that of disapproval and withdrawal of affection. The third style is induction, that is, reasoned approaches with children in which parents promote their understanding of morality by careful explanation, including appeals to the concern for the well-being of others. These three styles are common, successful approaches to disciplining children.

Basically, any development agenda should be permeated by a focus on the children's rights and well-being. Children must be put first as provided by the UN's Convention on the Rights of the Child of 1989. Putting children first on the public agenda, in terms of society's resources and time, is basic to the realization of their rights and well-being and to bring about progress. According to Joaquim Chissano, "While Africa has done well in improving access to essential services, a lack of quantity in these services, especially in education, is a threat we cannot afford to ignore if we are to prepare our children for the challenge of tomorrow, and if Africa is to participate meaningfully in the world economy."[41] What is important here is the collective action which we need to undertake for the well-being of the child. "The Africa we envision will not materialize without first ensuring the central place that children must have in society, without giving greater priority to other best interests in our laws and policies, or without listening to their voices."[42] On a promising note, children in modern Africa live longer and are better educated and protected than they were a decade ago. However, Africa is still a continent in which a large number of children die of preventable causes.

A development agenda for the good of Africa ought to be permeated by the rights and welfare of the child as outlined in the African charter

39. Fleming, *Piaget, Kohlberg, Gilligan,* 7.
40. Fleming, *Piaget, Kohlberg, Gilligan,* 22.
41. Chissano, "Foreword," xii.
42. Chissano, "Foreword," xii.

of the same name that was adopted on July 11, 1990.[43] Any human being under the age of eighteen is considered a child (Article 2). The noted charter is an African regional human rights instrument of the African Union (AU). What is distinctive is that it addresses issues which are peculiar to Africa but which were not taken into account in the United Nations Convention on the Rights of the Child (CRC), such as practices and attitudes which have a negative effect on the girl child; displaced persons due to internal conflicts; Africa's ethical dimension of community; and the particularly difficult socioeconomic conditions of the continent.

Reflection: Childhood Education

A child has a right to quality and integral education. The integral development of the African child can be promoted by restoring moral formation in the African family. This context contains the ethical dimension of community and ought to be taken into account in curriculum planning. According to Constance Bansikiza, "The African traditional moral values if revisited and well utilized can positively contribute to the revival of moral formation in Christian families in Africa that are in the crisis of moral formation."[44] In understanding the quality of education, programs ought to take into account a broader conception involving learners and outcomes.[45] There are five qualities of education I would like to highlight. The first is that of learners (children) who are healthy, ready to be involved in learning, and supported in the process by their families and communities.

The second quality is an environment that is healthy, safe, and protective; the war-torn environment does not contribute to quality education. The environment also includes the dimension of gender sensitivity. The resources provided have to be adequate and facilitate gender equality. To ensure children's rights and protect all children, various forms of discrimination, especially against girls, must be eliminated.

The third quality of education regards the content of the curricula and the materials used for the acquisition of fundamental skills Here the ethical dimension of education is crucial. At the advanced level, every technology used for educational purposes must be ethical not only for

43. OAU, *The African Charter on the Rights and Welfare of the Child.*
44. Bansikiza, *Restoring Moral Formation in Africa*, 71.
45. UNICEF, "Defining Quality in Education."

the good of the present generation but also for that of the not-yet-born. Ethics must, in the final analysis, define the character of education provided. Learning without values can be dangerous.

The fourth quality involves trained teachers who use child-centered teaching approaches in well-managed classrooms and schools as well as skillful assessment to facilitate learning and reduce disparities. The fifth quality concerns the results—the knowledge, skills, and attitudes acquired—which are related to national educational goals and the positive movement of society. It is important to note that the quality of children's lives before starting formal education greatly influences the type of learner they will be. This implies that school systems operate with the children who come into them. In some African societies, attitudes discouraging girls' involvement in education have been a considerable barrier to quality education for all children.

Early childhood education covers the teaching of children until the age of about eight. Parents are the child's first teachers, hence a prominent part of the early learning process. They also have important educative roles in the child's religious upbringing. As John Paul II states, "It is in the heart of the family that parents are by word and example . . . the first heralds of the faith with regard to their children."[46]

Children need to be taught to rationalize and be open to interpretations and critical thinking—for example, about challenging issues in the world they live, including basic issues of morality, faith, and science. According to Stuart Wolpert, "No media is good for everything. If we want to develop a variety of skills, we need a balanced diet. Each medium has costs and benefits in terms of what skills each develops. Technology is beginning to invade the art of play and a balance needs to be found."[47] Acknowledging its many positives, Kirima appeals for the proper use of mass media, observing that " [w]e should be on guard against the negative influences they have on our young people. People, especially young people and children, have to be made aware, initiated, formed, and educated in the language of media."[48] Unavoidably, children must be given at least rudimentary instruction in media ethics, especially in the use of internet: "for the sake of their children, as well as for their own sakes, parents must learn and practice the skills of discerning viewers and lis-

46. John Paul II, *Ecclesia in Africa*, 23.

47. Wolpert, "Is Technology Producing a Decline in Critical Thinking and Analysis?"

48. Kirima, "The Family," 218.

teners and readers, acting as models of prudent use of media in the home. As far as the Internet is concerned, children and young people often are more familiar with it than their parents are, but parents still are seriously obliged to guide and supervise their children in its use."[49] Let parents, as primary educators of their children, take the responsibility as the main instructors about the convenient use of media. This demands that parents train their children on the moderate, critical, watchful, and prudent use of media in the family.

The art of play also has its relevance in educating children. Play is the mental way that children learn to make sense of circumstances at a young age. They discover various roles, learn how things are linked, and learn to communicate and relate with others. And their thinking and mental development are impacted by sociocultural experiences. Cognition takes place within a social set-up, which means that our social experiences influence our modes of reasoning and evaluating the world.

We can identify some notable cases where the education of children promoted reconciliation. According to Alan Smith, "Ensuring the rights of the young generation who have grown up in armed conflict is not only a humanitarian concern, but is also of significant political importance in ensuring human resources needed to develop post-war societies and in the interests of national security."[50] After the 1994 Rwandan Genocide, a Faith and Reconciliation Commission was established. It was a large-scale justice system that provided an opportunity for conflict resolution through local means. The Commission worked in line with the International Criminal Tribunal for Rwanda to promote a process of healing the nation through the traditional courts called *Gacaca*. It has promoted reconciliation in the restorative sense. This is a model of transitional justice that promotes communal healing and rebuilding. It has facilitated channels for dialogue between victims, offenders, and communities by providing forums for those parties to come together and talk.

For many post-war societies, such as Rwanda, truth and reconciliation have proven to be successful concurrent strategies to bind up wounds of the past, to confront impunity, and to save the energies of the people focus on the pressing issues of national security. Traumas caused by war will not disappear by simply ignoring them. Compared to the Western model of the judiciary, truth and reconciliation commissions focus on

49. Pontifical Council for Social Communication, *Ethics in Internet and the Church and Internet*, 76.

50. Smith, "Children, Education, and Reconciliation," 3.

truth rather than criminal justice. Such strategies should be adapted to a people's culture and history. In response to post-conflict situations, there are other means that can be employed such as the Convention on the Rights of the Child (CRC), which protects children from involvement in armed conflict, and the Optional Protocol of CRC Articles 34 and 35, which protects against the sale of children, child prostitution, and child pornography.[51] These are challenging issues that need to be taken into account in thinking about a pastoral response for providing better education to children in post-conflict situations.

Pastoral Involvement of the Family in Education

It is important to acknowledge the impact of family involvement in the education of children: "Children benefit when parents and family members get involved in their learning and development."[52] According to the Charter of the Rights of the Family, "[p]arents have the right to educate their children in conformity with their moral and religious convictions taking into account the cultural traditions of the family which favor the good and the dignity of the child; they should also receive from society the necessary assistance to perform their educational role properly."[53] The implied right is inalienable, as Pope John Paul II points out: "The right and duty of parents to give education is essential, since it is connected with the transmission of human life; it is original and primary with regard to the educational role of others, on account of the uniqueness of the loving relationship between parents and children, and it is irreplaceable and inalienable."[54]

Parental involvement in education has been broken into four categories by Frances L. Van Voorhis and others.[55] First, there are learning activities at home that parents engage in. Second is family involvement at school. Third is school outreach to involve families—for example, strategies that teachers employ to engage families and make them feel welcome. Fourth are supportive parenting activities, such as rule-setting, instilling moral values, and nurturing their relationship with their child. These

---

51. Van Voorhis et al., *The Impact of Family Involvement*.
52. Van Voorhis et al., *The Impact of Parental Involvement*.
53. Van Voorhis et al., *The Impact of Parental Involvement*, 111.
54. John Paul II, *Familiaris Consortio*, 36.
55. Van Voorhis et al., *The Impact of Parental Involvement*.

are ways that the family can be involved in the education of children. "Parents from diverse background, when given direction, can become more engaged with their children. And when parents are more engaged, children tend to do better."[56] It is recommended that "parents associate with other parents . . . in order to protect, maintain, or fill out their own role as the primary educators of their children, especially in the area of education for love . . . ."[57]

What is needed is holistic education that takes into account the formation of character. As Mahatma Gandhi argues, "Education, character, and religion should be regarded as convertible terms. There is no true education that does not tend to produce character, and there is no true religion which does not determine character. Education should contemplate the whole life. Mere memorization and book learning is not education. I have no faith in the so-called system of education which produces people of learning without the backbone of character."[58]

There is general agreement that if pupils are to maximize their potential from schooling they will need the full support of their parents: "It is anticipated that parents should play a role not only in the promotion of their own children's achievements but more broadly in school improvement and the democratization of school governance."[59] Strategies to involve parents include providing them a voice and encouraging parental partnerships with schools.,

Regarding character, it is only with the heart that one understands rightly; what is essential is invisible to the eyes. Good character is about knowing the good, loving the good, and doing it. Pope Francis rightly points out that "the strengthening of the will and repetition of specific actions are the building blocks of moral conduct."[60] The role of formal education is not simply to provide information; its ultimate achievement is to bring about transformation.

Parents and schools can work together to raise moral children. Formative institutions can do even more to promote moral human beings than either can do working alone. In this way, a school community

56. Van Voorhis et al., *The Impact of Parental Involvement*. 111.

57. Pontifical Council for the Family, *The Truth and Meaning of Human Sexuality*, 114.

58. Rouner, "Can Virtue Be Taught in Schools?" 146.

59. Desforges and Abouchaar, The Impact of Parental *Involvement*, 7.

60. Francis, *Amoris Laetitia*, 266. See Ryan and Bohlin, *Building Character in Schools*.

consensus about values can be developed. Moreover, various opportunities can be created for parents to be involved in moral education programs.[61] Parents and schools should read from the same script concerning these important issues. Therefore, the foundation the family lays is very critical. Schools will have fewer problems if the parents have already done their part. Some children develop a sense of entitlement because of how they're raised. When everything seems to be about them, they may not see anything wrong with destroying school property, for example. After all, their parents will be on their side regardless of the offense they've committed. Under the general rubric of education, there are many good things happening but also many evil things, as evidenced by the overwhelming reports of school carnage and destruction. One example can be found in the research of Nyambura Owinyoin in *Caught in Between: Exploring the Complexity of School Vandalism.*[62] It describes a school that has suffered seven incidences of violence and challenges us to reconsider the choices we are making for ourselves and for our young people. It also suggests options to be taken into account by educators.

There is a growing phenomenon of parents being isolated from each other: "Today's mobile parents do not know who their neighbors are or who the parents of their children's friends are."[63] In this context, schools can bring parents together for face-to-face communication that will provide them a space to discover their shared values. In spite of the implied cooperation, parents are challenged to fulfill their parental responsibility. As Aidan Msafiri argues, "Today there is widespread parental irresponsibility and negligence of child education and moral formation. Most parents seem to overlook their role as the first and indispensable moral educators and formators."[64] There is a sort of imbalance indicated by the fact that "spouses are delegating their responsibilities of parental care to house girls/boys who take care of domestic formation and work, while in normal circumstances parents should not delegate their parental responsibility."[65] Parents have the responsibility to take care of their children.

61. Lickona, "How Parents and Schools Can Work Together to Raise Moral Children," 36–38.

62. Owinyo, *Caught in Between*, 15.

63. Lickona, "How Parents and Schools Can Work Together to Raise Moral Children," 37.

64. Msafiri, *Rediscovering African and Christian Values for Moral Formation*, 36.

65. Msafiri, *Rediscovering African and Christian Values for Moral Formation*, 28.

Parents can play an important role in supporting their children's academic achievement, and there is a strong relationship between students' achievements and family background factors, such as income and parents' education levels. "Even if parents are unable to assist their children with a specific subject or skill, they can still play a vital role by encouraging students feeling of competence and control and positive attitudes towards academics . . ."[66] The beliefs and expectations of parents seem to strongly influence children's motivation: "In other words, parents who are actively involved in their children's education and provide a stimulating learning environment at home can help their children develop feelings of competence, control, curiosity, and positive attitudes about academics, according to various studies."[67] This is crucial for avoiding scenarios such as parents helping their children cheat on national exams. In order to promote better education for children, the role of the family must be put at the center.[68] The Christian family is the center of re-evangelization, because it is the school for dialogue where virtues and values are learned through words and deeds in the context of the extended family, the clan, the tribe, and the nation. The family is where the ethical formation of children can be provided naturally.

Conclusion

In AL, Pope Francis states: "Parents always influence the moral development of their children for better or for worse."[69] The educational role of families is so relevant and yet increasingly complex. Parents have a distinctive obligation to prepare children and adolescents to face the risks of today's world. They have a vital role in the school to promote spheres of support, guidance, and direction. While it is true that families rely on schools for the sound instruction of their children, they cannot totally delegate the moral formation of their children to others. Parents' absence from their children's education in their children's education process leaves a fragile gap.

66. Usher and Kober, "What Roles Do Parent Involvement, Family Background, and Culture Play in Student Motivation?" 1.

67. Usher and Kober, "What Roles Do Parent Involvement, Family Background, and Culture Play in Student Motivation?" 2.

68. National Marriage Encounter Team, "A Letter to the Bishops of Zambia," 1–14.

69. Francis, *Amoris Laetitia*, 259.

Children's moral development involves reasoning about morality, their attitudes regarding moral issues, and their behavior when confronted by moral dilemmas. As the child's first teachers, parents are a prominent part of this early learning process. Thus, the quality of children's lives at home, before starting formal education, has a significant impact on the type of learners they can be.

Bibliography

AMECEA. "Families Truly Christian and Truly African." *AFER* 28:3–4 (June–August 1986).

Bahemuka, Judith. "What Does the Church Offer the Young People of Africa?" In *The Gospel as Good News for African Culture*, edited by Juvenalis Baitu Rwelamira, 103–118. Nairobi: CUEA Press, 1999.

Bansikiza, Constance. *Restoring Moral Formation in Africa.* Eldoret, Kenya: AMECEA Gaba, 2001.

Benedict XVI. *Africae Munus.* Nairobi: Paulines Africa, 2011.

Bujo, Benezet. *The Ethical Dimension of Community: The African Model and the Dialogue Between North and South.* Nairobi: Paulines, 1998.

Chissano, Joaquim. Foreword to *The African Report on Child Well-being 2013: Towards Greater Accountability to Africa's Children*, edited by the African Child Policy Forum, xii. Addis Ababa: ACPF, 2013.

Damon, William. "The Moral Development of Children." *Scientific American* 281:2 (August 1999) 72–78.

Desforges, Charles and Alberto Abouchaar. *The Impact of Parental Involvement, Parental Support, and Family Education on Pupil Achievements and Adjustment: A Literature Review.* Nottingham, UK: Queen's Printer, 2003.

Fowler, James. *Stages of Faith: The Psychology of Human Development and the Quest for Meaning.* San Francisco: Harper 1981.

Francis. *Amoris Laetitia: The Joy of Love.* Nairobi: Paulines Africa, 2016.

John Paul II. *Familiaris Consortio: On the Family.* Boston: St. Paul Editions, 1981.

———. *Ecclesia in Africa.* Nairobi: Paulines Africa, 1995.

Kirima, Nicodemus. "The Family." *AFER* 36:4 (1998).

Kirsch, Felix M. *Sex Education and Training in Chastity.* New York: Benziger Brothers, 1930.

Lickona, Thomas. "How Parents and Schools Can Work Together to Raise Moral Children." *Educational Leadership* 45:8 (May 1998) 36–38.

May, William. *Marriage: The Rock on Which the Family is Built.* San Francisco: Ignatius, 1991.

Msafiri, Aidan. *Rediscovering African and Christian Values for Moral Formation.* Nairobi: CUEA, 2010.

Nasimiyu-Wasike, Anne. "Child Abuse and Neglect: An African Moral Question." In *Moral and Ethical Issues in African Christianity*, edited by J. N. K. Mugambi and A. Nasimiyu-Wasike. Nairobi: Acton, 2003.

National Marriage Encounter Team. "An Open Letter to the Bishops of Zambia." *Catholic International* 2:19 (November 1991) 1–14.

Nyerere, Julius K. *Freedom and Unity*. Dar es Salaam: Oxford University Press, 1966.

Nzomo, Lydia N. "Early Childhood Development in Kenya: Keynote Address." In *Early Childhood Education for Holistic Development of the Child*, edited by Jacinta Adhiambo, et al. Nairobi: CUEA, 2013.

OAU. *The African Charter on the Rights and Welfare of the Child*. Addis Ababa: Organization of African Unity, 1990.

Owinyo, Nyambura. *Caught in Between: Exploring the Complexity of School Vandalism*. Nairobi: Paulines, 2008.

Pontifical Council for the Family. *Charter of the Rights of the Family*. Vatican: Libreria Editrice Vaticana, 2013.

———. *The Truth and Meaning of Human Sexuality: Guidelines for Education within the Family*. Nairobi: Paulines Africa, 1996.

Pontifical Council for Social Communication. *Ethics in Internet and the Church and Internet*. Nairobi: Paulines Africa, 2002.

Rouner, Leroy S. "Can Virtue Be Taught in Schools?" In *Can Virtue Be Taught?*, edited by Barbara Darling Smith, 139–55. Notre Dame, IN: University of Notre Dame Press, 1993.

Rwelamira, Juvenalis Baitu. *Traditional Moral Formation: Among the Bahaya of Tanzania*. Nairobi: CUEA, 2003.

Ryan, Kavin and Karen Bohlin. *Building Character in Schools: Practical Ways to Bring Moral Instruction to Life*. San Francisco: Jossey Bass, 1999.

Sacred Congregation for Catholic Education. *Educational Guidance in Human Love*. *L'Osservatore Romano*, December 5, 1983.

Smith, Ian. *Children, Education, and Reconciliation*. Florence: UNICEF Innocenti Research Center, June 2010.

Teklemariam, Amanuel and W. J. Akala, eds. *Effective Schools for the Twenty-First Century in Africa*. Nairobi: CUEA, 2011.

UNICEF. *Defining Quality in Education*. Florence: UNICEF International Working Group on Education, 2000.

Usher, Alexandra and Nancy Kober. *What Roles do Parent Involvement, Family Background, and Culture Play in Student Motivation?* Washington, DC: Center for Education Policy (CEP), 2012.

Van Voorhis, Frances L., et al. *The Impact of Family Involvement on the Education of Children Ages 3 to 8*. Baltimore: Johns Hopkins University, October 2013.

Vatican II. *Gravissimum Educationis: Declaration on Christian Education*. Washington, DC: National Catholic Welfare Conference, 1965.

Wolpert, Stuart. "Is Technology Producing a Decline in Critical Thinking and Analysis?" UCLA Newsroom, January 27, 2009. http://newsroom.ucla.edu/releases/is-technology-producing-a-decline-79127.

9

Amoris Laetitia and the Logic of Mercy and Integration in an Illuminative Church (Commentary on Chapter 8)[1]

STAN CHU ILO

"Illumined by the gaze of Jesus Christ, 'she [the Catholic Church] turns with love to those who participate in her life in an incomplete manner, recognizing that the grace of God works also in their lives by giving them the courage to do good, to care for one another in love and to be of service to the community in which they live and work'" (AL 291).

Introduction

My goal in this chapter is to propose some pastoral approaches for living the message of *Amoris Laetitia* (AL). I will begin by arguing that AL highlights the theological aesthetic which is operative in Pope Francis's other writings, which I would like to call "illuminative ecclesiology." I will interpret chapter 8 of AL as an extended commentary on the art of accompaniment, which Pope Francis proposed in *Evangelii Gaudium* (EG) 169–73. Three important themes are presented in this chapter, namely: how to interpret irregular unions or irregular conditions in marriages;

1. Some sections of this essay were originally published as "The Illuminative Ecclesiology of *Amoris Laetitia*," at *Political Theology Network*.

how to accompany those in such marriages and those in de facto unions through pastoral discernment; and how love and mercy can be adopted as a pastoral method built on the logic of integration. Pope Francis sees the logic of love and mercy as the means and end of all pastoral ministries directed to the service of those in difficult marriage situations. I will conclude the chapter with some pastoral proposals for living the message of AL in Africa and in the world church.

The Art of Accompaniment: Discerning and Integrating Weakness

I have proposed in a previous work that illuminative ecclesiology of Pope Francis offers the church in Africa and in the world, a Triple A pastoral method—accountability, accompaniment, and action.[2] I wish to elaborate on two of these in this paper—accountability and accompaniment. Accountability means that the church and all Christians have received creation and all things from God as an unqualified good. As a result, central to the mission of the church is to render account to God for all these gifts, especially the gifts of the least of the brethren who are close to the heart of God. The beauty of God is reflected in creation. "The revelation that God is the creator, the origin, and the ground and destiny of all creation is the ultimate basis for our affirming the truth (knowability) and goodness (lovability) and beauty (delightfulness) of all things. All things can be loved and enjoyed because they are created."[3] The beauty of God is not lost in creation in the face of evil, suffering, poverty, sin, and pain. Therefore, to give an account as an ecclesial practice is about how the church discerns, in the midst of the stories found in the contradictions and shadows of life, both in particular and universal contexts how and where God is present. In order to be an instrument for bringing light especially in the pains and sufferings of many people who are on the margins, an accountable church immerses herself in history. It is a church which seeks to encounter each person as a unique instance of God's beauty, and remains present to people in their places of pain. In this kind of church, no one is lost. Rather, like the Good Shepherd, the

---

2. See Ilo, "The Church of Pope Francis," 23–30; see also Ilo, *A Poor and Merciful Church*, 147–55.

3. Navone, *Toward a Theology of Beauty*, 1.

accountable church must take stock of all of God's children and go out in search of the lost, the forgotten, and the scattered children of God.

Accountability unites us to God who is the source of all things and for whom all reality and all persons count, no matter their situation or condition. There is a certain unique particularity to the union of all creation to God in how this is manifested and incarnated in the lives of individuals. The church is invited to see beauty in creation and to render to God a fitting praise by working hard in identifying instances in creation and in life where suffering and pain, injustice and structures of sin make it impossible for the beauty of God to shine out in creation. The accountable church is thus a church which cares for all creation; a church which is open to all people, and a church which has a merciful heart open to all people. It is also a church where people are embraced as beautiful unto God not because of their present condition but because of the intrinsic and priceless value of being created in the image and likeness of God. An accountable church is one which sees salvation and liberation as possible for all people especially those who are losing their way and those who are far away from God, truth, beauty, holiness, and love. An accountable church is one in which no one is lost.

The second aspect of this pastoral method is the art of accompaniment, which is the key with which I interpret chapter 8 of AL. Articles 291–312 could be summarized as the development of a theology of pastoral accompaniment as the praxis for ministry to families and for healing the suppurating wound in many lives. Accompaniment is what Pope Francis calls the "framework and setting" that will lead the church away from "a cold bureaucratic morality" in dealing with some of the sensitive and contested issues on marriage and family life in the church and the world today (AL 312). Accompaniment "sets us in the context of a pastoral discernment filled with merciful love, which is ever ready to understand, forgive, accompany, hope and above all integrate. That is the mindset which should prevail in the church and lead us to 'open our hearts to those living on the outermost fringes of society'" (AL 312).

Pope Francis proposes in this chapter some practices that will make it possible for pastors "to make room for God's unconditional love" in their pastoral ministry (AL 311). There are four steps for accompaniment, which one could identify in EG. I propose that these could help shed light on how Pope Francis appropriates them for developing pastoral practices in AL, which do not "water down the gospel" or empty the mercy God of its unconditional quality. The church can "empty the mercy of God" if the church's pastoral practices proceed from a mentality of rigorous severity, which can "put in doubt the omnipotence of God and, especially his mercy." Even though mercy does not exclude justice and truth, Pope Francis, however, teaches that "mercy is the fullness of justice and the most radiant manifestation of God's truth" (AL 311). Some of the four dimensions of accompaniment in EG include the following.

Seeing Others Through the Eyes of Mercy and Love

The first point is that accompaniment begins with Christians and churches looking "more closely and sympathetically" at people whenever it is necessary. Looking closely at humanity does not mean an obsession with "the details of other people's lives," which as Pope Francis points out is rooted in "morbid curiosity." On the contrary, accompaniment begins with pastoral workers and ministers looking at people's lives with "the personal gaze" of the Lord Jesus. This is with the intention of making present in the lives of people the fragrance of Christ and bringing Christ closer to the people and people closer to Christ (see EG 169).

When we look at people with the gaze of Christ, something fundamentally decisive and transformational takes place: it changes our optics about who the person is and about who we are in the presence of another. The words of Pope Francis bear repeating here: "The Church will have to initiate everyone—priests, religious and laity—into this "art of accompaniment" which teaches us to remove our sandals before the sacred ground of the other (see Exod 3:5). The pace of this accompaniment must be "steady and reassuring, reflecting our closeness and our compassionate gaze which also heals, liberates, and encourages growth in the Christian life" (EG 169).

However, Pope Francis also points to another important dimension of encounter with other people: the aspect of diversity where treating people differently or with equity is the demand of justice and mercy. This means that people are at different stages in their life's journey and the church should meet people where they are so that she can be all things to all men and women (1 Cor 9:19–23). There is need for diversity of approaches to encountering people because people's conditions and situations differ and their contexts might influence their response to God and thus challenge the church and Christians to be more creative in reaching out to people. Sometimes setting a general guideline or form for pastoral encounter with people may lead to dry and rigid pastoral ministries, which do more harm than good to Christians. There is need then to understand that to accompany people is to journey closely with them in total openness to God (EG 44).

Being with People Involves Respect, Trust and Openness to Mutual Transformation

The second aspect is about the method for accompaniment. Accompaniment is an art. This means that there is a method for being with people, walking with people and sharing in their lives, and openness to being touched by others. That method is modeled after the mystery of the Incarnation. By the mystery of the Incarnation, the Son of God entered into the chaos of our human lives, made a tent with us and assumed our human condition with all its pains and limitations in order to grant us liberation. It is similar to the African sense of hospitality or pitching a tent with another which is captured in an Igbo proverb, "may the visitor bring blessing and peace to his or her guest and when the visitor leaves may he or she go with greater blessing rather than a hunchback."[4] Here, sharing a home with another presupposes a prior intention to be open to the other in trust and love; it means openness to sharing in the blessing of the Lord, listening to the other, and being totally and readily available to the other in a spirit of humility, service, caring, compassion and support. This mutual indwelling or hospitality between a minister, for instance, and a parishioner; or between a social worker and a poor brethren presupposes that we are all learning and growing through each other and that every encounter in the pastoral ministry is a mutual exchange which creates a new event of meaning for both parties.

The art of accompaniment requires entering into other people's lives, leaving one's comfort zone and being-with other people from diverse spiritual, cultural, racial, national, and social locations, and meeting them as friends and as travelling companions. In a sense, the art of accompaniment is properly modeled for the church and ministers through the Trinitarian image of indwelling of the three divine persons. The three divine persons not only make a way for each other or travel with each other, but they participate in an intimate way in the life of each person of the Trinity in what traditionally has been called a sacred dance (*perichoresis*). In

4. On African hospitality, see Olikenyi, *African Hospitality*.

this sacred dance each divine person, while being a distinctive *persona*, shares in the life of the three divine persons and receives from each other the gift of love, which is the identity, and character of their divine nature. Mutuality, trust, respect, reverence, and shared participation are some of the qualities of the inner Trinitarian life. Indwelling of the three divine persons with each other becomes a model of accompaniment because it mediates the following characteristics which are needed in pastoral ministry—mutual respect, non-judgmental love and reverence for the other, solidarity with the other, collaboration and co-operation with each other, and participation or sharing in the life of each other.

This mutuality of relations built on trust, respect, and reverence manifest themselves in a pastoral context in such a way that the joys and sorrows of the other become the joys and sorrows of the minister. It is also an invitation to walk in the shoes of the other and to walk with the other so that they can assume responsibility for their own lives and attain their God ordained end. This is particularly necessary in setting the right focus and end of pastoral ministry, which is to connect people to God, to themselves, the world of nature and the world around them. It is indeed the integration of the person in such a way as to bring wholeness to the person so that he or she feels and experiences the grace of being loved by God and being a partner with God in the sacred dance of life. As Pope Francis writes, pastoral ministry is not simply a therapy, rather it is about how to bring people closer to God: "to accompany them would be counterproductive if it becomes a sort of therapy supporting their self-absorption and ceases to be a pilgrimage with Christ to the Father" (EG 170).

A New Way of Doing Pastoral Ministry

The third is that accompaniment is a new way of doing ministry in the church. It also changes how one sees the person of the minister and the one who is being ministered to. Pope Francis proposes a radically different approach to ministry through the art of accompaniment. As Richard Lennon rightly argues, since Vatican II, there has been a shift in pastoral ministry in the Catholic Church. This has shifted the focus of ministry from the identity of the priest and the superiority of the priest over the laity to a realization of the mutuality which should exist in a pastoral situation. Ministry is a mutual encounter and a two-way traffic. Furthermore, ministerial service is no longer the exclusive preserve of the ordained ministers and is becoming more specialized.[5] Both the minister and the person being ministered to are in a mutual relationship of respect and reverence, and both should be changed in the process of ministry and strengthened in their individual and ecclesial journey to God. Both the minister and the one being served are carrying wounds and have holes in their hearts in need of God's mercy and grace. This is why accompaniment is always a shared journey where both parties are touched by what is mutually seen and experienced in the journey. In EG 171, Pope Francis proposes some of the daily practices of pastoral accompaniment when he writes: "today more than ever we need men and women who, on the basis of their experience of accompanying others, are familiar with processes which call for prudence, understanding, patience and docility to the Spirit, so that they can protect the sheep from wolves who would scatter the flock. We need to practice the art of listening, which is more than simply hearing. Listening, in communication, is an openness of heart, which makes possible that closeness without which genuine spiritual encounter cannot occur. Listening helps us to find the right gesture and word, which shows that we are more than simply bystanders. Only through such respectful and compassionate listening can we enter on the paths of true growth and awaken a yearning for the Christian ideal: the desire to respond fully to God's love and to bring to fruition what he has sown in our lives."

Encountering God and a New Life

The fourth point to note about accompaniment is on the end to be sought in the pastoral setting. Pope Francis explains the goal of accompaniment in this way: "one who accompanies others has to realize that each person's situation before God and their life in grace are mysteries which no one can fully know from without. The gospel tells us to correct others and to help them to grow on the basis of a recognition of the objective evil of their actions (see Matt 18:15), but without making judgments about their responsibility and culpability (see Matt 7:1; Luke 6:37). Someone good at such accompaniment does not give in to frustrations or fears. He or she invites others to let themselves be healed, to take up their mat, embrace the cross, leave all behind, and go forth ever anew to proclaim

5. Lennan, "Ministry as Merciful Accompaniment," 142–44.

the gospel. Our personal experience of being accompanied and assisted, and of openness to those who accompany us, will teach us to be patient and compassionate with others, and to find the right way to gain their trust, their openness and their readiness to grow" (EG 172).

The beginning and end of all pastoral initiatives for accompaniment is a deep encounter in faith with God, a new experience of love, mercy, and grace, and new life in Christ through encountering the other. Accompaniment is about how we serve others after the example of Christ and how through serving others we inspire their hearts to service to their God and neighbors. Accompaniment becomes for Pope Francis, the new method for evangelization, which helps us to discern in the daily conditions of people the wounded face of Jesus Christ. The goal of all evangelization is achieved through a fruitful and faithful accompaniment when through our words, actions, and mercy we proclaim the good news to others who are hungry for God and for meaning and hope. Accompaniment is the incarnational praxis of mission for the church in present history. Accompaniment goes beyond legislating unchanging manualistic moral solutions to people's problems or fixed rules for resolving moral issues. Rather, it inspires people to be present to others, walk with them in love, and search together with them for the face of Christ in their daily struggles in order to find the footprints of God in their daily choices. It is the most effective means for leading people to conversion and to the fullness of life.

The Illuminative Church of Pope Francis and the Art of Accompaniment

The art of accompaniment is central to understanding the new paradigm of illuminative ecclesiology. Francis's illuminative ecclesiology puts a high accent on experience and beauty even in brokenness; moral clarity is no longer simply conceptual but performative and aesthetic. The church does not speak of herself or assume the moral high horse over her members and those outside the church. On the contrary, the church sees even an opposition to her teaching or its rejection by some of her members and the seeming abandonment of God by people as a summons to be a merciful church, which must see a light hidden in the face of people's rejection of God. This will help the church to walk with people and offer them an illuminating path to the saving truth which alone can satisfy the hunger of their souls while helping them to see the light of Christ in their doubts. The church is presented as the "seeing eye," which focuses her gaze on creation with the eyes of Jesus. This means that she sees in every reality the impetus to bring life where there is death; hope where there is despair and mercy where sin once prevailed. In this regard, the illuminative church brings the presence of God into every situation and sees every situation in the light of Christ. Nothing in this kind of church is outside the compass of God's love and mercy, and every situation in the logic of grace is open to being saved by love and mercy. The illuminative church is a light to the nations because she offers a mirror to the world for seeing the face of God. In the same light she also sees in the faces of men and women—especially those who are suffering—the face of Christ as in a mirror.

In his book, *The Name of God is Mercy*, Pope Francis makes a distinction between the "logic of the scholars of the law and the logic of God." The logic of scholars proceeds from pre-conceived and rigid notions of truth, purity, etc., whereas the logic of God proceeds from mercy and love and transfigures evil into good by entering into contact with sin (66). In EG, Francis calls on the church to adopt the logic of God, what he calls the "way of beauty" (EG 167), even in the contradictions and complexities of life. He invites the church to live in the truth by touching "the human heart and enabling the truth and goodness of the Risen Christ to radiate within it" (EG 167). In his first encyclical, *Light of Faith*, Pope Francis writes that illumination can be understood in many ways, but the key phrase for me is this; "Only when we are configured to Jesus do we receive the eyes needed to see him" (*Lumen Fidei*, 31).

Illuminative Ecclesiology in AL

Illuminative ecclesiology which I have outlined is central to the way *AL* discusses family life. In the introductory part of the document, Pope Francis writes that the synod was "both impressive and illuminating" (AL 4). In chapter 1, Francis teaches that in addressing the Christian family, the church must see things through the eyes of Christ because the light of Christ enlightens every person, even those in difficult situations or in irregular marriages (AL 60, 70, 78). In chapters 3 and 4, we see constant references to illumination and the opening of the eyes, such as when he writes, "The aesthetic experience of love is expressed in that gaze which contemplates other persons as ends in themselves, even if they are infirm, elderly, or physically unattractive" (AL 128). Indeed, love opens our eyes so that we can see the great worth of the other. The consent to marry each other, given through the promise made during the ritual of marriage between couples, "illumine all the meaning of the signs" of the sacrament (AL 214). Couples should allow their eyes to be illumined to see God's gift in the embryo from the moment of conception (AL 168). The language of sex education should be presented in such a way that it is an illumination for living in a mature way and embracing the joy of love (AL 280). The church and all Christians and family members must embrace the light of faith (AL 253) in order to see the goodness in everyone, especially those who are suffering and those who are weak and experiencing distress of different kinds (AL 296, 308).

As some of these passages suggest, Francis's illuminative ecclesiology affects the way he addresses controversial ethical issues related to marriage and the family because he wishes to show how the church can illumine both the truth of faith and the hearts of men and women to embrace the fullness of truth about life, marriage, and faith, through a faithful adherence to God. Gone are the divisive categories of the "culture of death" and the "culture of life" introduced by Pope John Paul II in *Evangelium Vitae* (33–65). In *AL* there is a broader and integrated understanding of human life not built on an anthropocentric priority but on a Trinitarian relationship of participation. Abortion (AL 170), birth and population control, polygamy, pornography, sexual exploitation, child abuse, etc. (AL 39–44, 53–57, 80–82, 135–41, 291–94), are rejected, but within the larger context of understanding that pastoral discernment and pastoral judgement and action must be connected to people's lives (AL 200–1). *AL* hearkens back to *Humanae Vitae* on the use of natural methods of regulating births, and it appeals to the natural law as grounding for the church's teaching on the nature and character of family and the goods of the family, gender differences, and the roles of mothers and fathers. In *AL*, however, natural law is seen as "a source of objective inspiration for the deeply personal process of making decisions" rather than "a set of rules" which impose themselves on the moral subject or on the church (AL 305). Same-sex unions (AL 250–51, 311–12) and the annulment process (AL 239–47, 291, 306) are still reinforced with teachings both from the *Catechism of the Catholic Church* and previous Popes, but there are no harsh, judgmental condemnations of people with same-sex orientations or divorced and remarried Catholics, nor is there an explicit insistence on excluding them from reception of Holy Communion (AL 301).

Pope Francis applies his illuminative ecclesiology to the life of the family through what he calls in chapter 8 the "logic of integration" (AL 299) and the "logic of mercy" (AL 307–12). The logic of integration is the principle that people should be enabled to exercise full membership in the church through participation in the life of the world and the life of the church. It is about being properly and intimately connected to God, church, and society no matter one's situation or condition. Integration is aimed at accompanying the family and every person in such a way that "they realize that they belong to the church as the body of Christ, but also to know that they have a joyful and fruitful experience of it" (AL 299). Francis insists that the logic of integration can be lived out through four movements:

a) accompanying people in their concrete personal situation, having the smell of the sheep;

b) pastoral discernment of each situation by being immersed in the situation with the person or family or couple (AL 79, 137–39, 234, 273, 297–98, 299);

c) dialogue with individuals (AL 300), by listening with patience to them and exploring with them the mitigating factors in that situation, and strengthening the process of repentance leading to the transformation of the situation;

d) affirming that all family members and people of God have a vocation to participate in the life of the church and in the life of the community.

Integration is about how "various forms of exclusion currently practiced in the liturgical, pastoral, educational and institutional framework, can be surmounted" (AL 299). To achieve this will require prayer, humility, respect for the church's "way of beauty," and attention to gradualism both in discerning and embracing this way of beauty, respecting the dignity and autonomy of individual conscience, and crafting through discernment the most effective means to reach the heart of people and lead them to God, love, service, and joy (AL 37, 303).

The logic of mercy, on the other hand, is not an attempt to depart from the ideal of marriage (AL 307) or of fidelity to the gospel. Rather, it is about how the church and her ministers and indeed the entire

Christian community should become facilitators of mercy and Goodness rather than arbiters of grace (AL 308). Francis makes an important point which might even sound contradictory: "Jesus wants a Church attentive to the goodness which the Holy Spirit sows in the midst of human weakness" (AL 308). The logic of mercy is a gift from God; it proceeds from the power of tenderness (AL 92, 127, 291, 305, 308) and it proceeds according to three movements similar to those of the logic of integration:

a) understand the situation and context of people, forgive freely (do not put in doubt the omnipotence of God and especially his mercy, (AL 311);

b) accompany people in their journey to God in their different situations through mercy;

c) bring hope and joy where there was once sadness, alienation, and death (AL 312).

On the Moral Judgment About Irregular and De Facto Unions: Some Tensions

Pope Francis in chapter 8 of AL wrestled with some of the most contested moral questions facing modern Catholicism since Vatican II—status of divorced and remarried Catholics, couples who live in de facto union without sacramental marriage and the status of same-sex relations. The contentious question is whether people in these kinds of relationships should be admitted to Holy Communion. These issues unfortunately have not been resolved even with the publication of AL. However, I think Pope Francis believes that human mysteries sometimes do not require the kind of "yes" and "no" answers which Cardinal Burke and three other cardinals posed to Pope Francis in their *dubia*.

Pope Francis lays down some principles in this chapter to guide the church and leaves the door open to local bishops and pastors to determine how to translate the principles into practices, which reflect the mercy and love of God. However, one can see in this chapter the tension in the text as the pope plays a balancing game trying to push for a more progressive interpretation of key teachings on marriage, while at the same time trying to keep the conservatives happy with an insistence on fidelity. Some key texts which show this tension can be pointed out as evidence for this assertion.

In the first article in this chapter (AL 291), Pope Francis sets clearly what he proposes about the pastoral approach to marriage when he calls the church a "lighthouse or a torch" which is carried to enlighten those who have lost their way. In this regard, the church is called to "accompany with attention and care the weakest of her children, who show signs of a wounded and troubled love." However, toward the end of the chapter, Pope Francis affirms that many people might be confused by the lack of clarity in the text and states as follows: "In order to avoid all misunderstanding, I would point that in no way must the church desist from proposing the full ideal of marriage; God's plan in all its grandeur" (AL 307). In the same article, he teaches strongly that pastoral discernment or accompaniment to understand people's specific situation does not imply any form of moral relativism, lack of fidelity to the gospel or a movement away from the ideal of marriage.

This tension is shown again in AL's teaching on the nature and property of marriage and exclusion from communion (see AL 306, especially footnote 351 and Canon 951). Pope Francis agrees with former Popes on the teaching on marriage when he writes; "Christian marriage, as a reflection of the union between Christ and his Church, is fully realized in the union between a man and a woman who give themselves to each other in a free, faithful and exclusive love, which belong to each other until death and are open to the transmission of life, and are consecrated by the sacrament, which grants them the grace to become a domestic church and a leaven of the new life for society" (AL 292). However, in the same article, he acknowledges without further clarification the existence of "some forms of union," which radically are opposed to this ideal and those which realize this ideal in a "partial and analogous way." He admits that the synod "does not disregard the constructive elements in those situations which do not yet or no longer correspond to her teaching on marriage," but he does not state what kind of welcome they should receive in the church but adds a footnote (AL 351) which proposes that their reception of communion is actually a help "in certain cases" for those who are not "subjectively culpable" in the face of the "objective situation of sin."

Three points are worth noting here: first, Pope Francis accepts that de facto unions (irregular marriages, same-sex unions, polygamous marriages, common law unions) contain some positive elements, which could serve as a point of entry for pastoral discernment and conversion. Second, he does not clarify how and why these kinds of unions are far from the ideal of Christian marriage. This lack of clarity creates confusion about the criteria to be used in pastoral discernment because there must be some common meaning or family traits, which should offer a starting platform for contextualizing pastoral praxis based on an objective teaching of the ideal proposed by the church.

Third, it seems that this lack of clarity was a deliberate teaching technique by Pope Francis to allow for dialogue and further conversations on these topics, which could help bring creative approaches for accompaniment. However, closer reading of the text shows that Pope Francis is more at home in AL with a more open and flexible interpretation of marriage with all its strengths and limitations. This approach adopts an open crack in understanding people's marital situation because it sees marriage as culturally mediated which demands more flexibility in interpretation of its nature and property rather than a fixed or rigid application of doctrine. This open crack can be perceived then as the cultural conditioning of all human actions in its natural state, which offers some tentative steps towards the transformation of human reality in the light of grace. Pastors can approach the couples through such cracks—which might reveal elements in their marriage that can lead to greater openness to the ideals of marriage; and elements, which will foster evangelization, and human and spiritual growth and elements which reflect God's love (Al 293–94). The pastoral approach proposed by Pope Francis is that of a welcoming church which should accompany couples in a journey similar to that which Jesus stimulated in the Samaritan woman by the well (John 4:1–26). This way, they can gradually move from where they are in their present situation, to the fuller expression of their marital love through the sacramental action of the church.

Pope Francis appealed to the moral principle of gradualism in encouraging pastors and the universal church to be patient with people in their different stages in life. Gradualism means that "the human being 'knows, loves and accomplishes moral good by different stages of growth'" (AL 295). Gradualism is similar to divine accommodation—*synkatabasis*— which proposes that God teaches people according to their different stages in life. God accommodates Godself to the human condition in order to encounter the totality of our history and culture in the ever expanding embrace of God. Gradualism, Pope Francis notes, is not "gradualness of law" but rather "a prudential exercise of free acts" by human beings in their attempt to understand the demands of the moral law and how to exercise moral agency within their own restricted condition.

From this principle, the pope proceeds to discuss how to accompany people in irregular marriages—various weaknesses and imperfections in people's marriage situation. This section seems to me to be the most incoherent of the whole chapter because ideas and themes are introduced without strong evidence or argument from Scripture, tradition, and magisterium to support them. It is very preachy—as is expected of an exhortation—but it lacks strong foundation from traditional sources for authenticating papal teaching in order to support what is being proposed as continuous with the church's doctrine and pastoral practices.

For example, AL rightly proposes that people should not be subjected to a life of being perpetually condemned and rejected as unworthy. The Pope's stance on this emerges from his own pastoral experience and encounters not only with divorced and remarried Catholics but also people in same-sex relations and in polygamous marriages (something AL 297 does not explicitly mention). However, a simple proposition that people should not judge others does not answer the question about the objectivity of moral precepts and the ultimate purpose of the moral demand. Christians make judgment based on revealed moral truth, which they perceive as valid for all times and for all people. Furthermore, such judgment must be distinguished in themselves as valid and applicable to particular situations without prescinding from the objective moral order whether the Christian passes such judgment or not. What is necessary is a moral clarity that people's moral failings or personal situation should not be the criterion for truth. Thus individual judgment of what is the objective moral truth relative to a particular situation or people's personal condition has a noetic and deontological status which is never attenuated by any moral judgment or condemnation or lack thereof about a person's choice made by an individual Christian or a church official.

Whereas AL affirms clearly that people's moral limitations or moral failures or personal situation should not be the criterion for moral truth or rectitude, it also affirms that such people can participate in the life of the church in many ways. It further proposes that divine pedagogy can help them to see the presence of grace in their situation. Specifically in AL 298, Pope Francis teaches that there should be "no overly rigid classification" which will shut the door to some creative approaches to personal and pastoral discernment of particular situations. This is because there are "no easy recipes" for addressing the mystery, joys, problems, and challenges of marriage and family life and of human life in general. Whatever the situation of couples, Pope Francis notes that there is need for pastoral discernment in order to accompany them with the suitable pastoral care, and the integration of people into the Christian community must assume a "variety of ways possible, while avoiding any occasion of scandal" (AL 299).

However, the pope was unequivocal in asserting that neither he nor the synod members can give definitive answers to these moral questions when he writes: "Neither the Synod nor this Exhortation could be expected to provide a new set of general rules, canonical in nature and applicable to all cases. What is possible is simply a renewed encouragement to undertake a responsible personal and pastoral discernment of particular cases, one which would recognize that, since 'the degree of responsibility is not equal in all cases,' the consequence or effects of a rule need not necessarily always be the same" (AL 300). He recommends for people who find themselves in these situations a "process of examination of conscience through moments of reflection and repentance" (AL 300) and listening to the gospel's call for conversion (AL 297).

What is evident in this section is that AL scratched at the surface of these contested moral issues without giving any definitive judgment or teaching. It does not answer questions about whether divorced and re-married Catholics should be allowed to receive communion, something which one could affirm in the positive as the full consequence of this papal teaching. It does not clarify the status of the homosexual person in the church and the sacramental status of a same-sex union entered into by Catholics. It does not give clear directives about the practices in some churches in Africa where divorced Catholics (who remain single) are not only denied communion but are also banned from holding any position in the church or sharing in any ministry. In some instances, children born to de facto union or those conceived outside marriage are often denied the sacraments. While the papal magisterium does not have all the answers to contested moral questions, the failure to take a stand on such weighty matters may give the impression that these issues are matters of personal judgment and pastoral creativity—Pope Francis proposes respect for individual conscience in the church's pastoral practices in certain situations (AL 302).

The danger of the slippery slope lurks in the horizon. This is not helped by the fact which is observable in Western societies that some of these contested moral questions became divisive for the very fact that they have been accepted as the norm in the West and legislated in the laws and constitutions of most Western countries. The failure to give clarity on

these issues has not helped the evangelizing mission of the church especially in the Global South where AL has left Catholics and pastors more
confused than they were before the Synod. This is even more challenging
in Africa where African Christians are being forced to defend the validity
of the Christian moral precepts vis-à-vis Islamic and African Traditional
Religious moral norms which have clear moral prescriptions, customs,
and cultural traditions about these questions.

Finally, the chapter concludes with discussion of the rules of discernment and the logic of mercy. The rules of discernment (Al 304–306)
and the logic of mercy (AL 307–312) grow from understanding people's
mitigating situations (AL 301–303). They call on pastors and the Christian community to step into the shoes of those living on the margins of
the church who find themselves facing locked doors and feeling alienated
from God.

Theological and Pastoral Foundations
for Marriage and Family Life

Chapter 8 of AL challenges us to seek some theological depth for any
pastoral method of accompaniment. In response to the *Instrumentum
Laboris* for the Second Synod on the Family, the Symposium of Episcopal
Conferences of Africa and Madagascar (SECAM) wrote of the importance of the Christian family in Africa; "studies of cultural anthropology
from several African nations have proved that Africans attach great importance to the family. They reaffirm what many Africans today already
embrace, that the family is a social and divine institution which expresses
deep human relationship and intimate encounters, constitutive of both
the identity of the individual and the community. The awareness of the
significant value of community and its intrinsic relation to the identity
and the fulfillment of the individual, is particularly of capital importance
to a given group or family. Thus, crises within the family have adverse effects on the church and society in Africa, as well as on individual identity
and commitment to achieving one's vocation and mission in life."[6]

In order to fully understand the challenges facing families and in
developing the praxis for family life and ministry, we must first begin
with a proper theological anthropology. This starting point will help the
church to embrace a pastoral approach to marriage and family life that is

6. SECAM, *The Future of the Family*, 16.

grounded on the principles of our faith and the traditions of the church, with sensitivity to diversity of cultures around the world. This will furnish the church and pastors with the foundation and model for Christian witnessing to the mystery of conjugal life and all the properties of the family as the domestic church. Marriage and family life are central to the vocation and mission of the church. This is because the Christian family not only mirrors the church but it also mirrors the depth of God who is the foundation of the proper theological anthropology for understanding human beings, cultures, and the ultimate goal of the moral order. What approach beyond proof-texting magisterial documents can be adopted in the light of the teaching of AL for helping Christians to appreciate the mystery of marriage and family life and for finding the inspiration to live fully this mystery in fidelity to God and to one another?

A pastoral approach must be sufficiently open to embrace new questions with sober discernment and humility. It must also resist the enslavement to ideologically-driven posturing and cultural pressures from the West which seek to reduce pastoral ministry to the family to those answers which are often the result of cultural contestations and social experimentations. This is why the African bishops in their response to the *lineamenta* write: "the Church in Africa calls on the universal Church and the global community, to be open to welcoming those values from the peoples of the Global South, on the importance of the family. Such values could help re-establish some anthropological, philosophical and theological foundations on human life and family; on the economy and the relationship to others, the world and God. These challenges, therefore, demand cultural alternatives whose values can have positive impacts on certain theories and alienating practices of contemporary cultures."[7]

The passionate, high-sounding theological and canonical battles, the spin the press put on every word which came out from the Synod on the family are all indications that marriage and family life are central to the mission and identity of the church. This was also reflected in the genuine concerns of most Catholics for a pastoral approach to marriage as reflected in the deliberations and propositions of the Synod fathers and mothers and the teaching of AL. However, marriage and family life are not simply the concerns of Catholics or Christians; they are the concerns of all peoples from other faith and non-faith contexts. Pope John Paul II was so prophetic about this when he wrote in 1981 that marriage is "the

---

7. SECAM, *The Future of the Family*, 21.

most precious of human values" and that "the future of the church and the future of humanity passes by way of family" (*Familiaris Consortio*, 86). In these simple but profound teachings, John Paul II gives us some foundational theological anthropology for a cultural and pastoral reflection and appropriation of God's design for marriage and insight on why marriage and family life is such a treasure for the Catholic Church. Let me highlight some of the theological anthropological principles which should be translated into pastoral practices in our parishes and domestic churches:

The first is that the teaching and practices of the church about marriage are not simply the result of cultural consensus or theological alignment of forces dictated by social change. C. S. Lewis was so prescient when he noted that any religion which marries herself to every cultural tradition will end up a widow. This is because cultures are the products of history—with its ebbs and flows—which embody some elements of truth. However, cultures are always limited by the fact that they are imperfect human creations which cannot embody the whole truth. The Catholic Church while being influenced by cultural traditions and cultural forces even in her history and development of doctrine has always excerpted herself from being imprisoned to any binding cultural tradition. Being a revealed religion, she marches on taking from each culture the "seeds of the Word" which help her to illumine the fullness of truth which Christians believe is revealed in the person of Christ. Therefore, if the church continues to shift her teaching according to the social experimentation of every age, she risks being simply one of many other cultural subjects on display lacking any form, any enduring truth, and any transcending invitation to humanity in our limitations to stretch our gaze beyond the limited horizons of history into the infinite horizon of God.

The second point to note here is that marriage and family life is central to the mission and identity of the church because it relates to human ecology. Pope Francis captures this very well in one of his speeches at World Youth Day in Brazil when he said: "There is neither real promotion of the common good nor real human development when there is ignorance of the fundamental pillars that govern a nation, its nonmaterial goods: *life*, which is a gift of God, a value always to be protected and promoted; the *family*, the foundation of co-existence and a remedy against social fragmentation."[8] John Paul II was the first to use the term

8. Francis, "Visit to the Community of Varginha."

"human ecology" in referring to the family when he wrote as follows in *Centesimus Annus*, 39: "The first and fundamental structure for 'human ecology' is the family, in which man receives his first formative ideas about truth and goodness, and learns what it means to love and to be loved, and thus what it actually means to be a person. Here we mean the *family founded on marriage,* in which the mutual gift of self by husband and wife creates an environment in which children can be born and develop their potentialities, become aware of their dignity and prepare to face their unique and individual destiny." Human ecology underlies the intimate connection between human well-being and the good of the rest of creation. It also points to the need to preserve the human person on this earth through right ethical and moral choices.

The third point is that the primary way of preserving humanity and creation is the priority of family. This demands a commitment to respect for life, and to serve the good of life at all stages, especially the vulnerable lives of the unborn, children, the elderly, the sick, and those who are poor and on the margins. This desire for the good of order, to promote, protect and preserve the common good is grounded in the natural law traditions, which are found in all cultures in different and varied ways. The goal of common existence on earth and the irreplaceable role of the family in bringing this about is not simply the invention of the church. However, the church's insistence that this can only be possible through a strong marriage and family life draws from multiple traditions throughout human history, especially through the teachings, priorities, and practices of the Lord Jesus, the early church, and the glorious traditions of families.

At every marriage, heaven unites with earth; the new covenant of love ratified through the self-giving sacrifice on the cross by the Lord is re-enacted. To marry, to love and to hold and cherish each other in marriage is to lose one's self-possession and to die to self and to rise again as a new person. Marriage is the flourishing of the primordial covenant of God with creation mediated in history through the Son of God, but now continued in the church and lived concretely through the Christian family. At every marriage ceremony, with the beauty of the Catholic liturgy and the various cultural traditions which have come to surround marriage, there is something glorious and deeply touching about the renewal of creation and the springs of a new heaven and a new earth. The origin, dignity, nature, identity, and destiny of marriage are irreducible to cultural configuration or legal positivism or juridical activism. Marriage is a gift from God; it is a vocation which God gives to mere mortals. We must enter into the mystery of God to understand and appreciate the mystery of marriage.

I believe that we need to recover the sense of mystery not only in marriage but also in the beauty of faith in daily life. This is the only way through which humanity can embrace the beauty and dignity of human life and the world of nature in general. The Christian life in all its mysteries and complexities is a beautiful way to God and to one another; it is the illuminative path of gratitude and joy. The deepening of appreciation of the treasure of the the Christian family should begin with recovery of the mystical dimension of the sacrament of matrimony. It requires also an appreciation of this mystical dimension as integral to embracing and living out the beauty of the Christian faith in daily life. There is an intimate connection between all aspects of the Christian life—marriage, morality, pursuit of happiness, and discipleship—when they are illumined by the truth of salvation and the economy of grace. Even though marriage is a natural institution governed by social conventions that emerged in the course of human history, the Lord Jesus Christ has ennobled married life and elevated it to the status of a sacrament and a covenant. Its inner essence can only be found through entering into the mystery of revelation of the truth of the gift of matrimony.

In this light, a proper pastoral approach must begin afresh with the priorities and practices of the Lord and a recognition that the sacramentality and sacredness of marriage are the gift of divine revelation mediated by the Lord. The church is only a witness to this revelation and not its moderator. Jesus is presented to us as faithful to his mission to the end and desirous for our ultimate salvation. He however, began this ministry as a little child at the heart of the Holy Family. He brings to us two models of families: the Trinitarian image and communion of love and unstinting self-giving which he mediates in his life, words, and deeds. In the Holy Family of Jesus, Mary, and Joseph, we see the human appropriation of this Trinitarian model which Jesus lived in simplicity, humility, and total fidelity to God in love and service to one another (AL 11).

The Trinitarian center of the Christian marriage reflects the ineffable love of God and the gift of divine life which in a mysterious way offers married Christian couples the inner source, grace, and form of the love which they are called to embrace in an indissoluble bond. It is through the mystery of marriage that our own origin and destiny to be like God becomes so concrete in all the properties and identity of marriage, which we find in their highest expression and instantiation in the

Trinity. Therefore, the Trinitarian image is the mirror through which we can enter into the mystery of the sacrament of matrimony in order to understand the beauty of marriage and the sacredness of the acts proper to the married life and its permanence, nature, identity, and properties.

When the Universal church or local parishes reflect on marriage or develop pastoral plans and programs for marriage, it is important to remember that we are standing on holy ground because every authentic Christian marriage is an image of the Trinity. This should inspire in every Christian a sense of gratitude for what God can do through the man and woman who offer their bodies to each other and to God to be used for the good of the church and the world. It should challenge the church to greater humility and care on how we are serving the true pastoral needs of the family. Above all, it should strengthen the Catholic community in her commitment to preserve the good proper to the Christian marriage in a divided world which constantly wishes to reduce Christian marriage to one of those cultural symbols which are open to constant revision, dictated by cultural pressure, judicial and legal positivism, social change, and cultural conventions.

Concluding Proposals: A Ministry of Mercy for the Church in Africa and in the World

Healing of Families

The need for ongoing healing in African families must be central to the ministry of mercy. There are many families who are torn apart by division and family feuds. Parents who are alienated from each other sometimes impose a heavy toll on their children by the way they treat each other. Communities are often broken apart because the constituent family units are not bonded internally. In many cases, the issue of land, inheritance, right of patrimony, ancestral curse, sibling rivalry, accusations of witchcraft and sorcery all create a negative atmosphere in African families and communities. The ministry of mercy must be directed to healing the family tree especially where ancient grudges, fear of ancestral curses, and hatred continue to hamper the health of families and make it impossible for God's grace to be incarnated at the heart of the family life. There is also the challenge of sickness, epidemic and diseases, especially HIV/AIDS, and the suffering and economic pressure imposed on many families in Africa by poverty and unacceptable social conditions.

The logic of integration called for by Pope Francis in AL should be implemented as a pastoral plan in Africa. But it means that African churches must examine the documents closely to discover some of the principles and practices within it which can help develop pastoral accompaniment for families in Africa. How can we integrate people into our churches without making them feel that they are the rejects of society? How can the merciful light of the Lord shine in the darkness and heal the wounds that many people carry in our communities and churches because of their marital situation? In many instances, these people abandon their faith or join other churches or simply lapse into new forms of paganism or eclectic spirituality with a high reservoir of anger towards the church and animosity to all things religious.

Those Who are Living in Polygamous Marriages

How are polygamists in Africa to be integrated into the church without inflicting further pain on the family? The SECAM document (42) calls for the development of "pastoral guidance towards the polygamists, which makes the church a witness of divine mercy." However, the document does not go far enough in suggesting concrete steps towards extending mercy to the African polygamist beyond a call for "conversion." The characterization of the polygamist as someone in need of conversion and effectively judging the polygamous to be "living in sin" is a negation of African culture. This also fails to appreciate beyond generalized ethical judgement the reason why polygamy still flourishes in many African tribal communities. This negative judgment and language is hard to sustain when this situation is viewed beyond a restrictive manualist moral teaching that ignores the cultural context of the polygamist and the plausibility structures that ground the choice of polygamy.[9]

The current practice in many African churches is to ask the polygamous man to choose one of his wives for sacramental marriage and then separate from bed and board with the rest of his wives and live with them as brother and sisters. How is mercy being shown to other wives who are not chosen? What kind of message is the church sending out to

9. See Bujo, *Plea for Change of Models for Marriage*, esp. 94–132. For a detailed African Christian ethico-theological analysis of polygamous marriages in Africa and why African polygamous marriages should not be equated with "the scourge of divorce" or "free-love" or a disfigurement of marriage (GS, 47), see Kisembo et al., *African Christian Marriage*, 85–116.

the children of the other wives in that marriage? If the church does not accept divorce, why does it actually promote for practicality purposes a form of divorce in a marriage which was contracted properly through African cultural laws and customs? But more importantly, what image of womanhood is the church promoting if the ultimate decision lies with the man in these circumstances?[10]

The Painful Condition of Divorced and Separated Catholics

In many African societies, there is a clearly-defined process and customary procedure for divorce and remarriage. The norms that govern these are different according to family traditions of each ethnic group and have some specificity within ethnic groups according to family groups or ancestral ties. The process in most cases goes through four stages: mediation, negotiation, reconciliation, restoration. However, if repeated attempts to bring the partners back together in marriage fail, the two families will mutually agree to end the marriage through a formal breaking of the covenant and the establishment of rights and duties between partners, their respective families, and their children. Once this process has come to the point of divorce both partners are free to remarry traditionally and there are clear customary specifications for just settlement with regard to property, alimony, and support for children. These settlements have their limitations in many instances, but there exist some duties and responsibilities that must be upheld if a marriage ends in divorce.

Many partners who have gone through this traditional process in Africa and have moved on with their lives and/or have gotten a divorce through the courts are usually not allowed back into the church and are

10. This approach to dealing with polygamy has consistently been rejected by African theologians and scholars, but most African pastors rigidly enforce this practice to polygamous families. Writing in response to the *linementa* of the First African Synod, foremost late African philosopher, Chukwudum Okolo bemoaned: "The practice in Africa so far has been for the polygynous husband to send away all, but one, of his wives lawfully married to him (according to the tradition of his ancestors) so as to contract an ideal Christian marriage. This is done in total disregard of the social, economic and religious effect it will have on the other wives. To Africans, this is unjust and inhuman and it has incurred the wrath of many polygynous husbands, many of whom have refused to heed the voice of the church on this point. To support them, one African theologian queried: 'How could they commit such an act of injustice against their wives lawfully married according to their own culture?'" Okolo, *The African Synod*, 27.

denied communion and excluded from holding any leadership position in the church. Beginning another process through the rigorous, time-consuming and expensive annulment process in the church seems to many Africans to be a rejection of the African approach to healing marriages in difficult situations or ending ones that have been irremediably damaged.

The annulment process, as my former bishop and foremost African canonist, Bishop Gbuji, told me in a discussion for this essay, is a negative act. In this light, annulment in my thinking is a negative juridical process meant to declare that the conditions and property of marriage never existed. The declaration of nullity in itself does not add anything new to the subjective condition of the partners or the healing of the wounds of separation—in many cases it opens a wounded memory. This is especially true in Africa where the process repeats in an imperfect way—through people (priests, defenders of the bond, judicial vicars, etc.) who may not be traditional mediators in the marriage or familiar with the stories of the couple—what was already settled traditionally. The declaration of nullity does not offer or add any new transformative or pastoral dimension to the objective condition of the couple. It is an imperfect rehash of what is already a holistic approach to resolving family disputes and failed marriages in traditional African marriage practices and rituals. The adoption of African approaches to resolving marital conflicts—mediation, negotiation, reconciliation, and restoration—and for ending marriages in place of legalistic annulment process seem to me to be a prospect which needs to be explored in the development of a ministry of mercy for the church in Africa especially in the light of the teaching of AL (AL 3). The church in Africa must be encouraged to integrate this four-fold process for healing of families in difficult situation as the inculturation of annulment in the church. This would help update the current Western juridical and legalistic process required by the Canon Law.

In a few dioceses in Africa, it is stated clearly that anyone who divorces for any reason whatsoever and remarries without an annulment cannot hold any position in the church and cannot receive the sacraments and if they die will not receive a church funeral. Divorce is seen then as a scandal rather than an unintended evil which happens sometimes because of the faults of the partners but in most cases as a result of the reality of sin and evil in the world which imposes limitations and imperfections on everything human. A ministry of mercy in Africa for families in difficult situation means that divorced and separated couples should not be demonized because a marriage covenant ended with divorce or separation. We all—married or single—in our different vocations know the wounds, hurts, and pain of failing at something to which we have invested so much energy, time, moral, and spiritual resources. People who have experienced divorce in their marriages are already going through deep hurts and carry deep wounds and are in dire need of healing and comfort. Imposing on them punishing restrictions and laying on them a burden of guilt and shame, as is the case in some instances, is a form of practical excommunication from the church which is opposed to the ministry of mercy.

The church in Africa must find a better way of accompanying those in difficult marriage situations which helps to integrate them into the church and society. A ministry of mercy which accompanies people in their journey through difficult marriage situations helps them to the beautiful way of conversion without imposing further spiritual burdens on them or minimizing the needed spiritual discipline and penitential path which ought to precede full participation in the sacramental life of the church.

The same attitude of mercy should always apply to children born out of wedlock who are often denied baptism, or in a few cases the punishment imposed on parents whose children marry outside the church, as well as women who got pregnant out of wedlock and those partners who have procured abortion. Many African men and women whom I have met in pastoral settings are carrying heavy guilt and painful burdens for violating the church's teaching on birth control, while some are having children without the material and emotional support they need to raise these children because of the church's teaching on birth control. The teaching of the church in these areas and the pastoral accompaniment which is needed must become essential to the ministry of mercy of the church in Africa. This requires a broader conversation in the churches and in families with a view to forming the conscience of the faithful on the teaching of the church and strengthening them to an adult faith (AL 37) which is able to make discerning choices with maturity, clarity, and hope in the grace of God and the assurance of mercy which accompanies us in our often imperfect effort to please God.[11]

11. The five-year research project, Churches' Research on Marriage in Africa (CROMIA) carried out in East Africa in the early 70s still contains the most comprehensive inter-denominational approach to some of the issues on the inculturation of marriage in Africa and the pastoral praxis of addressing some of the challenges facing

The Condition of Same-Sex Persons in Africa

It is important to note, that an open and accepting pastoral ministry, the kind that is recommended by AL does not mean celebrating same-sex marriage as a sacrament in the church. Marriage is understood in the Christian tradition as a vocation and not a right. Actually in many instances, people are often required as a result of religious vocation not to marry and to live a celibate life. On the other hand, there are our brothers and sisters who have same-sex orientation and who are living in the shadows and in pain. African churches must come to terms with the experience of many of her sons and daughters who self-identify as LGBTQ /SSA. Denying that these people do not exist or imposing draconian laws against the public self-identification of their sexuality is not consistent with the practices of pastoral accompaniment proposed by AL.

In this regard, I propose that every diocese should have an ongoing ministry and chaplaincy for same-sex persons. Such a ministry of mercy and love must find best practices—which are mediated through African moral tradition of inclusion and participation of all in the life-force—in the art of accompaniment for our brothers and sisters in their journey of faith. However, having a ministry to the LGBTQ or affirming their dignity does not in any way change the conviction of most African Christian theologians and Christians that marriage is between a man and a woman.[12]

African Christians in marriage and family life. I think that such an inter-denominational research should be commissioned more than 40 years after CROMIA with a specific focus on developing different African models for meeting these challenges and drawing richly from the experience of married couples and the religio-cultural context of their faith and life as Christians who wish to live fully their vocation as married couples. See Kisembo, Magesa, and Shorter, *African Christian Marriage*.

12. When it comes to opposition to same-sex unions in Africa, there is a common consensus among most African Catholic theologians that same-sex marriage does not meet the ideal of marriage in African understanding of the properties, conditions, features, and goals of marriage and family life and the abundant life of the community. A distinction is often made by those African theologians who like this author propose respect for the right of two adults to live together in a stable relation of friendship upholding a moral order which is protected by state law, and the sacramental union between two heterosexual persons whose common life approximates fully to African ideal of abundant life and ancestral communion. See for instance, Laurenti Magesa, "The Challenge of African Woman Defined Theology for the 21st Century" in Ndung'u, and Mwaura, eds., *Challenges and Prospects of the Church in Africa: Theological Reflections of the 21st Century*. For a robust deconstruction of a homogenous African theological view on homosexuality and detailed discussion of

There are many aspects of gay culture, like every other humanly constructed cultural behavior and lifestyle, which many African Christians find unacceptable. This does not mean that African Christians are opposed to an inclusive church and society where same-sex persons are treated with respect and dignity as children of God. The legalization of same-sex marriage in many Western countries, therefore, should not be considered as the universal norm for determining how societies outside the West should create an inclusive culture. Rather than charge African Christians as homophobic, churches of the North are called to listen to African reasoning on this human reality beyond the attempt to universalize same-sex marriage as the only path to creating an inclusive church and society. People and cultures are different. In this regard, a majority of African Christians, Muslims, and traditional religionists who hold different positions on gay rights or gay culture deserve to be respected.

In addition, the right of government to protect the rights of people with same-sex orientation must be upheld. At the same time, however, what the government does to protect the rights of same-sex persons is also open to discussion and moral judgment by religious subjects based on their apprehension of the common good and divine revelation. We should not close any issue simply through judicial activism or legislative fiats. Whereas governments has the right to change their interpretation of constitutional provisions about what constitutes the canons for living together between two adults in a stable union, many African theologians argue that the church cannot change those canons without violating divine positive law and putting herself in opposition to God. This calls for mature, slow, and honest dialogue and not simply the enactment of new laws either by the church or the state.

Finally, I must add that enforced rights do not often change entrenched attitudes. Rights are not tokens from one person to another but are claims which arise from who we are as equal persons before God. These rights also come with duties and obligations. Rights emerge from natural law discoverable through reason and from a community's identity and appropriation of the ultimate good through the ordination of the acts of members to laws which promote, preserve and protect the common good. However, there should be a place in every society for those who do not think like we do, who do not act like we do, and who do not

---

different African perspectives on homosexuality and same-sex relations from multiple perspectives see van Klinken and Gunda, "Taking up the Cudgels against Gay Rights? Trends and Trajectories in African Christian Theologies on Homosexuality."

look like us; this is the path to a better and more tolerant society. Thus accommodating same-sex persons is still a big challenge for churches in Africa and this calls for greater dialogue in African churches beyond what presently obtains.[13]

Holy Communion Is for Sinners and Not for Saints

Pope Francis did not give a final word on the reception of Holy Communion for those in irregular marriages, same-sex unions, polygamous situation, divorce, and remarriage, etc. The closest one can glean of his position on this is footnote 351 of AL when he writes: "In certain cases, this can include the help of the sacraments. Hence, 'I want to remind priests that the confessional must not be a torture chamber, but rather an encounter with the Lord's mercy' [Apostolic Exhortation *Evangelii Gaudium* (24 November 2013), 44: AAS 105 (2013), 1038]. I would also point out that the Eucharist 'is not a prize for the perfect, but a powerful medicine and nourishment for the weak' (AAS 47: 1039)." Further indications are found in AL 305 when he cautions: "for this reason, a pastor cannot feel that it is enough simply to apply moral laws to those living in 'irregular' situations, as if they were stones to throw at people's lives."

What is at issue here are Canons 915–16, 1331–32, and 1339, and the authoritative judgment of Pope John Paul II (*Familiaris Consortio*, 79–84) which states in different ways that those are to be excluded from communion who "prefer to contract a merely civil marriage and who reject or at least defer the religious marriage," and "divorced persons who have remarried." Persons in this kind of union are denied communion because according to John Paul II: "the Church reaffirms her practice, which is based upon Sacred Scripture, of not admitting to Eucharistic Communion divorced persons who have remarried. They are unable to be admitted thereto from the fact that their state and condition of life objectively contradict that union of love between Christ and the Church which is signified and effected by the Eucharist. Besides this, there is another special pastoral reason: if these people were admitted to the Eucharist, the faithful would be led into error and confusion regarding the

13. A very helpful comparative study of this question from a Hindu theological perspective which helped me to even widen my own understanding of the complexity of this human mystery is Talwar, *The Third Sex and Human Rights*. See Masiiwa Ragies Gunda, "Contemporary African Christian Thought and Homosexuality: Issues and Trajectories" in Ngong, *A New History of African Christian Thought*, 204–20.

Church's teaching about the indissolubility of marriage" (*Familiaris Consortio*, 84). This teaching has also been defended by the Congregation for the Doctrine of Faith in the 1994 letter, *Annus Internationalis Familiae*. Those who are excluded from communion are also to be excluded from holding any offices in the church according to Canon 1331–1332.

Pope Francis convoked the Synod on the Family because he felt that there is the need to find other means to help those in difficult marriage situations through a pastoral approach which opens the door to God's grace rather than denying them the gift of God's life through the sacraments. What AL is calling the church to do in this matter are the following:

(i) To accompany those Christians who have been traditionally denied Holy Communion with love and mercy. This requires listening to them, entering into their stories and accompanying them to explore the way forward with each person rather than to give a one-rule-fits-all law. This is the import of the new openness shown by bishops in Malta and Germany in their creative development of pastoral accompaniment through sacramental participation for those in these kinds of marriage situation. The church as a teacher of morals and the custodian of the truth revealed by God and the sacraments has a right to set the standard for her children consistent with divine positive law. However, the church should not reject people especially those who are most in need of God's love, grace and mercy. As a result, the church must provide adequate pastoral ministry to support those who do not rise to the ideal. Pope Francis is proposing a more personal approach rather than a legalistic one.

(ii) Pope Francis wants the church to look more at what Holy Communion does in the lives of the individual rather than being enslaved to the condition for worthy reception. When it comes to "worthy reception," one can aver that not even the holiest Catholic can truly claim to be worthy before God. This is why the church in her wisdom has put the Centurion's prayer before Holy Communion for everyone: "Lord I am not worthy that you should enter my roof, but only say the Word and I shall be healed." It is the prayer of all sinners before God. It is a prayer of the humble which affirms clearly that no Christian is righteous before God and that we are all in need of God's mercy. Even the words of consecration attributed to Jesus speak of "the blood poured out for sinners" and "the lamb of God who takes away the sin of the world."

The Eucharist takes away sin; it is the enactment in history of what was done for humanity on Calvary. The cult of the Eucharist and other associated Eucharistic devotion must take us deeper into divine mercy and invite those who are far away from God into the fountain of mercy. As Pope Francis said: "Who am I to judge?" Or as the Good Lord himself taught (John 8:7) "He who is without sin should be the first to cast the stone on the sinner." Pope Francis is drawing the attention of the church to the painful truth that the Eucharist, the greatest symbol of unity and love, has become one of the instruments for excluding people and provoking divisive debates in our churches, as was the case at the Synod on the family in 2014 and 2015 in Rome.

I have read many of the writings on this topic and classify them into two: first, those who make a defense within the wall which separates the pure and the holy in the church from those who are judged as unholy and impure; and secondly those who want a church without wall where sinners and saints can meet together and help in the healing of the wounds that sin imposes on our human condition. I will identify Pope Francis with the latter. This group wants to identify with the sinners and seeks an open crack to allow grace into the life of those who are weak, wounded, or weeping so that God can heal them through the ministry of the church. The point to note is that the Canon Law is an ecclesial tool meant to help Catholics to live in accord with God's will. It is a document of the church produced to help the church in her teaching, and sanctifying function. This is why it should be constantly renewed in the church's mission of illuminating the life of God's people with the truth of Christ. Holy Communion, as Pope Francis teaches, is not a trophy, which is given to those who have lived well or those who have run the race of life very well. Holy Communion is a remedy for sin; food for the journey of life. Those who need this remedy most are those who have sinned greatly and have come to Mass with wounds and brokenness in need of God's healing.

(iii) Pope Francis is also challenging the church to enter deeper into the source and context of this doctrine of excluding people from communion. What the Canon law states is that divorced and remarried Catholics are basically excommunicated from the church. However, when we look at the historical context of Paul who wrote about "receiving the body of Christ unworthily" (1 Corinthians 11:27–32) and the context of Justin who justified the exclusion of people from communion if "they do not believe what we believe" we might see the wide gap between the moral order which they wanted to preserve and what the church is enforcing in

excluding people from communion because of their marital situation.[14]
I do not think that Pope Francis is proposing that the communion line
should be a drive-through, even as the confessional line becomes shorter
and shorter. Rather, I think that AL is proposing a deeper and broader
understanding of what Holy Communion does in the life of people, with
greater respect for individual conscience and discernment as proposed
by St. Paul with a view to what the Eucharist symbolizes for the church
and God's people in the light of the intention of the Lord Jesus in instituting this Holy Meal.

Jesus did not intend the Eucharist to be a food for saints and perfect
people; otherwise he would not institute it for sinners here on earth. Jesus
intended Holy Communion to be a food of love and unity for the community and a remedy for sinners; a help for those on pilgrimage to God's
house, and a healing for those bruised by sins, evils, wounds, and the
burdens of life. Pope Francis is challenging the church to think of what
the Holy One who allowed the woman with the flow of blood to touch
his garment, who allowed the public sinner to touch his body and wash
his feet with her tears, would do if the divorced and remarried Catholics,
the prostitutes, the same-sex person entered into the dinner hall during
the Last Supper. Will he who said he came to seek and save the lost not
welcome to the table and grant his mercy, healing, grace, and unconditional and unmerited divine love to those who came searching for God
with wounded hearts and contrite spirits?

I am convinced that we as created human beings do not contami-
nate God by touching God in communion. When God comes in contact
with me and when I come in contact with God, it is not what is human
and sinful in me which affects God's holiness. Quite to the contrary, it is
God's holiness, grace, and power which change what is sinful and human
in a mysterious exchange governed by compassion and mercy. Indeed,
God takes away our sin if we come to God with a sincere, contrite, and
open heart.

This message is particularly worth reflecting on from the stand-
point of an African culture. I grew up in a very wonderful large family.
When my father became the monarch, our home became the home for

14. See Justin's Apology, "No one may share the Eucharist with us unless he believes
that what we teach is true, unless he is washed in the regenerating waters of baptism
for the remission of his sins, and unless he lives in accordance with the principles given
us by Christ. We do not consume the Eucharistic bread and wine as if it were ordinary
food and drink." First Apology in Defense of Christians, 66–67.

all members of the community where everyone was welcome to share in communal meals and celebrations. In my culture, you cannot exclude someone from a meal, especially if the person participated in preparing the meal. Any stranger who walks in is welcomed and invited to join the meal. Refusing to allow a guest to share in a meal is a grave sin against the spirit of the community and the ancestors. The same is also true for sacrificial meals and offerings made in shrines and libations to the ancestors. Everyone present is invited to share in the meal.

There may be people considered evil in the community but they are not denied a sharing in family meal. Culturally, extending an invitation to such evil people is actually a way of challenging them to embrace the spirit of participation in the community by purifying themselves of all evil intentions and actions which wound the spirit of the community and war against ancestral life. To exclude someone from participating in communal or ritual meal whether in shrines or in the homestead is to pronounce the person culturally dead. Such persons are not wanted in the community; to belong to a community is to participate in all the life of the community especially in meal fellowship. Participation is thus a central motif of African communal and religious life. It is an existential pillar for individuals and communities; to belong is to participate and this is so concrete in meal fellowships.

However, sometimes one may refuse to eat from a particular family's home if there is a fear that they could poison their guests. However, this is a rare occurrence, and the community ostracizes people who would kill or those who plot to kill if their lives cannot be reformed. Murderers have no place in African traditional society nor are people with murderous intents tolerated. One of the greatest challenges facing the churches of Africa with regard to the denial of communion in the Catholic Church to non-Catholics, divorced and remarried Catholics, and others is that it is very contrary and opposed to a core value of African traditional hospitality—food is to be shared between all who are present at a feast, event, worship, etc. The Catholic churches in Africa rather than reaffirming this doctrine with greater severity should begin a serious conversation on how to create for the world church an African model of inclusion when it comes to Holy Communion. This should go beyond the present pastoral incubus built over time by the legalism and rigorism of contentious Western church practices built around the reception of this beautiful gift of the Body and Blood of Christ, to which all are welcome.

The African approach will reject these binaries of those who are worthy and those who are unworthy, which grew out of the dualism in Western thinking that polarizes people between conservatives and liberals, the right and the left, sin and righteousness, saints and sinners.[15] In African thinking, there is always a third way, or rather an openness to healthy ambivalence which is capable of opening the door to a third and higher way. This means the inclusion of opposites through a conscious attempt to include everyone in vital participation. This is why in many traditional African societies, moral dilemmas and breakdown in intersubjective relations are always resolved through restoration, healing, and building up of community. The goal is always the participation of all in the vital force which unites the community. This is an ideal which may never have been realized in its fullness in the past nor in present circumstances, but it is a value which needs to be explored further by African churches in meeting the challenges facing families today. Is there some moral reasoning outside of Western thinking which can help the church to move away from a rigid and legalistic pastoral celebration of the Sacrament of the Eucharist? I think a deeper engagement with African hospitality and communal and inclusive participation in meals could offer a new illuminative way of embracing a healthy duality of both/and beyond the restricted and polarizing Western canonical either/or approach on this contested question.

Conclusion

What I have offered here are personal pastoral and theological reflections on what we can do as priests, pastors, teachers of the faith, pastoral workers, and members of the family of God in celebrating the beautiful gift of marriage and family life in our continent. This, no doubt, is an imperfect offering which I humbly present for further conversation and dialogue. However, what I have done is to highlight some important dimensions of the teaching of AL applied to our context in Africa.

There are many other challenges facing marriage and family in Africa—poverty, migration, disability, childless marriages, domestic violence,

15. See Paul G. Hiebert's important essay on how a Western two-tier thinking makes it impossible to find a middle point in most issues, and why voices from the South (and I will add from Africa) help the world church to find "the excluded middle" in both faith and morals. Paul G. Hiebert, "The Flaw of the Excluded Middle" in Gallagher and Hertig, eds., *Landmark Essays in Mission and World Christianity*, 179–89.

the rights of women within marriages, marriage in stages, inculturation of African marriage rites and rituals, the rising cost of celebrating marriages and funerals, etc.—which deserve greater treatment in our pastoral theology classes, and courses on Catholic Social Teaching, and faculties of education. However, these discussions must be translated into local parishes and dioceses.

The experience of those who actually live the married life must become central to the discussion of the pastoral care for families. Pastoral formation and ministry must speak to the context of those who are actually married, separated, divorced, or remarried, and must arise from that context in a real and effective manner. I am sure that if married people were the ones who formulated parts of the Canon Law on marriage, it might look much different from what we have today. It is obvious as Pope Francis wrote in the preface to AL (AL 3) that this Apostolic Exhortation has not spoken the last word on the vocation, mission, and challenges arising today from the gospel of family. What is needed is to translate the teaching of AL into a pastoral accompaniment that takes account of the different contexts of people. Above all, we all need the courage to seek new approaches to new problems rather than a reaffirmation of doctrines, and the same canonical discipline of the sacraments and unchanging pastoral practices as if they were developed historically without cultural mediation. The pastoral life is our own historically and culturally conditioned human development of concrete patterns and forms for realizing the mind of the Lord. With regard to marriage or reception of Holy Communion, our mothers and fathers in the faith in coming to the formulation of teaching and practices have always listened to the Holy Spirit because what the church does is always specified by the forces of history and openness to the movement of the Holy Spirit in history. We too in our days must ask the Lord for this Spirit to guide us beyond any enslavement to any cultural and doctrinal form.

Bibliography

Bujo, Benezet. *Plea for Change for Models for Marriage*. Nairobi: Paulines Africa, 2009.

Calvin, John. *Institutes of the Christian Religion*. Translated by Henry Beveridge. Peabody, MA: Hendrickson, 2008.

Francis. *Amoris Laetitia: On Love in the Family*. Nairobi: Paulines Africa, 2016.

Gallagher, Robert L., and Paul Hertig, eds. *Landmark Essays in Mission and World Christianity*. Maryknoll, NY: Orbis, 2009.

Ilo, Stan Chu. "The Illuminative Ecclesiology of *Amoris Laetitia.*" *Political Theology Network.* http://www.politicaltheology.com/blog/the-illuminative-ecclesiology-of-amoris-laetitia-stan-chu-ilo/.

John Paul II. *Familiaris Consortio.* Nairobi: Paulines Africa, 1982.

———. *Centesimus Annus.* Nairobi: Paulines Africa, 1994.

Kisembo, Benezeri, Laurenti Magesa, et al. *African Christian Marriage.* Nairobi: Paulines Africa, 2001.

Ndung'u, Nahashon W., and Philomena Mwaura, eds. *Challenges and Prospects of the Church in Africa: Theological Reflections of the 21st Century.* Nairobi: Paulines Africa, 2005.

Ngong, David, ed. *A New History of African Christian Thought: From Cape to Cairo.* New York: Routledge, 2017.

Okolo, Chukwudum B. *The African Synod: Hope for the Continent's Liberation.* Eldoret, KE: Gaba, 1994.

SECAM, *The Future of the Family: Our Mission, Contribution to the 14th Ordinary Assembly of the Synod of Bishops on the Family.* Accra: SECAM/SCEAM, 2015.

van Klinken, Adrian S., and Masiiwa R. Guda. "Taking up the Cudgels against Gay Rights? Trends and Trajectories in African Christian Theologies on Homosexuality." *Journal of Homosexuality* 59 (2012) 114–38.

10

The Spirituality of Marriage and Family Life in *Amoris Laetitia*

LEONIDA KATUNGE

Introduction

The importance of the family as a domestic church and concrete incarnation and fruitfulness of Trinitarian love in history has been the constant teaching of the church. Greater accent has been given to this centrality of the institution of the family in Africa in post-Vatican II African Catholicism with the Second African Synod's teaching on the church as the Family of God (John Paul II, *Ecclesia in Africa*, 63). In this light, pastoral and theological discussion on the importance of this institution in any society, particularly in Africa, has focused on the challenges it faces in a world of cultural diversity and the strains of social and economic pressures. These challenges among others were actually the reason why Pope Francis announced in October 2014 an Extraordinary General Assembly of the Synod of Bishops on the family on the theme: "The Pastoral Challenges of the Family in the Context of the New Evangelization," and an Ordinary General Assembly of the Synod of Bishops on the Family in 2015. These two synods and the deliberations on the family resulted in the publication of the post-synodal Apostolic Exhortation, *Amoris Laetitia* (henceforth AL), by Pope Francis in March 2016.

Chapter 9 of AL clearly states that Christians are called to express and to live the spirituality of marriage and the family in all circumstances of life. This can be expressed in various moments of prayer, catechesis,[1] and participation in the sacraments, among other moments. These expressions begin in the family and extend to the parish level lived in a life of communion, togetherness, and sharing. In the terminology of the Second Vatican Council, family life is a domestic church (*Lumen Gentium*, 11) where people learn and practice societal values together such as care for one another, consolation, hospitality, and respect of each one's dignity. Consequently, these aforementioned values require special attention in order to render family life possible and viable.

The Second Vatican Council calls this special attention "the spirituality of marriage and family" that has roots in the mystery of the Trinity. The Pastoral Constitution on the Church in the Modern World (*Gaudium et Spes*) has these opening words: "The joys and the hopes, the griefs and the anxieties of the men of this age, especially those who are poor or in any way afflicted, these are the joys and hopes, the griefs and anxieties of the followers of Christ" (*Gaudium et Spes*, 1). These words resonate in AL where Pope Francis locates the central teachings of this document within the wider compass of the life of the church and in dialogue with human experience which offers the church the phenomenological basis for living out her faith in history—the person of the world is the person of the church. It is for this reason that AL begins with a solid statement "the joy of love experienced by families is also the joy of the Church."

This essay discusses chapter 9 on the "the Spirituality of Marriage and the Family." I will summarize key themes from this chapter, then theologically reflect on these themes from an African perspective and conclude with some proposals and recommendations for the implementation of pastoral action and accompaniment of families in Africa.

The key themes in this essay are based on the spirituality of marriage and the family. Basically, we will have a look at the spirituality of marriage from supernatural communion to natural communion; from the understanding that God (divine) dwells in the real and concrete families. He still has his dwelling place among the families, despite their worries, sorrows, struggles, joys, achievements, etc. Love should be the uniting factor of the Family that calls God also to remain and be a source of hope for the family in all situations.

---

1. Francis, *Amoris Laetitia*, 287.

Another key theme is "gathering in Prayer in the light of Easter" despite the various sorrowful moments in life which every family passes through in each phase in a normal cycle of life. This should be taken as a moment of growth as it is in union with Christ who on the cross offered himself to all that such moments can be seen as instances of victory if taken in faith. Having such a conviction, God will alleviate and transform our sorrows as he did in the person of Jesus: "Moments of pain and difficulty will be experienced in union with the Lord's cross, and his closeness will make it possible to surmount them" (AL 317).

Then the spirituality of care, consolation, and incentive which is much needed in all families especially in Africa where the family institution is faced with so many challenges. This is the care, attention, and assistance motivated only by love and if the gift of love is missing, then all will be judging of one another, hatred, jealousy, and even feelings of being outcast from the family for some members which can lead to suicide, divorces, separations, etc.

My goal in this paper is to draw out the content and pastoral accompaniment proposed in AL with a focus on the spirituality of marriage and the family as the spirituality in AL.[2] This will be in the general sense of AL and specifically applying to the situation in Africa in search of solutions to some of the challenges they face and what will suit the people of Africa. This means showing how God journeys with his people in their daily experience, especially in the family. In other words, I would like to demonstrate how God is present in the joys and sorrows of the African Christian family and the kind of pastoral and practical spiritual acts that enjoin families in order for them to live out faithfully their marriage commitments and vocation.

Such personal and communal experience makes people feel God's love and communion unceasingly. Therefore, the spirituality of marriage and the family is the spirituality of love that flows from the Trinitarian family and dwells in the human family. This spirituality becomes incarnate in the communion of family through people's daily interactions and relations (AL 316). Of the challenges faced in marriages, the focus will be on those that hinder the living and expression of the spirituality of marriage. Let us then spell out the components of this spirituality of marriage and the family in the light of the papal Apostolic Exhortation, AL.

2. Francis, *Amoris Laetitia*, 315.

Commentary on the Spirituality of Marriage and the Family (AL Chapter 9)

The ninth chapter of AL is devoted to marital and family spirituality where the pope looks at four key elements in marriage life: a spirituality of supernatural communion, where the pope clearly states that "those who have deep spiritual aspirations should not feel that the family detracts from their growth in the life of the Spirit, but rather see it as a path which the Lord is using to lead them to the heights of mystical union" (AL 316). He then speaks of prayer in the light of Easter, of the spirituality of exclusive and free love in the challenge and the yearning to grow old together, reflecting God's fidelity (AL 319). And finally, the spirituality of care, consolation and incentive: the pope teaches that "all family life is a 'shepherding' in mercy. Each of us, by our love and care, leaves a mark on the life of others" (AL 322). It is a profound "spiritual experience to contemplate our loved ones with the eyes of God and to see Christ in them" (AL 323).

From the above, we can see that AL has its focus on God's love as an expression of communion and God's dwelling among people. In this way, Pope Francis observes this, "Today, we can add that the Trinity is present in the temple of marital communion. Just as God dwells in the praises of his people (see Ps 22), so he dwells deep within the marital love that gives him glory" (AL 314). Although the couple will enter *into* a marriage relationship aware of all the good things and challenges it entails, for those who are well prepared and who have Christ at the center will overcome all and lead a good Christian life. One of the implications of marriage is the formation of a family due to the love that one has for another. What constitutes a family and how this is presented is crucial in reading AL.

Pope Francis bases his definition of a family on some of the key church documents that had been written by his predecessors. In (AL 69) he states that Saint John Paul II in his catechesis on human love defined the family as "the way of the Church" in *Gratissimam Sane* (14), and in *Familiaris Consortio* (42) the family is seen as "the first and vital cell of society and still the ideal for family life." *Gaudium et Spes* (47) defines the family as "a community of love." *Lumen Gentium* (11) calls it "domestic Church" while *Apostolicam Actuositatem* (11) sees it as the first cell of society." Paul VI in *Humanae Vitae* (10) presents church teaching on responsible parenthood and defends conjugal morality. Saint Pope John Paul II in *Familiaris Consortio* (86), and *Evangelium Vitae* (94) says that "the future of humanity passes by way of the family." Pope Benedict XVI, in his Post-Synod Exhortation, *Africae Munus* (42) remarked, "The family is the sanctuary of life and a vital cell of society and of the Church." It is through the family that the society continues to exist and to function. This is the means through which the society operates and finds its meaning, though at times this may not be the case. Despite the fact that the marriage institution is of great importance in any society, we realize that the challenges this institution faces should not be taken as a valid ground to say that marriage has no meaning in the society.

AL having its focus on wounded families going through divorce, single parenthood, childlessness, violence, drugs, etc., looks at all families with the eyes of Jesus who loved all regardless of their situations. This love, although human at this stage, draws its origin from God's love: "Love one another, God abides in us, and his love is perfected in us" (1 John 4:12). The question here is: "how does this divine love incarnate itself in human life?" This question paves the way for God's love that reaches out through human love, a central theme of chapter 9 which I will unpack in the next section.

A Spirituality from Supernatural Communion to Natural Communion

The aforementioned key theme on, "human love" makes us transit from supernatural communion to natural communion in which God reaches out to the level of human beings and touches them in their day-to-day experiences both of joys or sorrows: "The Lord's presence dwells in real and concrete families, with all their daily troubles and struggles, joys and hopes" (AL 315). This means that the divine and Trinitarian love becomes incarnate among men and women in their daily interactions. This is expressed through human love in marriage.

In this way, the pope observes, "The spirituality of family love is made up of thousands of small gestures. In that variety of gifts and encounters which deepen communion, God has his dwelling place. This mutual concern 'brings together the human and the divine,' for it is filled with the love of God. In the end, marital spirituality is a spirituality of the bond, in which divine love dwells" (AL 315).

The positive way of experiencing God's love among people is really to reciprocate this love to neighbors as God does to each one of us. People have an obligation to love their neighbors as God teaches them in their life's experiences. Based on personal encounter with God, one must not forget to reciprocate the love that God has shown to him/her in his or her personal life to his or her neighbors. For this purpose, the guiding principle should be God's love as an intimate and personal encounter with God and others. Along this line, Benedict XVI observes, "Closing our eyes to our neighbor also blinds us to God" (*Deus Caritas Est* 16). Therefore, love should be the light that enlightens men and women in their relationships in order to discover God's presence in their life. Benedict XVI continues, "And that, at the end, love is the only light which can "constantly illuminate a world grown dim" (*Deus Caritas Est* 39). The bond of God's love guides us and compels us to show gratitude to God through concrete actions such as prayer.

Because marriage and family life on the African continent are facing many challenges, the African people highly value the idea that God reaches out, in natural communion, to each family at their time of need.

Gathered in Prayer in the Light of Easter

There are sorrowful and joyful moments in life; every family passes through each phase in a normal cycle of life. Here it's good to point out the reality that many families in Africa face. For instance, in many African families, there are joyful moments experienced when family members pray together, eat together, celebrate key moments in family achievements together like graduations, birthdays, marriage anniversaries, etc. However, there are also moments of sadness like death, infidelity, bareness, drunkard couples, lack of unity, etc., which should also be shared and be taken as an avenue of fostering unity and love in the family. As human beings, we have to embrace life in its completeness even in times of sorrow, divorce, barrenness, infidelity, etc. Christians accept these trials with difficulty simply because they tend to forget the place of spirituality in marriage and the family. It is clear that if they base themselves on the Paschal mystery of Christ, these difficulties and challenges will be transformed into moments of accepting suffering in Love.

This is in union with Christ who on the cross offered himself to all. Having such conviction, God will alleviate and transform our sorrows as he did in the person of Jesus: "Moments of pain and difficulty will be experienced in union with the Lord's cross, and his closeness will make it possible to surmount them" (AL 317). The moments of joys in celebrating marriage anniversaries, birthdays, graduation ceremonies, eating and praying together should be taken as key moments in the family's life to make the family strong when sorrowful moments arise like deaths, divorces, barrenness, and infidelity.

These moments in Africa are many when the couple faced with problems may feel alone. This is why some resort to witchcraft and medicine men to get solutions to their problems. Their religious observance is immersed in superstitious beliefs. They take traditional titles and even sue opponents to juju courts. There is syncretism, here rightly expressed in the poetic words of Bolaji Idowu:

Oh! Unhappy African Christian,
Mass in the morning,
Witch doctor in the evening,
Amulet in the pocket,
Scapular around the neck![3]

These words were also echoed by Cardinal Francis Arinze when he said that "Many Christians at critical moments in their lives have recourses to practices of the traditional religion, or to 'prayer houses,' 'healing homes,' 'prophets,' witchcraft or fortune tellers . . ."[4] However, to the married couples in Africa and all over the world, prayer is a moment of experiencing and living God's strength in order to meet the challenges in their marriage and family life.

It is a time of telling God their worries, difficulties, and troubles in view of God's light and assistance. Finally, it is a time of renewal of their marital commitment in remembrance of their marital seal or covenantal seal: "There, the spouses can always seal anew the paschal covenant which united them and which ought to reflect the covenant which God sealed with mankind on the cross" (AL 318).

It is obvious that the example of deep spiritual life of the married couples inspires their children to have a deep relationship with God. The connection couples have with God that is being emphasized in AL serves as a model not only for children born and raised in the family, but also for neighbors and others within the wider extended family structure. Family spirituality is a form of witnessing to the gospel of love. Thus, I will propose that living an authentic family spirituality and celebrating the

3. Idowu, *African Traditional Religion*, 182.
4. Arinze, "Pastoral Sttention to African Traditional Religion."

gospel of love is a veritable evangelical medium for initiating the children into a life of prayer with God.

It also offers the Christian family a golden pathway to unity in the bonds of family prayer and participation in the Eucharist as one family. This togetherness is already a sign of God's presence and dwelling among the family. In this way, the family continues to play her role of being "a domestic Church" (*Lumen Gentium*, 11) as underlined by the Second Vatican Council. Christian families in Africa are being summoned by AL to embrace all their sorrows and trying moments with the eyes of hope. The salvific event of Christ is present as a source of renewal in all families and always offers them a new beginning in the face of all kinds of situations that challenge their faith and sometimes shake the foundations of their family life.

A Spirituality of Exclusive and Free Love

The key word here is fidelity, or better, the spousal relationship of belonging to one another. The married couples daily live out their love toward one another. This belonging means living in love from the heart for one another. You can always tell what a person loves by what he or she devotes himself or herself to most passionately. What a person values most is reflected in his actions and motivations.

The love commanded here in marriage life is that of a husband and wife loving one another as God loves us. We should notice that the love commanded here relates to both outward deeds and inward attitudes: "You shall not hate your brother *in your heart*" (Lev 19:17). A marriage that is based on exclusive and definitive love, becomes the icon of the relationship between God and his people and vice versa. God's way of loving becomes the measure of human love as Pope Emeritus Benedict says in *Deus Caritas Est*, 11.

Marriage is also the experience of belonging completely to another person. Spouses accept the challenge and aspiration of supporting one another, growing old together, and in this way reflecting God's own faithfulness. This love of the heart is based on God's faithfulness and this calls for the couple in marriage not to possess each other and consider the other as personal property but in love and faithfulness bear with each other. In this way, the pope observes, "This happens when each spouse

realizes that the other is not his or her own, but has a much more important Master, the one Lord" (AL 320).

The understanding of belonging is one of the important elements
in marital life. Spouses are called to love one another in a personal way.
However, they should always remember that their first call is to love God
who is, above all, the Source of love. Such distinction and understanding liberates spouses from deviation or divestment: "There is a need to
help them to a certain 'disillusionment' with regard to the other, to stop
expecting from that person something which is proper to the love of God
alone" (AL 320). In such a case, human beings are reminded of their place
and should respect God's place as well. It is a place of inclusive and free
love where all married couples and their children should express their
love to one another, freely giving out all they have as Christ did, despite
the challenges faced in marriage.

A Spirituality of Care, Consolation, and Incentive

A spirituality of care is a spirituality of hospitality, attention, and assistance. For this reason, the Second Vatican Council calls the family "the
nearest hospital" (AL, 11). Under this name, the family should fulfill its
task of being a place to welcome people without discrimination. The care,
attention, and assistance are motivated only by love. Spouses in their mutual interactions express this love through gestures such as an embrace,
a word, and a look (AL 321). At the end of the day, spouses feel and
experience God's care through their ordinary acts of assistance and care.
The pope states, "Marital fruitfulness involves helping others, for 'to love
anybody is to expect from him something which can neither be defined
nor foreseen; it is at the same time in some way to make it possible for
him to fulfill this expectation'" (AL 322). Such treatment and approach
builds up a culture of hope that will make people grow together as both
a family and a society.

Growing and building a society together requires that people culti-
vate attention toward one another. Being attentive to one another, especially in the family setting, requires that one asks himself this question of
Mark: "What do you want me to do for you" (Mark 10:51). Consequently,
people will develop and live a culture of tenderness in which everybody
expresses the joy of being loved (AL 323). In this way, the family and

society fulfill their mission of being "a domestic Church and a vital cell for transforming the world" (AL 324).

Fulfilling the task of a domestic church and a vital cell for transforming the world, the family must have enough roots in the teaching of the Master. This implies that spouses must understand the teaching of the Lord on marital life in order to fulfil their responsibilities as a domestic church. In this regard, the Holy Family of Nazareth is offered by AL as the model that should inspire spouses in building with God's grace families which mirror the faithful and sacrificial love of the Holy Family. For this purpose, each member of the family should avoid judging others, especially those who are in frail situations (AL 325).

This is actually one of the major challenges faced by Christian couples in the universal church given that other than caring and consoling those who are deemed to be "outcasts" in the church, we judge them and even go to the extent of excluding them from society and more so, from the church where they are supposed to be accommodated and accepted. It is time for the church in Africa to think of a way of incorporating these people who are left out, and though this may take time, one day it can be realized.

There are several incidents that we have witnessed especially in the church in Africa where so many of our sisters have been secluded from society due to prostitution. In Mombasa-Kenya, we have had cases where many women who engage in prostitution have been labeled as "outcasts" even at the church level and this has made many shy away from going to church. There are some religious men and women who have formed an association of rescue centers where they help the women to accept their situations and get them back to their homes and place them in jobs; actually many are working at the same center. As such, people can give testimony. I recall one of them telling me, "I have the courage to go out to the beaches to look for my sisters who engage in prostitution as I have come to rediscover that we are God's children and this is not what he created us for!" Such words were touching, but at the end, one realizes that the church in Africa needs to afford these people some care, console them in their different situations, and feel with them when they falter.

In conclusion, we can rightly say that AL addressing the issues of spirituality in marriage and family engages in seeing the centrality of the family and marriage life as a bond that is sealed by the love of God the Father, Son, and Holy Spirit. This is spirituality from a supernatural to a natural union where the Trinity is at the center of marriage and the union between a man and wife where the Holy Spirit is present in the temple of marital communion. Henceforth, those who have deep spiritual aspirations should not feel that the family detracts from their growth in the life of the Spirit, but rather, see it as a path the Lord is using to lead them to the heights of mystical union.

This is only achievable by living the light of Easter; united in Christ and illuminated by him. In the moments of joys and sorrows, difficulties and worries, he is there to care for them. In times of sorrows, difficulties, etc., family prayer is a special way of expressing and strengthening the paschal faith (AL 318) with the culmination in the Eucharist. With this, all is possible as Jesus is called upon to assist in any difficult moment.

Then in marriage, all are called to love one another and to live exclusively for the other just as Christ lived for the church. This will help the couple realize that each lives for the other and hence no more jealousy, competition, struggles, misunderstandings, etc. Then, the spirit of forgiveness, care, and feelings for one another will take the right place; peace, joy, and harmony will prevail in families.

Reflection on the Spirituality of Marriage in an African Context

From the above characteristics of this spirituality that unfolds in marital life, we realize that the church in Africa, in the course of living the spirituality of marriage, is faced with various challenges that may hinder this institution from expressing marital love and living the paschal Mystery to the fullest. The church has always been an institution that gives some guidelines on living the Spirituality of marriage and family life. The church is called to accompany families in these challenges with love, pastoral care, compassion, and guidance from experience and guide them by sound teaching.

AL underlies the importance of the family and marriage life by a strong emphasis on deep spirituality for Christian families. The importance of "family prayers, catechetical instructions, evangelization, frequent reception of the Eucharist, gathering in prayer in the light of Easter and other sacraments should be emphasized,"[5] as stressed by Cardinal Francis Arinze. However, taking all these into consideration, we should also bear in mind that this institution is still faced with a series of challenges and all members should be encouraged to bear with one another

5. Arinze, *Christ's New Homeland.*

in love. These challenges affect the general good and happiness of members of the family. Hence, there is a need to focus on these challenges in the African context.

AL focuses more on love as one of the ways to accommodate everybody in the divine plan. This invites people, especially pastoral agents, to develop more and more attitudes of compassion and respect toward people who are viewed as "unacceptable" by the church, who live in situations of "sin" such as divorce, homosexuality, single parenthood and breakdown of marriage and separation. While these issues may not be as contentious in Africa as they are in the West, the church in Africa must constantly be watchful and proactive in guiding married couples on sound sexual and conjugal spirituality, while guarding the young from embracing social experimentations of the West which are constantly unraveling a world that faces the anthropological crisis of understanding what it means to be human.

There are various pastoral challenges that the families in Africa are facing that call for accompaniment and pastoral support of the families. The issues of infidelity, poverty, diseases, barrenness, etc., call for the church's urgent attention, if we want at all to have faithful and responsible Christians for tomorrow's church. There are good and bad moments in life. AL calls her members to accompany the couples in various moments of life; in times of joys and sorrows. In the spirituality of marriage and the family, the pope and bishops underline some important elements that can assist Africa to embrace these challenges with hope, especially in these areas: *polygamy, dignity, communion, fidelity, divorce, and hospitality, preparation for marriage, taboos, same-sex marriages* and *barrenness.* Let us deepen the understanding of some of these elements.

Polygamy: Africa is waiting for solutions to its problems, especially that of *polygamy.*[6] AL 53 rightly mentions that "some societies still maintain the practice of polygamy," but it goes further and states that, "it is legitimate and right to reject older forms of the traditional family marked by authoritarianism and even violence." It follows that many authors observe that the Papal Exhortation, AL deals more with Western than African issues. Polygamy is a respected form of marriage in many African cultures, but as Cardinal Onaiyekan says, "this does not mean that every African male married to more than one wife . . . or polygamy, was ever

6. In most of African cultures, polygamy is a cultural reality whereby people marry many wives for various reasons such as prosperity, wealth, and sometimes for faithfulness in marriage.

considered the norm, or the ideal."[7] Spirituality would ask, how do these church members or those in polygamous marriages experience God in their lives?

The issue of polygamy also comes in where a polygamist decides to embrace the faith and seeks to be admitted into the church. The practice has been that they can be admitted into the church: but not in full communion, as they cannot receive sacraments until they have conversion of their marriage (Marriage Act: Kenya 2014, section 9). This means choosing one wife out of many and the question that remains is: what of the rest of the wives and their children? John Cardinal Onaiyekan, says that this has been a "difficult demand especially to justice and many remain as they are trusting in the mercy of God, without asking to receive communion, regardless of their good intentions."[8]

In the actual sense, despite the fact that the church has set such regulations, some of these people are married according to the local customs awaiting solemnizing of their marriages. If roles are given to these people in the church, their passion for the renewal of marriages can be awakened in the course of time, to turn to the right way of the sacraments. This can be a platform that the local churches can adapt in such a way that all who are not active members in the reception of the sacraments, especially the Eucharist, can be made to feel as active members of the society. This calls for mutual understanding by the ministers and those who in various parishes have felt as if they are left out. Let each diocese have a plan of action for such people to call them for seminars, workshops, and conferences where they can even meet those who are receiving the sacraments and share their life experiences. There is a possibility that even such people have no impediments at all and the problem may be lack of knowledge.

We also realize, in some cases where people have knowledge, that they are already excluded from the church and they don't feel that they belong anymore and they are not ready to take any active role in the church. Thus, the church in Africa should have these people accepted in the church and get them involved in small Christian communities (SCCs), parish leadership, etc. The measures that any diocese or parish may take should be the spirituality of "*care, consolation, and incentive.*"

On *dignity*: Africa is invited to treat women with respect. This is what AL stresses stating that there are some positive developments in

7. Onaiyekan, "Marriage in Our Contemporary World."
8. Onaiyekan, "Marriage in Our Contemporary World."

the respect of the dignity of women in some parts of the world but still it states ". . . some unacceptable customs still need to be eliminated. I think particularly of the shameful ill-treatment to which women are sometimes subjected, domestic violence and various forms of enslavement which, rather than a show of masculine power, are craven acts of cowardice" (AL 54). Here the stress is placed on the recognition of women's rights and their participation in public life, in some countries much remains to be done to promote these rights. In some cultures, pastoral practices such as holding posts of leadership (i.e., chairpersons, secretaries, catechists, and even choir members) in the parish need to be done in view of promoting these rights and making women have a sense of belonging and acceptance. In some African cultures, women are viewed as less human compared to men. In this case, the spirituality of the papal exhortation will assist Africans to develop a culture of respect of each one's dignity, especially on the women's side, principally in cultures where matters to do with barrenness are attributed only to women and never to men. A recent case in Kenya had to do with a woman who suffered serious bodily harm and whose hands were chopped off when her husband, who claims she cannot bear children, attempted to murder her—yet he is the one who had fertility complications![9]

The church in Africa, faced with such a scenario where the dignity of women is not respected, should take recourse to the Scriptures and learn the virtues of inclusiveness and avoid being judgmental.[10] The church should come to the realization of respect of women and sacredness of *all* people, a guiding principle when they seek justice and peace. To uphold the religious and social values of peace and justice, the church must condemn violence against women as a pertinent sin against the Creator. As theologians, we should address threats to human dignity. We must work together to enhance all that dignifies even the most marginalized, stigmatized, and vulnerable beings in the society. Every human person is created in the image and likeness of God and if we all realize this, the church in Africa will be the best place where the dignity of women will be respected in the home, parish, nation, and continent as a whole. This section will look at the role of women in the society and their involvement in church matters. In my work with women I've found that African Christian communities are realizing every day the greater impact of women in

9. Habil, "Battered woman says why she remained in abusive marriage."

10. John 4:1ff. Jesus and the Samaritan woman where this woman was seen as an outcast in the society due to her sinful nature but Jesus accepted her in her condition.

social development and their critical role in the work of small Christian communities in local contexts.

John Paul II on the occasion of an the International Conference "Twenty-First Century Slavery—The Human Rights Dimension to Trafficking in Human Beings," addressed a letter on May 15, 2002 to Archbishop Jean-Louis Tauran. In the letter, the pope wrote: "The trade in human persons constitutes a shocking offence against human dignity and a grave violation of fundamental human rights. Already the Second Vatican Council had pointed to 'slavery, prostitution, the selling of women and children, and disgraceful working conditions where people are treated as instruments of gain rather than free and responsible persons' as 'infamies' which 'poison human society, debase their perpetrators' and constitute 'a supreme dishonor to the Creator'" (*Gaudium et Spes*, 27). Such situations are an affront to fundamental values which are shared by all cultures and peoples, values rooted in the very nature of the human person.

On *community*: realities such as a marriage in Africa are never a personal affair. Rather, it is always a communal affair.[11] This means that the choice of who to marry comes from the family of the man in most African societies, but we have cases in Africa where this is the opposite. Examples of these communities include "the Luapula in Zambia, the Ashanti and the Akan in Ghana, the Ila in Zimbabwe, the Yoruba and the Bidjogo in West Africa and in the north there are the Tuareg people and the Kabylei."[12] We have also the Makonde of Mozambique, the Zaramo and Luguru of Tanzania. This is also a common norm among the Yao, Nyanja and Lomwe of southern Malawi. These are matriarchal societies where females hold primary power, and predominate in roles of political leadership, moral authority, social privilege, and control of property at the specific exclusion of men, at least to a large degree. Very often, the man appears passive in the choice of his spouse in traditional African societies.

---

11. Mbiti upholds community participation as essential in marriage: "In other societies, it is the young people themselves who make their own choice and afterwards inform their parents about it. Then the parents and relatives begin the betrothal negotiations. Since the individual exists only because the corporate group exists, it is vital that in this most important contract of life, other members of that corporate community must get involved in the marriage of the individual" (Mbiti, *African Religions and Philosophy*, 136).

12. Mbiti, *African Religions and Philosophy*, 136.

Due to the social, political, economic, and academic changes, today we will realize that even in Africa, community life has been affected. Once marriage was considered a family affair; it has now turned into a personal business and has actually become a matter of international concern where bodies like the United Nations have seen these arranged marriages and early marriages as abuse of human rights. There was for instance, The UN Resolution on Child, Early and Forced Marriage that was adopted on November 21, 2014, where it was agreed upon including, *inter alia,* among other resolutions "to enact, enforce and uphold laws and policies to end the practice; Promote and protect the human rights of all women and girls, including their right to education and to have control over and decide freely and responsibly on matters related to their sexuality."[13]

In this way, Mbiti rightly observes, "In other societies, it is the young people themselves who make their own choice and afterwards inform their parents about it. Then the parents and relatives begin the betrothal negotiations. Since the individual exists only because the corporate group exists, it is vital that in this most important contract of life, other members of that corporate community must get involved in the marriage of the individual."[14] For this purpose, the papal exhortation invites Africa to go beyond a limited cultural self-understanding of mere and superficial understanding of communion. This means that Africa should respect the freedom of spouses in the making of the spousal choice. On the one hand, such clarification will define the roles of the community and on the other hand, the roles of the individuals who want to engage themselves in marriage.

Another danger in the choice of spouses is greed or self-interest. The traditional way of choosing spouses engenders a selective spirit among families. As a fact, rich families marry among themselves and poor families are victims very often. In making reference to AL 317, we note:

> If a family is centered on Christ, he will unify and illumine its entire life. Moments of pain and difficulty will be experienced in union with the Lord's Cross, and his closeness will make it possible to surmount them. In the darkest hours of a family's life, union with Jesus in his abandonment can help avoid a breakup.

13. Hamilton, "Girls Not Brides."
14. Mbiti, *African Religions and Philosophy,* 136.

As such it will be in community. Hence, we are faced with a situation where many people are excluded from this participation in community due to their marital status and conditions. Thus, communion with these people, involving them in church matters, electing them as leaders in the SCCs and even recognizing them in the parish set up can make them have a different view of life and feel a sense of belonging.

On *Fidelity*: this is a value that is held with high regard in Africa. In terms of marriage, this may be a value that has been misunderstood and it seems that it is a requirement that binds only women. In most of the African societies, it seems that men can be unfaithful and can even go to the extent of keeping concubines if they are married, but it is different for women. Cultural double standards and make it difficult for women to be liberated and allow men to embrace a life of infidelity at the expenses of cultural protection.

This may seem to be a vehicle of injustice and in response to it, the papal exhortation should enlighten African societies to apply and advocate for justice, i.e., equal treatment between men and women. Fidelity should be lived by both spouses in order to avoid realities such as divorce and breakdown in marriages. Africans need to develop a culture of real love, respect, and understanding, especially toward women who are very often culturally victims. This as a result will enhance marital life and people will express their spirituality and take role on various matters that pertain to marriage spirituality.

On *hospitality*: Africa should use the papal exhortation to uproot the issue of tribalism among her people. Tribalism has become one of the destructive elements that is slowly destroying the structure of most African societies. In the light of the papal exhortation, Africa should develop and widen its understanding of hospitality. Hospitality should go beyond geographical boundaries especially in marriage alliances. The mystery of Christ the Risen One should be experienced by all regardless of their church.

The element of hospitality also calls for accepting each other as brothers and sisters even in an area where people are from different ethnic groups. Unfortunately, the so called "outsiders"— those who are not members of some communities where we live—are not accepted. Even in intermarriages, some men have been reported to be deserted by their family members for marrying women from outside their cultures. In Kenya, for example, during the 2007/8 inter-ethnic clashes, it was clear that so many people who lost lives, homes, and property were seen as outsiders and foreigners. In fact, it was reported that, "They were seen as 'strangers,' 'foreigners,' 'outsiders,' and as 'invaders' who had gone there to displace the 'rightful' owners of the land and were not welcome. Anything that could be done to expel them—had to be done. And that included killing them. It became an orgy of killings."[15]

The attacks in the Rift Valley and Coast Provinces in Kenya and the inflammatory language used by the instigators of this kind of violence to inflame passions among the indigenous people in those provinces had striking parallels to what happened in Nigeria in the nineteen-sixties, particularly in the language used by Northern Nigerian leaders about the Igbos who had settled in their region. As Representative Mallam Mukhtar Bello stated in the Northern House of Assembly during the February–March 1964 session, just two years before the massacre of the Igbos in that region:

> I would like to say something very important that the Minister should take my appeal to the Federal Government (controlled by Northerners) about the Igbos . . . I wish the number of these Igbos be reduced . . . There are too many of them in the North. They are just like sardines and I think they are just too danger-ous to the Region.[16]

And so was the case of Rwanda during the 1994 genocide which left half of the nation dead, and to significant loss of property. All caused by lack of hospitality and accepting one another as brothers and sisters.

A spirituality of care is a spirituality of hospitality, attention, and assistance. For this reason, the Second Vatican Council calls the family "the nearest hospital" (AA 11). It's true that Africans are known to be hospitable people, despite the fact that the current trend of life has influenced this value.

On *Barrenness*: The emphasis placed on childbearing when preparing individuals for marriage has often trumped the importance of unity between spouses. For Africans, children were and are more valued than unity in marriage. Many women (and some men) suffer the indignity of being referred to pejoratively because they cannot or have to struggle to have children. In addition, this inability to have children often becomes a license for unfaithfulness and even polygamy in Africa even among the Christians whose faith is not strong.

15. Mwakikagile, *Kenya*, 155.
16. Mwakikagile, *Ethnic Politics in Kenya and Nigeria*, 120.

Divorce was once unheard of in Africa but now it is so common that some couples don't want children and those who by chance get pregnant choose to go for abortion. Africa had a great influence from the western countries and Kenya, in particular, due to advanced technology that propagates Western values and culture. Today, abortions are very common even among Christians who have forgotten that children are a gift from God. Christians should not forget that in the *Catechism of the Catholic Church*[17] and even in the Rite of Marriage, children are to be received as a gift from God and have to be accepted lovingly and be brought up according to the law of Christ and his church. It is for this reason that even in Christian marriages where the gift of children is not given due to barrenness, couples should recall this commission and understand barrenness should not be a cause of divorce, as divorce is contrary to the example a community must set for bringing up children according to the law of Christ and his church.

The church in Africa has the mentality that a man will be regarded a responsible man if only he has children, at the expense of forgetting the teaching of the church that children are gifts from God and in case they fail to have children, then they should look unto God. This should also be part of the program in the courses of preparation for marriage.

Pastoral application of AL in Africa in relation to the Spirituality of Marriage and Family

After the study above, one may ask: what's new, if anything? And how will AL speak to the church in Africa, and to be precise, to the church in Kenya today? Looking at the exhortation from the perspective of the church in Africa, borrowing from the words of Cardinal Wilfrid Napier of Durban, South Africa, I can say that, "What is new about this exhortation is its tone."[18] He went further and said that, "There is no one-size-fits-all" approach and "local churches are urged to adapt church teachings from the synod to their particular circumstances," noting, for example, that "different cultural understandings of marriage within South Africa would give the church here different challenges to those faced by churches in other parts of the world."[19]

17. CCC, 1652.

18. Napier, interview on *Amoris Laetitia*.

19. Napier, interview on *Amoris Laetitia*.

Pope Francis has admonished church leaders in the world, "Don't hide behind the veil of magisterium!" (AL 3). Instead, we need to pay close attention to the unique elements within African cultures that allow the church in Africa to engender innovative pastoral solutions to family life and marriage with sensitivity to local needs and traditions (AL 3). There is a great opportunity here to be creative!

The following examples are explanatory of the pastoral application of AL in Africa, based on some recent matters that I am handling as a theologian and a pastoral agent, as well as some experiences shared by my co-workers. These examples involve the challenges faced in marriage and family life in Kenya that lead to the lack of living the marriage spirituality.

In St. Theresa Catholic Church, Eastleigh, Nairobi, there is a couple I have journeyed with who have been married for the last forty years. The husband is biologically sound and fertile but the wife is barren and as such she cannot bear children. The wife asked the husband to marry another woman so as to bear children for him but interestingly the husband told the wife that the ends of marriage are not only children. According to this man, if God blesses them with children in the marriage, it will be a blessing but if not they can still celebrate their life together as a couple. This is what actually is making this couple happy and still moving on. Even though they may consider adoption, what I observed was the picture of a deeply spiritual couple at home with each other and with their gift of each other. However, the opposite is also possible. One week ago a wife was almost killed by her husband in Machakos County, Kenya,[20] as he claimed that she could not bear children when in fact the contrary was true that it was he who was impotent. He openly claimed that he wanted to kill her as it was a taboo for the family to have a woman who could not bear children. Thus, we can see the challenges posed by what barrenness can mean to some people in the African culture where children are not only received as a gift from God but as a source of fame and wealth.

I am presently handling another case here in Kenya where a couple agreed to come together in marriage even though the lady's ovaries had been damaged in an accident when she was eighteen years old making it impossible for her to conceive. Talking to her, she says that, "my beloved fiancée knows of my case and he is ready to take me as his wife because he loves me and he is ready to adopt a child because we cannot have our own child." This is one of those cases that always makes me think that

20. Habil, "Battered woman says why she remained in abusive marriage."

they should be emulated by people in the African context where many people are discriminated against because of issues like these.

Nonetheless, in AL, all these different situations should be a matter for reflection and "our contemplation of the fulfillment which we have yet to attain also allows us to see in proper perspective the historical journey which we make as families . . . keep walking together . . . never lose heart because of our limitations, or ever stop seeking that fullness of love and communion which God holds before us" (AL 325). African families facing challenges like barrenness and even assaults and battering must be supported by the church in Africa to embrace the message of AL and the spirituality of fruitful love through other means beyond procreation. This will require a deeper cultural knowledge on the part of the church in Africa to fully respect and appreciate the social and cultural location of our young people today and how they make meaning about marriage, children, and the construction of the future through ancestral ties and lineage. Communion with those who find themselves in such a situation and the church has to lay structures which are inclusive. Those women who don't have children should be given the duty of taking care of the Sunday school children, PMC, catechesis, as well as the youths both in the SCCs and in the parish as "mothers." Such a way will help them to feel that they are in the company of children whom they lack.

Another case at hand is polygamy. In May 2014, Kenya's president, Uhuru Kenyatta signed into law a bill on marriage that had long been debated. Section 3 of the Act defines marriage "as a union between a man and a woman in either monogamous or polygamous marriage." Looking at this definition, it is clear that there is room still for polygamy and this is the reason why section 8 of the same Act talks of the conversion of marriage for those who want to move from one system of marriage to another and more precisely from the customary marriages to either Hindu, Christian, or Mohammedan marriages. We can see from our African situation, polygamy is a challenge even for Christian families where a man has more than one wife, contrary to Scripture teaching and even some cases of polyandry where a woman has more than one husband. There is also the so-called "special marriages" like surrogate, wife inheritance, woman-to-woman marriages, etc. These are common practices in Africa. In my pastoral work, I encountered a lady in Mbenuu Village in Makueni county, Kenya, who had this to say on her status as a first wife and having two other co-wives, "It is clear that I am the first woman in this house and there are two other younger ones. The priest told me I cannot receive the sacrament of Eucharist as I am not married in Church and yet the cat-echist said for me to marry in Church the other two women have to die or my husband has to make a choice of leaving the two and marrying me."[21]

Polygamy is one of the greatest challenges facing marriage and fam-ily life in Africa. It is commonplace in many parts of Africa especially where the first marriage produces no children—especially male progeny. In some cases, because the man does not wish to be excluded from Holy Communion, he may also marry the second wife secretly or simply keep her as a partner without formalizing the marriage. This is what we call in Swahili "*mipango ya Kando*" or in English "concubines" where a man is known to have one wife but he has another lady incognito. This is a common practice, and we see cultural and religious practices come to a point of contradiction.

Faced with the challenge of same-sex marriages, there has to be a point of reflection in some of the continents where this has been legal-ized. South Africa is the only country in Africa where same-sex mar-riages have been legalized. However, in my pastoral work I encounter many people who are struggling with their sexual identity in East Africa. In one case which I am currently working, one couple has been married for nineteen years now and unfortunately, the wife has been suspicious of her husband's behavior only to find out that even before marrying her, he had another "wife" who happens to be a man. They have been in a relationship for the last thirty years since they were in college. The man tells this woman that he married her because he had to but that if the church allows for same-sex marriage, he would be the first one to marry his same-sex partner. It is true that most Africans say that same-sex mar-riages are against their cultural values, so it is not actually an issue of re-ligious values but cultural ones! However, there are examples of Africans who have same-sex attraction whom I encounter in my ministry. The question is: What will the church in Africa do in this situation?

It is clear from AL that in all these situations enumerated above, in marital life, the couple should be accompanied and be supported by the church. This is following the call of AL to love and care for one another as brothers and sisters. Pope Francis reminds us that, the family "has al-ways been the nearest 'hospital'" (AL 321) where all are called to heal the sick spiritually, psychologically, emotionally, etc. It is in the family as a domestic church where parents are called to "become their children's first

21. Mama Magdaline Katheu, Mbenuu Village, July 2016.

teachers in the faith" (AL 16). This is extended to the parish where the pope states that, "The main contribution to the pastoral care of families is offered by the parish, which is the family of families, where small communities, ecclesial movements and associations live in harmony" (AL 202). As such, in a family where the spirituality of marriage is lived and expressed, when challenges like disease, barrenness, death, and widowhood occur, the entire family will be united in the light of Christ the Risen Lord. There will be a spirit of care and love in the family. Forgiveness will take precedence in all matters. AL 27 states that, "Love also bears fruit in mercy and forgiveness." Most of the broken families, we realize, are caused by lack of forgiveness as the couple keep count of the wrongs committed by the other and when one cannot bear any more, then he or she decides to quit. We should learn that, "When we have been offended or let down, forgiveness is possible and desirable, but no one can say that it is easy. The truth is that "family communion can only be preserved and perfected through a great spirit of sacrifice . . ." (AL 106).

In cases where no children are born in marriage for the parents then, ". . . we know that this can be a cause of real suffering for them. At the same time, we know that "marriage was not instituted solely for the procreation of children . . . Even in cases where, despite the intense desire of the spouses, there are no children, and marriage still retains its character of being a whole manner and communion of life, and preserves its value and indissolubility" (AL 178).

As such, the church does not allow divorce and the couple are called to bear with each other. God's love for humanity is eternal, so also is the love for one another that should be free and without conditions.

The challenge of HIV/AIDS: HIV/AIDS has also to be addressed in living the spirituality of marriage in the African context. When I was teaching a Masters students' class on marriage one of the students asked me, "How can the marriage formula remain as it is with its statement 'in sickness and in health till death do us part' when we know that the scourge of HIV/AIDS has to be seen as a serious problem?" Should the marriage rite be amended due to the scourge we have in Africa of HIV/ AIDS? I think we have had cases where people are married and they are sick and are living together. What solution does AL have for such a couple? These are common cases and an archbishop in Kenya is reported to have advised such couples to use condoms so as to continue with their sexual relationships. This was not taken positively by some of the Christians in Kenya. Upon his death, this was a point that was repeated by many in the media in Kenya. What will the church say of such cases? I met a certain catechist in Tanzania. This man[22] was a victim of HIV/AIDS as well. His state worsened. His physical deterioration became a serious issue to many villagers because they considered his disease as a curse from God (John 9:2). However, he pleaded with us that the church should allow him to marry another wife in order continue his progeny because the first wife was sterile. The priest did not allow him to marry another wife, rather to remain faithful to his wife. Compelled by his cultural belief, the man decided to move to another village where people did not know him in order to have another wife capable of giving him children.

I visited one HIV treatment center in Kenya. This center provides patients with medicine, food, and accommodation. The majority are women. At some point, I had a chat with some of them confidentially. Most of the women faced serious problems of love in their marriages. One explained to me her marital issue. She said this: "The center gives us many things to solve the basic problems of our life. However, one problem is never resolved. This problem is love. This means that I have a husband and children. My husband knows well that I am HIV positive. However, he continues to force me to make love with him. If I told him that I am sick and must avoid the spreading of AIDS to him and the children, his first reaction would be to go to other women. Imagine, at this age and with this disease, who will take care of me? To avoid any problem, I always give in and satisfy him. Despite this, my husband still goes always out to other women and using my disease as a reason for him to do so."[23]

What solution will the church in Africa have for such cases? Will she allow the concomitant couple to use contraceptives so as to safeguard the marriage? This is one of the challenges among others with which the pastoral agents in Africa have to sit and seek for a lasting solution. The solution which is presently being offered to these brothers and sisters in the continent does not seem to be adequate for meeting this challenge. This is why greater dialogue needs to be held in the African theological academia and in our parishes and chanceries on finding a pastoral accompaniment for these brothers and sisters or else we will lose more Christian faithful hiding under the canopy of magisterial teaching rather than seeking African solutions to the challenges that face marriage.

22. Man "X," catechist of one of the outstations in Igunga, Tanzania.
23. Woman "X," "Marriage Issues: Joys and Sorrows," Personal notes.

The question remains: How to apply practically the teaching of love and of communion found in AL in these aforementioned cases? The document proposes *mercy* and *understanding* above all virtues. The pope observes, "All family life is 'a shepherding' in mercy. Each of us, by our love and care, leaves a mark on the life of others" (AL 322). Furthermore, he continues, "It also keeps us from judging harshly those who live in situations of frailty. . . . Let us keep walking together" (AL 325).

With these, the spirituality of marriage and the family intends to remind the church of her mission: to be *a nearest hospital* (AL 321). This underscores relevantly that families need *understanding* and *acceptance* above all. Being *a nearest hospital*, the church must welcome everybody without any judgment or condemnation.

In our African parishes and societies, the church can achieve her mission of being *a nearest hospital* in being attentive to all those who approach her pastors or ministers. Here, the pope reminds pastoral agents strongly of this; "In such difficult situations of need, the Church must be particularly concerned to offer understanding, comfort, and acceptance, rather than imposing straight away a set of rules that only lead people to feel judged and abandoned by the very Mother called to show them God's mercy" (AL 49).

Having such a principle of mercy, understanding, and acceptance in mind, pastoral agents are called to heal families and even facilitate healing processes. By accompanying difficult families (as in the three cases of HIV above) to embrace acceptance and understanding despite HIV or diseases, the church will assist spouses to find ways and means to keep fidelity and love as they first promised at their wedding. We all know that it is very difficult to make families understand such a teaching of love and of communion, but by God's grace, all is possible as Mary believed it well at the annunciation: "For nothing is impossible to God" (Luke 1:37).

There are so many Christians who do not receive the sacraments in the church for various reasons. They do suffer in their situation because they would wish to but they are barred from reception. They are active in church activities, in the SCC, parishes as well as in their families, but they need to have a revival in their faith through the reception of the sacraments, especially the Eucharist, through which each Christian encounters Christ personally and in a more intimate way.

Another key challenge that the church is confronted with these days is divorce. The Catholic Church does not permit divorce for valid sacramental marriages. In fact, a valid sacramental marriage is impossible to dissolve.[24] In marriage, the two become one flesh in a union joined by God (Mark 10:8). Jesus speaks about divorce: "Therefore what God has joined together, no human being must separate" (Mark 10:9). So, for a marriage that meets the requirements of being a sacrament,[25] divorce in the Catholic Church is not possible. There are moments of crisis in a couple's relationship that destabilize the family and "may lead, through separation and divorce, to serious consequences for adults, children, and society as a whole, weakening its individual and social bonds" (AL 41). There are some people who have opted to separate and stay apart but this is not actually the original plan of God in a marriage. As John Paul II rightly says, in *Familiaris Consortio*, "separation must be considered as a last resort, after all other reasonable attempts at reconciliation have proved vain."[26]

The Synod Fathers noted that, "special discernment is indispensable for the pastoral care of those who are separated, divorced or abandoned. Respect needs to be shown, especially for the sufferings of those who have unjustly endured separation, divorce or abandonment, or those who have been forced by maltreatment from a husband or a wife to interrupt their life together. To forgive such an injustice that has been suffered is not easy, but grace makes this journey possible. Pastoral care must necessarily include efforts at reconciliation and mediation, through the establishment of specialized counseling centers in dioceses."[27]

There is a need for spiritual nourishment for those who are divorced and as the *Relatio Synodi* stated "divorced people who have not remarried, and often bear witness to marital fidelity, ought to be encouraged to find in the Eucharist the nourishment they need to sustain them in their present state of life. The local community and pastors should accompany these people with solicitude, particularly when children are involved or when they are in serious financial difficulty."[28]

The pastoral agents have a mandate to accompany the divorced and help them to understand their situation according to the teaching of the church and the guidelines of the bishop as most of them do not understand the implications of such divorces. In every diocese, there is

---

24. See Ortiz, "Catholic Marriage."

25. See Ortiz, "Catholic Marriage."

26. John Paul II, *Familiaris Consortio*, 184.

27. Synod of Bishops, *Relatio Synodi*, 47.

28. Synod of Bishops, *Relatio Synodi*.

need of an office to cater to the pastoral needs of such people, so as to have them feel as members of the body of Christ even after divorce. The Church is the first family where a Christian will belong by virtue of baptism. So even after the annulment of the marriage, the same Christian family should welcome the brother or sister who has annulled her or his marriage and make them feel as members of the community. This is to avoid instances where those who have annulled their marriages seem to be less Christians than thy were before annulment.

Annulment also needs our attention. An annulment (formally known as a "declaration of nullity") is a ruling that a particular marriage was null from the beginning—that is, something was gravely wrong at the time the wedding vows were made and it prevented a valid marriage from coming into existence. But with Pope Francis's clarification and shortening of the process of annulments, couples have all reasons to rethink their marriage before applying for annulment, lest we have many marriages breaking from the fact that the Church has made it look like an easy exercise. Of course, measures should be taken that any marriage that is celebrated should be valid to avoid occasions for annulment. However, in case it happens, then the couple should be instructed appropriately by the church.

Conclusion

In conclusion, we can say that the spirituality of the family as a unit, as a domestic church, irrespective of its form or shape, is still being developed in Africa. A true family spirituality is one of relationships. It can and should include the individual, the person as a member of a family, but the ideal should encompass experiencing God in the family in its diversity with its different stages and types of relationships.[29]

Married people should reflect God's love in their daily interactions through the practice of some societal values such as hospitality, fidelity, attention, prayer, care, and above all, their bond of love as expression of God's Trinitarian communion. All the challenges of life should be looked to as moments of growth and the opening to new avenues of growth based on Christian values.

Reading AL, one may conclude that the document deals more with Western issues than African ones. This should not be the reason to

---

29. Rowland, "*Amoris Laetitia* and a Spirituality of Family Life."

discourage pastoral agents from making use of AL in their pastoral work. Nevertheless, Africans should select some of the elements that can assist them to clarify their African issues of divorce, infidelity, barrenness, and polygamy among other issues. Clarification of some cultural elements in the light of AL may greatly assist Africa to move forward on such issues as human dignity (especially of women), fidelity, communion-family, and hospitality. With such an approach and reading, AL can address everybody in their respective cultures and worldviews.

The parishes and dioceses in Africa should arrange for courses for couples newly married, and even the long established couples, to remind them of their responsibility as parents. Family prayers and the reception of the sacraments should always be emphasized at the family level as the family is an active agent of evangelization, within itself and with other families. This is also in relation to the SCC and then extended to the parishes and dioceses.

There are also some people in the same church who cannot be admitted to the sacraments, such as those who have divorced and remarried (see *Familiaris Consortio* 84). The call here is that the church should not abandon such members. She invites them to read and listen to the proclamation of the Word of God, to take part at Mass, to persevere in prayer, engage in works of charity, and acts of penance.

The doctrinal aspect is not only the *telos* of this document. The *telos* of the document is what many in Africa will find difficult: the invitation to be open to the realities of family life and thus respond primarily from a place of mercy. Responding from the place of mercy does not mean blind forgiveness but the preparedness to help reintegrate and accompany those who find themselves outside the teaching of the church. Mercy is the hermeneutic of AL. That is a real challenge for Africa because it is asking for dialogue, listening and a certain vulnerability on the side of the church. In fact, Pope Francis cites John Paul II in *Familiaris Consortio*: "Pastors are obliged to exercise careful discernment of situations."[30] It is interesting to note that here a *mandamus* is given to pastors. It is from the doctrinal position of the church, coupled with the knowledge and compassion for the specificity of each case that the African church can respond adequately and pastorally in every circumstance. That rattles us as Africans because it means that not all questions are going to be met by an immediate answer.

30. John Paul II, *Familiaris Consortio*, 84.

Bibliography

Arinze, Francis. "Christ's New Homeland: Africa." Preface to *Contribution to the Synod on the Family by African Pastors*, translated by Michael J. Miller, 7–12. San Francisco: Ignatius, 2015.

———. "Pastoral Attention to African Traditional Religion, Letter of the Pontifical Council for Interreligious Dialogue to the Presidents of Episcopal Conferences in Asia, the Americas, and Oceania." November 21, 1993.

Catechism of the Catholic Church. Vatican City: Libreria Editrice Vaticana, 1992.

Francis. *Amoris Laetitia: post-synodal apostolic exhortation on love in the family*. Vatican City: Libreria Editrice Vaticana, 2016. http://w2.vatican.va/content/dam/francesco/pdf/apost_exhortations/documents/papa-francesco_esortazione-ap_20160319_amoris-laetitia_en.pdf.

———. "Catechesis (11 February 2015)." *L'Osservatore Romano*, February 12, 2015.

Habil, Evans. "Battered woman says why she remained in abusive marriage." *Daily Nation*, August 2, 2016. https://www.nation.co.ke/news/Battered-woman-says-she-stayed-on-to-save-marriage/1056-3326414-tytvefz/index.html.

Idowu, Bolaji. *African Traditional Religion: A Definition*. New York: Orbis, 1975.

John Paul II. *Ecclesia in Africa*. Nairobi: Paulines Africa, 1995.

———. *Familiaris Consortio: On the Role of the Christian Family in the Modern World*. http://w2.vatican.va/content/john-paul-ii/en/apost_exhortations/documents/hf_jp-ii_exh_19811122_familiaris-consortio.html.

Katunge, Leonida. *Death and its Celebrations among the Kamba People of Kenya*. Saarbrücken, DE: Lap Lambert, 2016.

Mbiti, John. *African Religions and Philosophy*. Oxford: Heinemann, 1990.

Mwakikagile, Godfrey. *Ethnic Politics in Kenya and Nigeria*. Huntington, NY: Nova Science, 2001.

———. *Kenya: Identity of a Nation*. Pretoria: New Africa, 2007.

Napier, Cardinal Wilfrid. Interview with Catholic News Service on *Amoris Laetitia*, April 8, 2016.

Onaiyekan, Cardinal John. "Marriage in Our Contemporary World: Pastoral Observations from an African Perspective." In *Eleven Cardinals Speak on Marriage and the Family: Essays from a Pastoral View Point*, edited by Winfried Aymans, 63–72. San Francisco: Ignatius, 2015.

Ortiz, Andres. "Catholic Marriage." *AboutCatholics.com*. http://www.aboutcatholics.com/beliefs/catholic-marriage.

Rowland, Toni. "*Amoris Laetitia* and a Spirituality of Family Life." *Marfam Marriage and Family Life Renewal Ministry*. https://www.marfam.org.za/amoris-laetitia-spirituality-family-life-t-rowland/.

Synod of Bishops. *Relatio Synodi: The Pastoral Challenges of the Family in The Context of Evangelization*. Vatican City, 2014. http://www.vatican.va/roman_curia/synod/documents/rc_synod_doc_20141018_relatio-synodi-familia_en.html.

Subject Index

abortion, 105, 126n20, 140, 210, 226, 255
accompaniment
    as an art, 205–6, 208–12
    counterproductive aspect, 206
    God encountering, 207–8
    illuminative ecclesiology, 208–12
    pastoral, 117–18, 206–7
    people's lives, 204–5
    weakness, discerning and integrating, 202–8
accountability, 202–3
addictions, 48
Adibe, Gregory, 109
adoption, 106, 116, 256
Africa
    Akan culture, Ghana, 72–73, 82
    Amoris Laetitia and, 144–45, 217, 255–63
    Bahaya community, 190n36
    Catholic population, xvii
    cosmology in, 138, 140, 144, 148, 150
    Dinka culture, South Sudan, 148
    diocesan synods in, 57
    as a diverse continent, xv
    Esu culture, Cameroon, 73, 90
    existential life situations, 151–52
    family importance, 217
    God, family, and community, 98–99
    Gurunsi culture, Upper Volta Ghana, 72

Hausa tribe, 150
Igbo culture, Nigeria (*see* Igbo culture, Nigeria)
issues facing families, 64
marriage cultural practices, 39, 39n73, 146, 219
Synod of Africa, 56, 82–84
Teso culture, Uganda, 74
worldview, 137, 143, 146, 150, 158, 171, 190n36
Yaamba culture, Burkina Faso, 73
Yoruba culture, Nigeria, 13, 74, 126, 130–33, 150
Africae Munus (Benedict XVI), 35n60, 60, 142, 241
African Christian Initiation Program (ACIP)
    generally, 15, 157
    on "lost generation," 174
    mission of, 175–76
    vision of, 177–78
Afro-Christian faith, 82–84
Agbona, Femi, 74n23
Akan culture, Eastern Ghana, 72–73, 82
alcoholism, 48
Amoris Laetitia (AL)
    African reception of, 144–45
    biblical foundation, 19, 33–34
    biblical-theological interpretation, 20–25
    dubias, 15, 212
    generally, 2–3

Scripture Index

OLD TESTAMENT

Genesis

Exodus

Leviticus

Deuteronomy